THE CIRCLES OF LIFE

Wisdom is carved in failures, pain, and tears

ENHANCE EDITION

BERNARDO A. ARANGO

INDEX

Ecclesiastes 3:15: That which has been, is already; and that which is to be, has already been and God restores that which has passed away.

BIOGRAPHY

Biography: Library of Congress of the United States of America.

Biography: Library of the Congress of the United States of America.

The Bible

Wikipedia: the free encyclopedia

The father speaks to his children

Graphics, art, and design: Bernardo Arango through A.I

THANKS, AND DEDICATION

I am deeply grateful to the Creator of the universe, whose divine inspiration is evident on every page of this book. I also thank Jesus (Yeshua Hamashiach), our brother, teacher, and Savior, and the Holy Spirit for bestowing me the gift of writing, conducting workshops, delivering conferences, and producing well-received CDs worldwide. It is a profound privilege to dedicate myself to the purpose for which we came into this world. I hope this book will inspire a deeper reflection on life's cycles, stages, and levels and that every reader will experience a more profound connection with themselves, God, and the world around them.

I also dedicate this book to my wife, Conny, for her patience, love, and understanding, as well as to my children, Sebastián, Stephania, and Christian. I extend my thanks to my family, friends, and acquaintances. With your support and engagement, I believe this book will help us all realize that each of us has a mission on this planet.

Allowing our light to shine and taking it wherever needed starts the evolution toward a better world. I am grateful to all the people and experiences—both positive and negative—that have shaped my existence, as each has contributed to my wisdom through successes, smiles, tears, failures, and frustrations. It is through our struggles, pain, and tears that wisdom is carved into us, and I want you to know that your experiences, no matter how challenging, are valuable and contribute to your growth and wisdom.

PREFACE

This book invites you on a transformative journey to the heart of the human experience. Life, a marvelous spectacle, unfolds in different circles or levels we choose to inhabit. We are the protagonists in this existential stage, where our emotions and decisions shape our story. For some, life is a lesson that inspires them to discover their brilliance. For others, it becomes a stage of frustrations and toxic emotional wounds, plunging them into ignorance and pain.

Human reality is woven with a spectrum of emotions—from joy to sorrow, love to hate. Our mission is to evolve and transform, yet we often find ourselves trapped in a whirlwind of toxic emotions. The global pandemic reminded us of our fragility and the importance of our connections.

We are an expansive species capable of harm and destruction. We fish and hunt more than we need, pollute the water we drink, poison the air we breathe, and cause unnecessary conflicts and wars. We destroy our surroundings and ourselves, pretending to live happily in darkness, ignorance, and self-destruction.

Everything that begins has an end; life is a continuous cycle of births and deaths. Our actions and choices leave a legacy that transcends our existence. As we advance through this play of life, let us remember the words of the wise: do no harm to others, keep a clear conscience, and seek balance in our existence.

I invite you to embark on a journey of self-discovery, personal growth, and greater awareness. Along this path, we will explore our spiritual dimension, an underutilized resource within us all, through neurology, psychology, science, and spirituality. This journey will motivate you to grow and engage with the world in a more aware manner.

This book is not a psychological treatise, nor does it aim to change the world (far too complicated). It is an invitation to change our perception of the world and ourselves. As we share this journey, I aim to release the wisdom I have gathered and inspire you to make the slight difference we can in our lives. Let us look to the horizon and seek ways to improve instead of lamenting the past where nothing can be changed.

One of the secrets to a healthy and peaceful life is to maintain a clear conscience and find inner peace. Our happiness depends not on others but on our choices and thoughts. We unleash our divine potential by choosing to believe in God and ourselves. Our mind, like a magnet, attracts what we think. So, let us carefully select our thoughts to build our desired reality, empowering us to be in control of our happiness.

«In the journey toward a full and meaningful life, let us cultivate love, a clear conscience, and inner peace. »

INTRODUCTION

Navigating the Circles of Life is an awakening to self-realization—a journey inward toward wholeness.

In the pages of *"The Circles of Life,"* we will embark on an introspective journey through the mind and heart, exploring the emotions, values, and gifts that lie within us. We will navigate the concentric circles that represent our existence, recognizing the inherent duality of life: joy and sorrow, love and disappointment, abundance and poverty, wisdom and pain, peace and violence.

As captains of our destiny, we wield the power to steer our lives and set our course. The decision of which circle to navigate is ours and ours alone. We can opt for the serene waters of love, the fiery intensity of passion, the murky fog of fear, the confining walls of trauma and self-deception, the hopeful light of faith, or the barren wasteland of negativity.

Breaking free from limiting circles. However, the currents of life sometimes pull us into undesired circles. These circles could be the fear of failure, the belief that we are not worthy of love, or the habit of self-sabotage. We forget our power to change course and find ourselves trapped in repetitive patterns, conditioned by past thoughts, actions, and experiences. These circles may seem inescapable, as though an invisible force ties us to situations and relationships that neither nourish nor propel us forward but instead hold us back.

The key to transformation and liberation lies in understanding that these cycles and the people within them are not sentences but opportunities for growth and transformation. The first step toward healing is taking responsibility for our journey and acknowledging that, with the support of a higher power or our own inner strength, we are the creators of our reality.

Escaping the circles that confine and control us demands a journey of self-discovery, transformation, and faith. We must confront our limiting beliefs, face our fears head-on, and step out of the comfort of the familiar. It's crucial to understand that this process requires patience, perseverance, and a profound willingness to change, awakening our inner power and fostering a sense of hope.

Through this process of self-discovery and liberation, we reclaim the power God has given us and take control of our destiny, freeing ourselves from human oppression. We cultivate an elevated consciousness, heightened awareness, and spiritual connection, creating new love, abundance, and personal fulfillment circles.

You possess the power to liberate yourself from the circles that bind you. You have the freedom to navigate towards the life you yearn for. The journey to self-realization demands courage, determination, and faith. Trust in the process and strive with resolute steps toward the life you deserve. It's essential to recognize your worth, irrespective of others' opinions. With genuine faith, you can achieve great heights.

This book invites you to actively participate beyond being a passive reader. It allows you to write and reflect on your positive and negative experiences, exploring your life, world, relationships, and faith.

"Our existence is a journey of encounters, transformation, and purpose. Learning to accept, correct, and heal is part of life."

A BRIEF ANALYSIS OF THE HUMAN BEHAVIOR

Human beings are diverse in personality, mood, and behavior. Without a doubt, we are strange creatures, for many lived at the tail when we were born to be at the head. No one asks to be born, but we don't know how to live, and even less do we want to die. If only people were as happy as they pretend to be, as in love as they claim, and as sincere as they express; these are just words and appearances. Many wish to receive everything without cost, offering what they don't have and promising what they cannot fulfill.

We lack knowledge of our origin and greatness, which leads to emotional and spiritual imbalance. We lose our sense of humanity and the transcendent purpose of our lives, becoming mere clowns of existence. Our understanding seems clouded as if an invisible force pushes us to be something we are not. We forget the true purpose of our existence and the greatness that lies within.

Some exhibit inexplicable thoughts and behaviors toward themselves and their loved ones. Others live angry with their past, ruining their present. Some fight with the living and only makes peace when those people pass away—they discard the living into a hole but request a proper place for them in death. They distance themselves and become angry with a loved one while alive but cling desperately when that person dies.

There is rarely time to visit and cherish a family member while alive, yet they have the entire day to see them after they've passed. Some criticize, offend, and speak ill of a loved one yet sanctify them in death. They have no time, energy, or strength to care for a loved one when they're ill, yet they punish themselves with guilt when that person dies.

Years can pass by without speaking to a loved one, yet when they die, people weep, lament, apologize, and pay posthumous tribute. The dead often receive more value through flowers, admiration, and respect than the living. This paradox of human behavior, where remorse usually outweighs gratitude, is a testament to our strange and complex nature.

It's a curious aspect of human nature that we don't offer a single flower to someone while they're alive, but we shower them with roses and bouquets when they're gone. We live with resentment and anger toward family members, only to ask for forgiveness once they've passed. This paradox underscores the profound value of relationships, a lesson we should have learned from the pandemic and recent years. Family truly does matter.

Others spend their lives lamenting missed opportunities to move forward yet do nothing to stand out. However, they envy and criticize the sacrifices of others, not realizing they cause their misfortune. Many desperately seek peace and forgiveness but cannot forgive themselves or others, living in constant internal conflict. Some spend their lives working hard and sacrificing, only to waste their health and amass money that will later be used to try and recover their well-being. We genuinely do not know how to live!

When we see someone rise, improve, and excel in life, we demand even more from them and criticize them for not reaching the perfection we secretly desire for ourselves. Even stranger is when someone uses excuses to live in misery, justifying their setbacks and lack of understanding while complaining about missed opportunities—without realizing they are an opportunity. This highlights the importance of the pursuit of balance and purpose in life, a key to making life more meaningful and discovering the actual dimension of our existence.

What can we say about those who fail, refusing to be both students and teachers? They always look for someone to blame and never admit their mistakes. Even more peculiar is that when they can't find anyone to blame, they blame God, deepening their misfortune and curse. It appears humanity is content to walk in darkness. Most people waste their lives satisfying fleeting desires, pleasures, and needs, filling a tank that only pleases the senses.

At the same time, we weave a massive web of lies, yet we always demand the truth. What won't a person do to ruin their existence? After living entirely on errors, filled with leaps into the void, they realize too late that they never did what truly mattered, begging for just a few more days of life. In other words, people do not live—they merely survive.

We only value what we have in its absence. Human behavior is curious: we only appreciate people and things when they're gone or can no longer enjoy them. For example:

- *Time:* We think we are immortal until we face death.
- *Air:* It's always been free, but we only value it when it's scarce.
- *Family*: We miss and cherish them only when we are far away or after we lose them.
- *Children:* We complain when they are young but long for their childhood when they grow up. We wish we had taught them differently and relished their early years.
- *Parents:* We argue with them, but when they pass away, we desperately wish we could turn back time and give them one more hug.

We complain about what we lack and forget to enjoy what we have. Yesterday is gone, tomorrow is uncertain; the only thing we have is the present. Don't wait to say, "I love you," fight for your dreams, or give hugs and kisses when you can no longer. There's no sense in saving smiles, embraces, kisses, gratitude, and faith for later.

Now is this moment. Ask for forgiveness and forgive. Enjoy the sunshine while it shines, the rain as it falls, the kisses while they are given, and the laughter when it comes. Suffering is a part of life, but happiness is a gift we must not waste. Don't wait until you are at the edge of death to appreciate life. Live fully in the present.

Awakening Consciousness: I extend a heartfelt invitation to embark on an introspective journey, a transformative adventure into the depths of your soul, spirit, and mind. This journey can illuminate and give profound meaning to your existence. It's a journey that can turn the ordinary into the extraordinary, for humanity was born to elevate the world, to make it a more dignified, beautiful, and magnificent place. Yet, many are trapped in the cycle of satisfying created needs and traumas, unaware of their potential to transcend.

Our unsatisfied pride and endless erratic behaviors are merely reflections of emotional wounds and a life without direction. This book is just a collection of intertwined words, some already read, others already heard. But it goes beyond the letters, inviting you to reflect on the constant repetition of your toxic emotions and mistakes, each time with greater intensity.

My perspective is unique, and I write to help you realize that, though you have ears, you do not hear; you have eyes, you do not see; though you read, you do not understand. I invite you to awaken the greatness that resides within you. The ultimate purpose of this book is to show you that living with purpose is not just worthwhile; it's essential. You can learn from the wise, for those who listen and increase their knowledge gain skill and give value to their existence by helping others grow.

These pages will motivate you to generate better ideas. The actual encounter is with yourself, your soul, and God. The rest is up to you. Let's live by flourishing our virtues and abilities, allowing our actions to speak for us, not our words. Remember, greatness resides within you. S*o, wake up and help transform the world*!

When we speak in our favor, it's often out of vanity and pride. Let's make our lives worth living by letting our inner light shine, a precious gift from the Creator. Don't let yourself be just another name, leaving behind no mark or shadow worth following. If you don't do it, who will? If not now, when? Remember that some life opportunities come only once and never return.

We must be aware that sometimes, we must make decisions that hurt the heart but bring peace to the soul. Life changes, and we must recognize that the time to change and start anew is now! Conquering life is about learning to live it.

Some things will remain undone if you don't do them because we are each unique. So, dare to challenge yourself—you were born to be great. Grow with the universe, which is constantly evolving. Escape the darkness and let your light shine as an inexhaustible source of inspiration to be shared and used wherever needed.

- *Were you born for mediocrity?*
- *Were you born to fulfillment?*

"You can choose how to live your life, so why live in suffering?"

THE CIRCLE OF THOUGHT

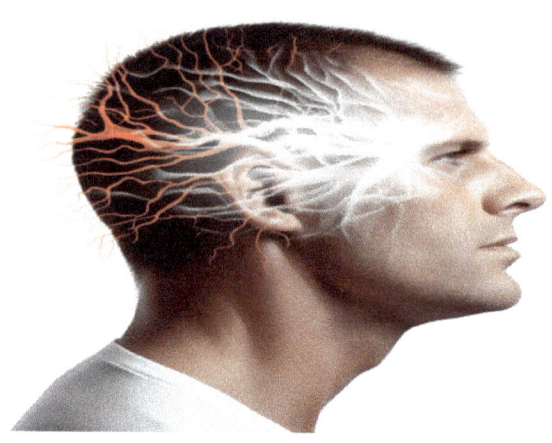

In science, philosophy, theology, and psychology, if there is no **analysis and creation,** without our thinking, nothing can exist. This indicates that it is tough for a human being to be without a brain and reasoning. In fact, the whole essence of what we are as human beings begins in our head, the brain, and intelligence. Everything begins within our brain, defined in the first Hebrew word in the bible, *bereshit*.

Bereshit, translated into Greek, means genesis; in English, it means origin or beginning. *Bereshit* has its origin from two Hebrew words, *"be"*, means (<u>inside</u>), *"reshit"* means <u>first, beginning, it</u> comes from the same root *"rosh"* which means (<u>head or main</u>). They are united in a phrase; the result is the word bereshit, which means beginning, beginning, and origin, indicating that everything begins inside our head. God began to conceive a universal plan, analyzed his spiritual world of ideas, and created a material world. He united spirit with matter, making it rich and diverse, endowing it with life, soul, and intelligence.

In this way, our universe was preconceived by God the Father and is thus formed.

In resume, we were first ideas and then reality. From that moment on, the universe's evolutionary development can be seen. It was part of the universal plan initially devised by the creator and masterfully interpreted by science. *Bereshit in Greek means genesis, which means "origin,"* the beginning or process of generation. Translated, **genesis** = *origin* equals *beginning* or *beginning*. This is just the first word of the Bible in Hebrew, which raises the intriguing question: what will the other words in the biblical texts reveal?

God created everything from nothing—and you, too, have the potential to transform your reality! The creation story is not just a biblical tale; it is a powerful blueprint for personal growth. Just as light was born from darkness, you can illuminate the dark corners of your life, sparking hope and optimism.

Do you want to harness the divine spark within you to create your moment? Discover how Bereshit's wisdom, a beacon of light, can guide you through life's challenges and inspire new beginnings. Imagine a world free of toxic emotions and where your dreams come true. The divine spark within you is the beginning of great things, Bereshit's wisdom is there to support and guide you every step of the way.

The Mind: A Universe of Transformative Power. With its extraordinary ability to think, our mind is a canvas where imagination and understanding converge to create. This transformative faculty encompasses various mental activities, from abstract thinking and reasoning to creativity and emotions. Everything that springs from our mind, abstract, logical, artistic, or creative, is a 'thought.' The essence of the mind lies in its power to turn ideas into realities, enabling us to experience, produce, and live through the various dimensions of our existence.

Reasoning is the cornerstone of our humanity, shaping our lives and defining our existence. Through reason, we become the authors of our stories, the protagonists of our journey. Our reflections, influenced by our perceptions, feelings, and experiences, form the core of our lives, giving us the power to shape our destinies.

Our mind acts as a filter for our decisions and actions, leading us towards good or bad. Our reflections can shape our destiny, but they are also significantly influenced by the environment in which we live, grow, and receive education. We are the product of our thoughts, and it's crucial to carefully evaluate them before taking any deliberate action, being mindful of the impact of our surroundings.

- Before putting on a shirt or an article of clothing
- Before boarding a bus, taking a cab, or driving a vehicle
- Before starting a conversation
- Before buying a cell phone
- Before going to the gym
- Before making a dinner
- Before reading or writing
- Before going to lunch
- A student applies his mind to learn, understand, and retain information, preparing for a successful future.

It's not the body that makes decisions but the mind; all our actions are directed by how we think. I invite you to observe your daily actions. You will notice you first think about what you want to do, and then it turns into action. This shows that if even the smallest things are possible, you can dare to think big. Better results are sure to follow. You have nothing to lose and everything to gain. Reflect and act, for thought is the seed of action and change. Knowing who we are is essential, but living it is even more important.

Everything that exists first forms in the mind. Every act and action we take first passes through the brain, which is analyzed, stored, and then transformed into action. From this, we can understand that in human beings, the brain, body, soul, and spirit are deeply interconnected, forming an inseparable unity. Without this connection, we would be empty beings. This concept holds true in psychology, biology, science, and our emotional lives, providing undeniable insight into the nature of existence.

Example:

- An athlete uses their mind to visualize success, develop strategies, and overcome obstacles during a competition.
- A musician Uses their mind to perform a piece of music with precision and emotion, conveying feelings through the notes.
- A doctor: Apply their knowledge to diagnose diseases, develop treatments, and save lives.

We are the product of our thoughts, which, in turn, attract what we focus on into our lives. Therefore, it is crucial to be mindful of and nurture our thoughts with care. Just as shadows follow the body, thoughts accompany actions, and those actions define our identity.

Often, we realize that our negative thoughts can cause more harm than any external enemy. Where we place our attention and energy is where our heart truly resides. This highlights the importance of cultivating positive thoughts and building meaningful connections with others, as they are our most valuable treasures.

Imagination is a potent and dynamic faculty; it is a *'wild child, the creasy of the house"* that can lead us from joy to sorrow, laughter to tears, and song to weeping. It thrives in creation, destruction, and distortion. Yet, it's vital to harness its potential, for when mastered, it can lead us to uncharted territories of inspiration and motivation.

Imagination is not a solitary force; our visual, auditory, and emotional perceptions activate it. It's a participative process that engages us in creating our realities.

For just as a person thinks and acts, so too do they determine their entire being, their sexuality, their professional life, their work, their destiny, and everything that will be their actual life.

Truth resides within us; it's what defines us as human beings. The *external is circumstantial*; the *internal is definitive*. In life, nothing happens to anyone that they don't, in some way, want to happen. This realization empowers us to be masters of ourselves in all our endeavors, to take control of our destinies, and to shape our lives.

Examples:

- An athlete: Cultivates positive thoughts of victory and perseverance to overcome obstacles and achieve their goals.
- An artist: Nourishes their imagination with images, sounds, and emotions to create works of art that inspire and move others.

A lack of critical thinking can lead to inaction and apathy. It's the key to unlocking personal growth and development. We will stagnate if we do not objectively analyze situations and reflect on the consequences of our actions. Thinking is acting, an infinite process that propels us towards change and growth. Those who live without reflection don't truly live. Thought and reasoning are the foundation of all existential human actions.

We live in a world where materialistic ideas like money, power, and sexual desire have a considerable influence. However, obsession with these ideas can lead us to weakness and ruin. History is full of examples of people who have fallen from grace by pursuing these goals excessively. Instead of focusing on the material, we should aspire to cultivate higher values such as compassion, creativity, and love. These values can guide us toward a more fulfilling and meaningful life.

Confronting and mastering thoughts of sexual desire and excessive ambition are among the most significant challenges a human being faces. This journey of empowerment allows us to understand the mind as a powerful tool for personal change and growth.

Thought is the source that brings actions into reality, whatever those actions may be. If you can understand how the brain works, you can change anything within yourself; as a person thinks, so is their life. We must remember that the human mind is the greatest masterpiece of God's creativity. For example, we interpret what we see and feel based on what resides in our minds and hearts.

- Nudity is not bad; bad could be what you think of the body you see naked. I analyzed that in the beginning, nudism was our natural way of living (Adam and Eve lived naked); nudity is a symbol of purity and perfection with the Creator.

- Money is not bad, but what you do with it can be harmful. Because the one who loves money will never be satisfied, the one who loves riches will never have enough of it.
- Cocaine and antibiotics are not bad; they are made to relieve pain. But the use you might make of them could be bad.
- Iron and steel are excellent, but the use they are put to in the manufacture of life-depriving weapons is terrible.
- It is not bad to live long; what is terrible is not knowing how to live.
- It's not wrong to wish you had a lot, but what you do to get it might be wrong.

Consequently, we can affirm that most of the evils we suffer are caused by man himself. For this reason, if we notice something that does not go according to what we want, we must act. In this way, you can give more sense to your life projects and rethink your plans. I analyzed the following: no matter how much technology the human being can develop, he will never be able to invent a system as solid and reassuring as an effusive hug and some sincere words said with love. Likewise, we spend most of our existence inside our heads. Therefore, we must make it a healthy place to live well.

Gandhi, in a few sentences, summed up what attracts thought. *"Watch your thoughts, for they will become acts. Watch your acts, for they will become habits. Take care of your habits, for they will become character. Watch your character, for it will shape your destiny, and your destiny will shape your life."*

Your closeness and faith in God, the way you perceive Him and relate to Him, yourself, and others, determine your future. If you lack God, seek Him. Neale Donald Walsh, the author of

Conversations with God, explains this beautifully, and I want to share it with you.

The law of opposites states that to experience something, we must experience its opposite. If we don't know the cold, we don't know the heat; without knowing the day, we do not know the night. This same law applies to our self-discovery and personal growth. To experience and understand who we really are, we must first face and experience what we are not.

It is not enough to know who we are; we must live it in our existence. Neale Donald Walsh explains that, in general, the opposite of what we want or seek will appear first in our lives as a prelude to achieving our goals. At this point, many people give up, abandoning their dreams and feeling frustrated at not achieving positive results, not realizing that they are only one step away from achieving it.

At this moment, we must relax, put aside the anguish and fear, and move on. We must get the best out of ourselves, knowing we are on the right path and about to see our dreams come true. As Neale explains, "If you are light and part of the sun, to experience yourself requires darkness, where you can discover your true strength." Now, I invite you to ask yourself the following questions.

- Why and for what purpose do I think?
- Why do I do what I do?
- What is the most important thing in my life?
- Do I know myself well enough?
- Why and for what purpose do I exist?
- What is the meaning of my existence?
- Do I feel true love?

Answering those questions will help us awaken our consciousness. We all desire better goals and personal fulfillment by meeting the needs of freedom, security, and love. True freedom speaks to us of evolution, understanding, consciousness, and spirituality, thus freeing us from what imprisons us.

"If you direct your thoughts well, you can direct your life well."

THE CIRCLE OF LOVE

What is Love? This question has intrigued philosophers, poets, writers, and lovers since the beginning of time. Millions of words have defined it, but what does it mean to you? Beyond theories and concepts, love is a deeply personal and unique experience, as diverse as the people who live it. It's a journey we all embark on, each with exceptional understanding and expression.

From philosophy to poetry, love comes in a thousand forms. Are you one of those who seek a love of service, physical, compliments, or time? Perhaps you feel more complete in one of them, but that does not entirely define love. Love is not divided, but we do so by pigeonholing it into labels. Your unique experience and expression of love are valid and accepted.

If you feel that love has been lacking in your life, it's time to reflect on yourself. Often, our perception of love is influenced by experiences and limiting beliefs. Are you allowing past wounds, such as betrayal, rejection, abuse, deception, or abandonment, to dictate how you love and how you let yourself be loved?

Are you living the love you desire or settling for emotional crumbs? Love is not a constant search but a cultivated state of being. An inner journey leads us to discover our true potential to love and be loved. To start this journey, you can begin by reflecting on your past relationships, identifying patterns or limiting beliefs, and seeking professional help. Let's look at what true love can be without emotional wounds or unnecessary makeup.

When love finds you and calls you, let yourself be mesmerized and seduced by its charm. And when it wants to caress you, get away from the world and enjoy its sweetness and tenderness because love is not a relationship. It is a state of being a precious gift from the Creator. When love speaks to you, you must believe it, even if its voice breaks your dreams, in the same way, that the waves shake the peace and the stillness of the beach, shaking the roots of your soul.

Love makes us dream, makes us grow, and is excellent. It also shrinks, weakens, and gives us strength; it is rational and irrational madness. It is noble and infinite, the most dynamic and powerful force we can have. Fear does not visit love either; the sun's rays hurt it, and the night can damage it.

Love, just as it makes us smile and cry, polishes and shapes us like a sword, is made with pure fire. It kneads us until we become flexible with fire, pain, and sweat; it pulverizes us until we become wheat. Love does all this to know the secret of our soul and make us accomplices of its delights. It is like a volcano on fire inside that, when let out, provokes an explosion of feelings.

Love's only desire is to fulfill itself, not to possess or be possessed, because love is enough for itself. Love is patient, waits

its turn, and knows how to arrive because it is not simply about who is with you. It is rather about who steals your thoughts and makes you dream. Who makes you grow and makes you tremble at the mere thought.

Love can do anything; it makes us overcome all obstacles and forgive anything. In what is wrong, there is also love because we do not see the flaws or mistakes. To love when everything is fine is easy but a test of difficulties. For this reason, it can be affirmed that there is no love without history since love also seeks to mature.

Love is the alliance of the heart and not business; it is understanding, not selfishness; it is a dream, not insomnia. It is an act of faith, not a lie; it is a motivation, not an emotion; it is a choice, not an obligation. It is an enchantment that not only makes the being tremble but also ignites the soul, undresses the spirit, and calms the being.

True love often involves moments of suffering—not because love itself is suffering, but because avoiding pain may mean missing the chance to experience genuine happiness. The capacity to love deeply is closely tied to our ability to face and overcome hardship, as each trial allows us to love with greater authenticity. This is why it's said that those who have never suffered for love may never have truly loved. Ultimately, true love nurtures and renews itself, strengthened by every challenge it endures.

Don't let the outside world define what love is. For some people, sex is love, confusing it with emotions and moments of pleasure. With sex, the only ones who fall in love are hormones, like fireworks that go off, make noise, and sparkle for a moment, only to die, leaving silence and loneliness. For most people, love and passion go hand in hand, but it does not define it. It would be hypocritical to ask for a sexual response to demonstrate love because love has a supreme value above pleasure and everything else. Thanks to love, there is no middle ground, just as there is no middle ground for God.

Mistrust, pride, arrogance, arrogance, too high ego, and fear are the most significant flaws that exist in the path of love. Because they obstruct the door of understanding, confusing the navigation in the sea of feelings. Trust and tolerance allow us to feel it and live it fully. In love, every action of good faith is reasonable. However, it is in the trust where its most significant strength lies: its fullness, growth, and sustenance. It makes us feel an infinite security that invites us to immerse ourselves in the eternity of feeling, living, and loving with determination.

When the trust of love is broken, it is the same as when a piece of paper is torn; no matter how hard you try to fix it, it will never be the same. It causes distance, estrangement, and difficulties in expressing feelings and communication. No matter what you do, there will always be suspicion and mistrust. For this reason, you should continually strengthen trust in love and not use rudeness, anger, or lies. Do not hold grudges or resentment; love is kind, patient, and generous.

The opportunity to love is for everyone, so if someone respects and loves you, never fail him. In this life, you will never meet the same person twice. Because by circumstances of destiny, some only show up once to teach us a lesson that, when learned, the pain disappears, leaving lessons in the heart.

The purpose of living on this planet is to love, rectify, transcend, and help others. If you cannot love, do not hurt; do not block the path in search of love. The most fantastic dreamer is the one who believes in unconditional love. Likewise, it is better not to have debts with anyone, only to love one another, because when love comes, it transforms lives.

HOW TO DISCOVER LOVE

How do we discover love? When we know that we love or are loved, without falling into false illusions or sentimental slavery or moments of emotional romanticism that pass fleetingly. There are fleeting and intense passions that are confused with love; they make us fall into a labyrinth of crossed emotions, confusing our being. True love will never be fleeting simply because God's love is not fleeting. True love requires patience, domestication, and tolerance. Likewise, the loving poet within us comes out to express what he feels. He is the one who tells us that love must not be forced or obliged but must be conquered.

The eyes are the reflection of the soul and its lamp. That is true love without nudity or artificial cocoons. It is where the couple grows together—without imposed blackmail, providing sincere happiness, where each one is important in constructing happiness. It is not based on literature or the opinion of others but instead on experience and our personal feelings. We are sharing with the spouse in an effort and dedication to build better days than the previous one. Thanks to this, there will be a beautiful intimacy and collaboration that, together with love, always grows more.

Love is a precious feeling that, when it comes, we cannot let go.

I feel love when my care for my partner is reciprocated, when I am the apple of their eye, as much a part of their body as they are of mine. Just as I care for my mouth, hands, and feet, I perceive the same care from my partner towards me. The belonging of love is like the flowers that belong to the tree, and the tree belongs to the earth.

It is to enjoy a union inseparable from the truth, a beautiful and just bond, in an eternal connection between the necessary and the pure. When he becomes the security, and she becomes his weakness, she becomes a universal delight to the joy of our hearts. And, even better, when they tell you, "*I am distracted because all my senses are busy dreaming of you.*"

In the madness of love, we often throw ourselves into it as if jumping into an abyss without calculating how far we fall. We don't see it as madness but as dreamers, unquestioningly believing that this love will give us the wings to fly to the love we've dreamed of and longed for. We may have clarity and know we could fall at some point, but we don't care. This belief in the transformative power of love drives us and makes us leap.

Sometimes, we believe it's better to love and lose than to have never experienced love out of fear of not reciprocating. If there is anything eternal and sacred, love is a beautiful and joyous experience like God, who turns it into a holy feast for his delight. When you feel the fire of love in your heart, with a single cry, you can say: "I am in the heart of God!" pure, absolute, and unconditional love because the Creator loves us with a love that transcends all human understanding!

And how it is written.
"*No eye has seen,*
No ear has heard,
No human mind has conceived,
What God has prepared for those who love him."

Love is also written with a "T" for time to dedicate to the loved one, quality time, understanding, and flirting. The time to know how to love is a personal choice; it is like the beginning of everything. I invite you to write what true love means to you in your own words. To me, love is.

_____

_____

_____

_____

_____

_____

_____

Likewise, we should love with grace, our neighbor with genuine love, and the best qualities we have. To love the one who loves us is to be reciprocal. However, to love with grace transcends us. To give to those who do not deserve it, to help those who do not ask for help but need it, to love those who do not ask for love but need it. To be mindful of the marginalized, the despised, the hated is to love. Jesus of Nazareth, in all his works, taught us what grace is.

«_Love and family are the bedrock upon which we build our ongoing journey of self-improvement and the preservation of humankind._ »

THE CIRCLE OF ACTION

"From words to deeds, there is a long way to go." This phrase, known by many and ignored by others, is correct. You can have good ideas, the best plans, and a defined goal, but if you act, something can be achieved because the action describes it, not the emotions. Action is the key to turning your dreams into reality. If you find the link between the two, you learn to live with yourself. With action, what we know is useful; remember that even the most minor action is better than the grandest intention.

Thought creates ideas, but the mind, the body, and the action achieve the purpose by driving and activating them. Here is the difference between the action of the active and the mediocrity of the passive. The mediocre always delay starting a new project until they feel 'ready. ' The comfortable prefer to stay in their comfort zone rather than take a risk. And the fearful, who is too scared even to consider the possibility of failure. These are the ones who want everything by inertia without doing anything to achieve an idea. They always delay a concept until they can demonstrate that it should not be done, or it cannot be done, or it is too late to do it; what hypocrisy!

Between thought and action, there are two bridges: the first is called decision, and the second is called time. In the decision, you take the idea to act, and your potential is measured in the time limit to obtain results. You must be aware that the power of a decision can changes your life and the lives of those around you, so it is essential to analyze the course of action.

You must Keep in mind that people look for ways, methods, and activities to achieve the purposes of their interest. However, the most crucial purpose should be self-improvement. We must remember what is essential, not to be better than others, but to be better than yesterday. Therefore, you must watch your heart closely, without lying to yourself, because from it springs the truth of life or the deception of life.

WHAT PREVENTS AN IDEA FROM BECOMING A REALITY?

Unquestionably, it is the fears, the insecurity, and the ideas of what cannot go right. Fears get in the way, indecisions abound, and speculations overflow into nothingness. Talking a lot without doing anything is a grotesque spectacle that causes regret. Some can but do not use or lend the axe, letting opportunities go. The risk-takers are the lucky ones who, despite the obstacles, have dared to fight for their ideas and make them come true. You analyzed your world; you enjoy the Internet, television, cell phones, movies, literature, cars, airplanes, computers, etc. We have all this thanks to the characters that, with madness or not, have dared to act. They materialized their ideas regardless of the number of failed attempts, and they risked everything to achieve it. Let's analyze several examples.

Thomas Edison, the inventor of the light bulb, made over 5,000 attempts before realizing his idea. Edison is the most prolific inventor in history, with 1,903 patents (an unsurpassed record). If this inventor had not implemented his ideas, electrical technology might not be where it is today. So, other great people have courageously turned their ideas into action, as they were and are.

- Nikola Tesla, inventor of the induction and alternating current motor.
- Johannes Gutenberg, with the invention of the printing press
- Charles Tellier, with the invention of the refrigerator (the fridge)
- Alexander Graham Bell, with the invention of the telephone
- Michael Hart is considered the father of the e-book.
- Wilson Greatbatch, creator of the pacemaker, the inventor who has saved the most lives in the past 50 years.
- Steve Jobs invented the Apple computers, the iPod, the iPhone, and the iPad, revolutionizing technology.
- Bill Gates invented the Windows operating system.
- Elon Musk, creator of PayPal, Tesla, and SpaceX

The list is endless, thanks to the fact that God has allowed the arrival of great geniuses to help us evolve. Those mentioned above are a reference to make the difference that thoughts and ideas put into action have results. If these brilliant minds had not dared, we would not have the advances and comforts we have. This indicates that an effort determines a thought becoming an idea. Anything else is just dead thoughts, ideas blown away by the wind.

I invite you to write down your ideas and the action plan you must make them a reality. I have the following ideas.

_____

_____

_____

_____

_____

_____

The plan I have for realizing my ideas is.

_____

_____

_____

_____

_____

We must understand that good ideas, with action, lead us to the triumph of goals, not emotion. Likewise, the secrets of success and inner peace live within each one of us, something that invites us to analyze, improve, and dominate toxic passions. Also, we know we have greatness and the capacity to transform our existence, so why not transmit it to others? So, contributing in this way, we can improve the creation, making our environment a pleasant place, better to live in, and, why not, with the whole world.

«Remember that you have more possibilities when you decide to act than when you must react».

THE CIRCLE OF GRATITUDE

Are you someone who finds it hard to give or say thank you? Do you even shy away from personal recognition? If you avoid expressing feelings of gratitude, this may indicate emotional harm—whether due to past traumas and fears or perhaps an inexplicable sense of selfishness or pride. If this resonates, I invite you to open yourself emotionally to the expression and manifestation of gratitude, showing that your heart remembers.

Gratitude enriches all areas of life: physically, mentally, emotionally, and spiritually. It fosters positive attitudes that enhance daily life. Adopting this habit would be transformative, as gratitude is one of the greatest gifts we can give, capable of uplifting lives through a simple shift in attitude.

Expressing thanks brings change, as gratitude is closely linked to happiness and well-being. Those who practice gratitude experience more positive emotions, savor good moments and are healthier. They face difficulties with resilience, enjoy stronger friendships, and lead a higher quality of life compared to those who are ungrateful or prideful.

Expressing gratitude is more than just having a mouth full of words and saying, ***"Thank you."*** We must learn and know how to give it, without this action making us think we need a delicate or special treatment raising arrogance. The act of gratitude is a language the deaf can hear, and the blind can see. To know how to give recognition is to say: "I recognize and accept you for what you are, for your spirit, for your way of being, and for the special way in which you contribute to enriching my existence, helping me to overcome the moments in which I sink into incomprehension and despair."

Gratitude, when expressed, is a significant form of recognition. It's not enough to feel it in silence; we must let it be known. When someone receives our gratitude, it sparks a feeling that encourages them to continue their positive contributions. This is because the meditation of the heart is the cause of understanding. Few values are as significant as the recognition of our fellow men through gratitude. When given with the heart, it is the best gift we can provide, and with this action, we make it worth twice.

When we express sincere gratitude to someone who has done us a favor, given us a gift, or helped us in any way, we encourage them to continue their acts of kindness. By making them feel valued and appreciated, we inspire them to keep the door open for future interactions, as we never know when we might need their assistance again. Gratitude is a powerful tool that fosters a sense of connection and belonging, reminding us of the importance of human kindness. Whether it's thanking a friend for their support, expressing appreciation for our pet's unconditional love, or acknowledging the help of a stranger, gratitude enriches our lives and strengthens our relationships.

Gratitude is deeply intertwined with mindfulness and awareness, catalyzing personal growth. By nurturing a grateful heart, we become more attuned to the positive aspects of our lives. When we practice gratitude, we not only appreciate the kindness of others but also recognize and value our strengths and accomplishments. Self-gratitude is not about narcissism; it's about self-compassion and self-care. We boost our self-esteem and resilience by acknowledging our efforts and celebrating our successes, inspiring us to strive for greater heights.

The transformative power of gratitude is truly remarkable. It has the potential to reshape our lives and the lives of those around us, making it a practice of immense value and impact.

Gratitude is intricately linked to love, joy, and peace. It's a simple yet profound practice that uplifts our spirits and deepens our connections with others. By nurturing gratitude, we become more resilient, compassionate, and fulfilled, shaping our reality with the powerful thought of appreciation.

With gratitude, there is no room for complaining, regret, grudges, pride, or sadness. Gratitude attracts appreciation, just as positivity and joy attract joy. Gratitude works like a magnet; that is to say, with attitudes of gratitude, you draw happy, positive, grateful, and well-being people to your existence. It is impossible to attract good and positive consequences to your life if you are ungrateful because discontent and ungratefulness will always bring negative situations.

The day has 24 hours, the hour has minutes, and the minutes have seconds, so God has given you the gift of 86,400 seconds today. I ask you: Have you used some seconds to say thank you for something? We should live in gratitude; there should be only one recommended excess on this planet: "excess gratitude." Today, I thank God for the gift of life, for the air, the water, and the earth; thanks for the planet because I breathe, I walk, I see, I talk, I work, I am in good health, I laugh, and I am giving one more day of life. For my family, my work, my health. Thank you for what I am and am not, what I have, and the hope.

To thank God for the Father "Hashem" in our way, we need more than emotions and a mouth full of words; we also need action and deeds with true faith. We have many things to be thankful for; giving is feeling gratitude and love. I give thanks by helping orphans and lonely children, clothing the homeless, feeding the hungry, helping the sick, and visiting the imprisoned.

In other words, we are helping God with the most disadvantaged creation. We must understand the environment, the world where we live, and what we do. We must make paths as we go, and why not? We must shine our inner light and take it wherever it is required. Likewise, illuminating the lives of others gives more value to the existence of this planet. He invited you to express how you give or would like to thank God and those who have helped you.

I show appreciation as follows.

_____

_____

_____

_____

_____

_____

I am thankful for it.

_____

_____

_____

_____

_____

_____

To be grateful is to be aware that happiness also depends on how we perceive others, our relationship with others, God, and ourselves. We must learn to develop feelings of love and understanding enlightened by reason, seeking more significant goals.

May this guide us in overcoming selfishness and pride, which are significant obstacles to a healthy life with others. Moreover, the pleasure of meeting a grateful person is so great that it is worth the risk of not being ungrateful because he walks humbly, and God in his heart leaves footprints wherever he steps.

«To give thanks and to know how to show it is to be worth twice because giving thanks speaks well of the heart and of the one who possesses it. »

THE CIRCLE OF REPENTANCE

Repenting is recognizing a mistake by changing one's attitude, thought, and opinion. It is retracting, rejecting, regretting, forgiving, asking for forgiveness, rectifying, and correcting past wrong or improper actions. Some acts torment our conflicting conscience, which sometimes defends us and sometimes accuses us without letting us live in peace. And sometimes, we regret and cry, but these are only temporary emotions.

When we sincerely repent, we first examine our actions with a conscience. Second, we rectify and change our attitude; third, we make amends. In this life, all things that come out of us, whether good or bad, also come back to us. So don't worry about what you will receive; worry more about what you will give. If true repentance exists within you, you will experience the best medicine and relief that the human soul and emotions have. This healing and relief are the rewards of true repentance, which requires heart, mind, attitude, and life changes.

What's done is already done; from the past, we can't change a second of what was done. In fact, nothing can be changed, but we can regret the time wasted with the wrong people. Regretting mistakes and errors is always a good start, with the idea of changing thinking and attitude toward feelings of guilt. True repentance is not only about acknowledging mistakes and errors.

Instead, it goes further, rectifying and changing attitudes and rewarding with what is right. Because it is never too late for a just reparation and to make a change in an intimate, emotional, and spiritual experience that manifests itself outwardly by opening the eyes of the soul. To discover God's wonders in you, you must know that there is nothing more valuable and liberating than true repentance. It is a transformative power that changes consciousness and lifestyle, inspiring and motivating us to become better versions of ourselves.

It is like a metamorphosis, with a change of judgment, convictions, and dedication. Along with the change comes some pain; there is no change without pain; you must accept it and know how to overcome it. Let go of everything that prevents you from getting out of the emotional and spiritual ballast. We all make mistakes; that is the mark of being human. But thanks to this, we learn from our lessons, which can become opportunities. We must repent and correct because we deserve chances to make things right in this fleeting and fabulous life. Learning from our mistakes empowers and enlightens us, guiding us toward a brighter future.

We must remember that asking God for forgiveness is one thing (*spiritual absolution*) that forgives us out of love and consideration, and asking forgiveness from a human being is

41

another. Problems with another human being must be solved with the one who has committed the offense or fault. Likely, God does not want to get involved in a matter you have caused with all your intentions. That is something that you must resolve. You must exhaust resources with that person and then pass them on to God.

Then you will have no one to accuse you before Him. Remember that if we are accused of God, he is a just judge. The bible says, "But God is the judge: He brings one down, he exalts another." he will be severe because being severe is the only way to be just [1.] It also says, "Settle matters quickly with your adversary taking you to court. Do it while you are still together on the way, or your adversary may hand you over to the judge, the judge may hand you over to the officer, and you may be thrown into prison [2].

Now, if you repent from your heart and ask for forgiveness from the one you offended, but the one you ask forgiveness from does not forgive you and does not want to do so because he expected something else or because of pride.

Therefore, the one who does not forgive will remain in his emotional and spiritual prison. That is no longer your problem; the one who does not absolve you will live with his conscience for blocking his search on the path of sincerity and reconciliation. Each one will live according to his conscience and actions. Yours can be at peace because you have sincerely sought forgiveness, even if you have taken off a great weight.

I invite you to deeply examine your conscience about the acts and actions you wish or need to repent. Doing an act of "*mea culpa*," I sincerely recognize.

_____

_____

_____

To recognize the pain, I will go to

_____

_____

_____

1. I   regret   having offended._____ I need to reconcile and ask for forgiveness.

2. I repent of. _____ and in the name of God, I ask your forgiveness for all that I made you suffer.

3. I deeply regret._____ and I say this because you and I deserve a better life.

4. I   regret, _____and I apologize for my actions. I promise to compensate you as much as possible for the damages caused.

5. Deeply,   I   regret   it. _____and I need your forgiveness, please forgive me.

I deeply regret it.

_____

_____

_____

_____

_____

Now, you can commit yourself.

---I commit myself to correcting and changing my attitude because I deserve a better life.

Without terrible memories, hatred, or guilt that binds me and chains me, I commit myself to retraining and coming out of the spiritual closet.

---I ask God to send his light within me, to make it shine and be helpful. I will no longer cling to material things but to knowledge that will elevate my conscience and soul.

--- I will seek what makes me grow internally, learning to live the present with a promising vision.

---I have learned that every being evolves in the sum of its struggles, positive or negative. This helps me to develop spiritual sensitivity and contribute with better resources in favor of myself and those around me and, why not, the whole world.

--- My God, help me with the part I must play on this planet and correct my mistakes.

--- Give a little brightness to my existence, making a slight difference. --- I will focus my eyes on the horizon, see what I can do to improve, and not look back where I can no longer change anything.

"Forgiveness is necessary for the development of consciousness and spirit."

THE CIRCLE OF GREED

Greed has several names, such as covetousness, rapacity, and greed for money. It leads human beings to commit deceit, murder, betrayal, hoarding, theft, stinginess, and arrogance. Greedy people live only for themselves; they are not interested in anything or anyone but their pettiness. His greed has no limits, so he never has enough. He admires everything he accumulates, enjoying it by sight without knowing that his greed is his prison. He forgets that he is a mortal being like all of us who live on this planet and ignores that a mother's womb molded his being and that he needed nine months to be formed, failing the torments of his mother in childbirth.

A greedy person is never satisfied with his lot or what he has because stinginess dries up his soul, closes his understanding, and isolates his existence. The more frugal the person, the more he has, the more unhappy he is, and, in the end, he dies in spiritual misery. Because he accumulates riches but does not enjoy them, and if he ever does any good, he does it only out of carelessness. He is constantly inventing schemes to surprise and abuse people with low incomes and unwary when they expose his cause and need.

Greed, a wicked and perverse vice, never satisfies its insatiable appetite. It is incompatible with peace, which should be a cause for concern. What good is it to gain the world if you lose your life and soul in doing so? What good is it to accumulate riches if, along the way, you lose love, values, heart, emotions, and joy? What good is having many possessions if you can take nothing when you die? Greed forgets that it is incompatible with peace, and it is most likely someone who doesn't even know it will enjoy everything it accumulates because greed loses everything by wanting everything. This vice sow's evils such as disloyalty, deliberate betrayal, bribery, theft, and corrupting all causes.

Because greed sows all the evils such as disloyalty, deliberate betrayal, bribery, theft, corruption, and all causes, desire puts a price on most human wrongs. It expends inordinate energy to accumulate money and power. Greed is cunning and deceitful; it can change its appearance to engage in the struggle between virtue and vice, to pretend that virtue has its price.

Unfortunately, it cannot hide its claws; in the end, it always reveals itself by falling under its weight. He ends up dragging sacks full of pettiness, symbolizing his baseness. He does not consider everything material in this world a vain illusion without knowing that he has no value for the hell he goes to.

Where is the limit of Greed? Nowhere does the greedy ever have limitations. He is blind in the abyss, disconnects himself from everything, and locks himself in his dark labyrinth. Some go into psychosis, distorting reality. Others reach psychopathy, and they do not connect emotionally with anyone.

The moment comes when the greedy person, immersed in his pettiness, forgets that he needs the standard air, the same air we all breathe. He forgets that he was in diapers and needed care to survive; he ignores the fragility of his being. For the miser, money and its accumulation are insatiable, as insatiable are man's eyes. What do you think they will ask you when you pass the threshold where we all go? Do you think they will congratulate you; do you think they will ask you?

--- Hey, tell me, how many properties did you own?

---How many vehicles did you buy?

---Congratulations on all the money you accumulated and the fame you had, and what did you do with all that?

---Of all that he accumulated, what did he take with him? Nothing, right? ***What foolishness, ignorance, stupid?***

---He let himself be dominated by his pettiness and his baseness, losing all control, and just so you know, everything I accumulated, someone else will enjoy it.

The miser is miserable with himself; with whom will he be generous; he cannot even enjoy his own money without knowing that no one is worse than he who tortures himself. The miser even skimps on food, and at his table, he goes hungry. He even skimps on the purchase of a mattress and buys the cheapest, without considering that he will rest a significant part of his life.

The natural enemy of greed is charity; it devours it, just as the big fish swallows the small fish. Such greed is known as the disguise of capitalism or, instead, as the excessive wealth of powerful nations. Confusing the belief of feelings where one fights for one's benefit is a petty theory that man uses to justify his pride, selfishness, and excessive ambition without limits.

Greed leads to the exploitation of the most vulnerable, including children, the homeless, widows, people with disabilities, and older people. It fosters the exploitation and enslavement of the needy, promotes prostitution, and steals the faith of many. This betrayal of faith, caused by greed, is a profound injustice that should invoke moral outrage. Greed ignites wars that claim innocent lives and betrays the Creator, crucifying Jesus again and again with pain more profound than those who drove the nails.

All this happens without the greedy considering when their hour of death will come, unprepared to account for their actions. They try to justify everything in a confused narrative of love and betrayal, faith and lies, goals, promises, and abandonment.

Throughout history, greed has been responsible for the fall of empires such as the Spanish, British, Byzantine, and Roman. It has led to family betrayals, land theft, and wars. The slave trade, land theft, and violence in the name of wealth are products of greed. Leaders and the powerful have needlessly shed innocent blood due to this insatiable desire for more.

Greed begins the chaos, and we remain in turmoil. It seems that through greed, we will all exterminate ourselves. This dire situation calls for a collective reflection and a change in mindset. We must recognize the destructive nature of greed and take responsibility for our actions to prevent further harm.

You can use the following lines to examine what you have and how you have achieved it. My greed is,

_____

_____

_____

_____

Everything I've gotten greedily; I'm going to use it in.

_____

_____

_____

_____

Analyze consciously and realize there is no reason to be stingy. There is no point in deprivation, comparisons, or negativity. You can improve by examining your conscience and committing to yourself and God to obtain an actual change and, thus, see and enjoy life's wonders.

"On this planet, there is enough to satisfy the needs of all, but there will never be enough to satisfy the greed of some." (Mahatma Gandhi).

THE CIRCLE OF PAIN AND SUFFERING

From the moment we emerge from the womb, pain greets us with our mother's cries of labor. Yet, in that same instant, life gives us an unexpected gift: the joy of being born. This duality, this dance between pain and pleasure, is an undeniable reality in the vast ocean of human emotions.

Pain, a reflection of our fragility, is an inevitable part of life, manifesting in countless ways. Yet, those who bravely transform their pain into learning and growth can discover forgiveness, healing, and liberation. Instead of allowing pain to become a consuming cycle, we can find joy despite its challenges.

On our emotional journey through life, we all encounter difficult times. Fearing suffering only gives it more power over us.

Avoiding it doesn't make it go away but rather amplifies it. At some point, we must confront it, no matter how painful. Each of us carries our burdens, our battles. While we can't always change the circumstances that cause us pain, we can choose the attitude with which we face them.

For example, imagine a climber scaling a steep mountain. The path is fraught with obstacles, falls, and scrapes that cause physical pain. However, as they ascend, they also experience a deep satisfaction and joy in contemplating the beauty of the landscape and the sense of accomplishment in overcoming each challenge. The journey, with its pain and happiness, is beautiful; the key is to find the strength to keep going, learning, and growing with each step.

I feel pain and suffer for what.

_____

_____

_____

_____

_____

What causes me the most pain and nostalgia is when.

_____

_____

_____

_____

_____

Abandonment, abuse, and aggression, in any form, leave deep scars on the soul. Deception, injustice, and violence inflicted by those who should care for and protect us, such as parents, siblings, family, friends, or even strangers, can mark us forever.

These traumatic experiences, from the earliest stages of life, do not discriminate. They can affect anyone, regardless of age or gender. The emotional wounds they leave behind go beyond physical pain, shattering our innocence and sowing resentment and coldness. They are silent cries of affliction that echo through time, gaining strength as we journey into adulthood.

Emotional damage can inflict wounds that cause deep pain, but the cruelest are those that deprive us of thoroughly enjoying life. These persistent wounds never cease to bleed, and the accumulated pain transforms into a bitterness that takes root in our being, affecting both body and mind. It becomes an invisible entity, making us feel trapped by dark feelings, surrounded by pain and bitterness, trapping us in a cycle of pain and darkness.

The weight of suffering is natural but knowing that these feelings lead us nowhere is even heavier. The unconsciousness of those who hurt us only increases our burden. However, experience teaches us that learning is the only retribution for this pain. The true victory is striving to live, heal, and find light in the darkness.

People who abuse you and mistreat you do so because you may not fully value yourself. It's essential to know your worth and how much you can shine. Abuse comes in different presentations and teaching packages. Physical abuse appears when they mistreat your humanity and mock or offend your actions.

Even more painful is when others transform our pain into a morbid spectacle. However, the sufferings and torments that leave a deep mark are those caused by the people we love. For this reason, any additional pain seems bearable and insignificant when we suffer. Just as fire forges a sword, suffering forges courage, giving rise to hope and faith. It's a reminder that even in the darkest moments, we have the potential to transform our pain into strength and resilience.

In the depths of our being, we know that he who has not suffered knows nothing, has not lived, knows nothing of good or evil. He who does not know misfortune does not know happiness does not know men. It is like he who has not suffered for love; he cannot say that he has loved and does not know his feelings, limits, or himself. Suffering and love have a great capacity for redemption, which some of us have forgotten, and others do not know.

Who can be the same after the loss of a son, a daughter, the loss of a father, a mother, or a loved one? Who can heal the pain of this nature without leaving wounds and voids? When will it be possible to erase from the soul those happy memories of the past that now bring pain and suffering? When can we come out of blindness and open our eyes to discover the wonders of God's will?

There is no reason to look for suffering, but if it arrives and is part of your life, do not let it stay for long. Look it in the face; face it with all you have, with all your strength, with all your being, with all your anger, with all your faith in God. Challenge your limits and exploit your capacity for self-improvement and rebirth. Thus, you will be able to overcome, and you will learn that from pain and suffering, the root is born that gives you the strength and courage to master the difficulties of your existence. I invite you to express what you will do to overcome pain.

KEYS TO OVERCOME PAIN AND SUFFERING

Emotional pain is distressing and causes sadness, hopelessness, and anxiety. To stop the emotional pain and suffering, we can take steps to soften its impact, especially when we become aware of its existence. The National Center for PTSD and Anxiety and

Depression Association of America suggests these keys to overcoming emotional distress.

- Understanding what causes suffering
- Initiate a therapeutic process
- Learning to be resilient to stress
- Empathize with others
- Develops effective communication
- Strengthen your problem-solving skills
- Set realistic goals and expectations
- Learn from both success and failure
- Be compassionate and contributing
- Lead a responsible life based on a series of sensible values.
- Feeling the strength and need to help others.

On my part, I recommend you read my book "Emotional and Inner Healing Workshop," based on my experience giving workshops, retreats, and conferences. Besides following the recommendations, if you have faith, you can also practice forgiveness. Forgive, attend workshops, seminars, and retreats, and above all, surrender your suffering to God and pray with all your faith because prayer and trust are our strengths and God's weakness. Now, I invite you to write down how you will overcome pain and suffering.

To overcome pain and suffering, I will do the following.

_____

_____

_____

_____

From now on, I will no longer suffer why.

_____

_____

_____

_____

_____

--- My God, why is it that no human being can escape the experience of suffering?

---- I ask you to help me understand the meaning of what we neither want nor to understand.

---- Deliver me from the sorrows of life, where I have a source of life and reflection instead of suffering. To understand that he who suffers everything can dare everything.

--- For I may receive blows from life, suffering from love, betrayal from a friend, but I expect only blessing from you, my God. Therefore, I ask you to listen to my lament, embrace me, and touch my heart and pain.

"God is my light and my salvation; whom shall I fear? God is the stronghold of my life; who can make me afraid?" (Psalm 27:1).

THE CIRCLE OF ERRORS AND MISTAKES

- To err is a human
- Anyone can make a mistake
- Where there is no good advice, anyone can fall

These words capture a shared human experience that transcends cultural, ideological, and societal boundaries. We all make mistakes in medicine, politics, government, religion, education, family, work, or personal matters. No one is immune, and claiming otherwise would be untruthful.

The pivotal question is not about the mistake but our response to it. Do we step up and take ownership of our actions or seek a scapegoat? Do we delve into our thoughts, our principles, and our feelings? Equally important is to ponder over why we make mistakes. We make them for one or more of the following reasons:

- Errors of omission
- Intentional or culpable errors
- Errors due to forgetfulness
- Errors due to ignorance, lack of knowledge, or inexperience
- Careless errors
- Errors due to negligence
- Errors due to pride and arrogance
- Out of fear and trepidation
- Stubbornness or stubbornness
- Lack of faith

Errors are a natural part of the human experience; they are mistakes and missteps in our actions, concepts, or decisions. All human beings make mistakes at some point in their lives. However, how we react to errors can vary widely. Some of us respond with fear, self-blame, self-rejection, and frustration when we recognize a mistake. Various emotions invade us when we do not recognize a mistake. Instead of recognizing it, we ignore, deny, or hide it.

There is often a lack of general awareness of the seriousness of mistakes; we have lost the ability to evaluate the long-term consequences of our actions. Many people act as if they are perfect and avoid recognizing their mistakes. However, making mistakes is an inevitable and universal reality. Ignoring them is a normal response for those who lack clarity of mind or self-awareness.

Occasionally, we recognize that we have done something wrong and made a mistake, and doing so is the best start to improve. Man is the only rational being who dares to step in the same hole twice and even more; we find it hard to assimilate. Likewise, it is the only way to learn because the only man who never makes a mistake is the one who never does anything and, as a result, has nothing, does nothing, and is nothing.

We cannot eradicate the mistakes and stupidities committed. However, we can evaluate the causes and thus be better prepared to prevent them. Mistakes are part of the very nature of human beings; that is to say, there is no mistake that is not human, and there is no human being who does not make mistakes. They are life teachers that teach us what not to say or do. They teach us that somebody can transform difficult times into opportunities; they teach us how and when to do things. The worst thing about making a mistake is to justify it without a valid reason. Instead, it should be used as a sign to improve things.

By making mistakes and errors, we fall into an existential abyss. We can go to psychological therapies, seminars, and workshops, but we only do something *if we rectify it from the heart*. Consequently, we repeat cycle after cycle and then cycle after cycle, going round and round in the same abyss without being able to get out. We are conscious *when we recognize this mistake, and all apologize, but we repeat the same mistake and keep apologizing*.

We apologize for continuing to make the same mistake; in *the worst case, we add more mistakes*. These reactions are what we call regrets, so we continue because *we are part of humanity, following the same repetitive cycle of errors*. All these actions result in intense, adverse, and excruciating emotions. We need to wake up!

Therefore, whoever makes a mistake and does not correct it is making two since it is better to admit a mistake than to fix it with stupidity. We make mistakes by nature; the bad thing would not be to make them, nor should we see all mistakes as foolishness, blaming ourselves. If you do nothing for fear of making a mistake, you are closing the door to the opportunity to learn how it is done.

For this reason, if you want to see something extraordinary in your life, you must first recognize its smallness by appreciating the occasion. To waste time is to lose the most valuable thing in life because opportunities only pass through our lives once. Even many goals will remain outside, navigating in the spiral of doubt. This is because you discover an unknown truth whenever you make a mistake. As human beings, we make mistakes and will continue to make them.

This is because all attempts have risks. These become more dangerous they are. Moreover, no matter the time or the size, every mistake made is always saddening, but let's keep in mind that failures are not forever. Life offers us different opportunities to continue growing as people. Many find these opportunities in our mistakes, thanks to the fact that they have discovered another way of doing things.

In educating children, we make mistakes; some do it with the preconceived idea that later they will receive a reward from them, for example, that they will help them to live better economically and give them better care for the effort for having given them education, etc. We must keep in mind that the purpose of providing education and improvement is for the children to be free in thought, choice, and deed and not to fulfill the whims of their parents. Now, if the children, out of responsibility and love, help care for their parents in adulthood, they will be blessed.

About people who change partners frequently. They may have two, three, or more partners in ten years. Undoubtedly, something is wrong with them and with their partners. This is because we are unaware of the accumulation of mistakes in their lives. Some live mindlessly with pride and arrogance, the leading food of failure, frustration, and loneliness.

They are unaware of their emotional wounds and do not find the dimension of their existence or the maximum motivation for achieving their goals. To achieve this, you must first do one of the most challenging tasks of a human being. That is to study himself and accurately recognize in the heart and conscience, asking himself several questions:

- Who am I?
- What am I doing here?
- What is the purpose of my existence?

Nobody likes to be reminded of the amount of mental garbage they have accumulated. Since we want to believe that we are right, it is more that nobody is correct and that the only ones who are right are us—a big mistake to commit to other bigger ones. We must make a truthful and sincere mental scan of our conscience, beliefs, words, and actions.

For this reason, we must learn to be patient. For example, if a grain of wheat does not sprout in one day, do not expect the sun to rise at midnight. Every matter has its time and its way. Patience is the art of knowing, and he who knows how to wait understands that frustration and pain disappear when the lesson is learned.

It is simple to live life, but as human beings, we like to complicate it; we are specialists in looking for problems, frustrations, and conflicts. However, the biggest and most serious mistake we can make is to face an error with a *negative attitude*. What can we say about an even bigger mistake when another person qualifies for the failures? The passion of knowing how to live is admitting errors; if you have never failed, you have not lived with intensity. Now, I invite you to analyze the following.

All successful people have always made mistakes that they turned into opportunities by trying many times. For example, they did not allow others to manipulate their emotions and goals.

Walter Disney, the creator of Walt Disney Park, worked in a newspaper, and the director fired him for "lack of ideas, creativity, and imagination." He even declared bankruptcy five times before creating the world's largest and most famous recreation park.

Alexander Fleming discovered penicillin by mistake. He left one of the flasks in his laboratory open for a few days, and a mold invaded it, which Fleming discovered could kill bacteria. He researched and created penicillin, an antibiotic that has saved millions of people.

Michael Jordan said, "I've missed over 9,000 shots in my career, I've missed almost 300 games, 26 times I've been trusted to take the game-winning shot, and I've missed it. I've failed repeatedly in my life, and that's why I'm successful." If Michael Jordan had been graded on his mistakes, he would never have been what he is.

Change for the sake of change is the same as crying for crying's sake; you won't achieve much with that. Do not venture to be a dream sewer if you do not harvest. Do you know what your path is? Or walk for the sake of walking? I urge you to define your path clearly, list your mistakes and attempts, and use them to make your idea, work, studies, and project a reality. Have you made mistakes and failed at something?

- Do you recognize these mistakes?
- Have you corrected them?

I recognize that I have failed for the following reasons.

_____

_____

_____

_____

_____

No matter how often I fail, I promise to carry out my project, idea, and work. I will try as many times as necessary, believing in my abilities and God. I am confident that every matter has its time and how, and mine is now! I will not allow pessimism to invade me; the only thing that will not allow me to reach my goal is to do nothing. Every human has time to lose and win; I have decided it is my time to try and achieve my goal, project, and dream now, not later. Opening a new path, I will do everything to get out of stagnation, and I will start with

_____

_____

_____

_____

_____

Your luck depends on the circumstances you are creating at this moment. Human beings can generate bad or good luck by avoiding mistakes. We must be prepared and intelligent enough to recognize luck. Technically, you are lucky, but if you do not have the preparation to recognize and receive it, you have nothing; remember that **"*coincidences do not exist.*"**

Everything happens for a reason, and you should also remember that whoever lacks God lacks everything, and whoever has God lacks nothing. Where there is faith, there is love; where there is love, there is peace; and where there is peace, there God is, and where God is, there is happiness.

"And I say unto you, Ask, and it shall be given you; seek, and ye shall find; knock, and it shall be opened unto you. For everyone who asks receives, and he who seeks finds, and to him who knocks it will be opened." (Luke 11:[9-10]).

THE CIRCLE OF DECEITS AND THE LIES

Let's travel back in time and compare our experiences with the present. Along this path, we'll uncover the lies and deceit hidden behind various masks. These falsehoods seep into every aspect of our lives, from personal relationships to business, education, work, and faith. But amidst this web of deceit, one thing remains clear—the value of truth in our relationships. It's the foundation of honesty and trust and what we should strive for in all our interactions.

Some call it a trap, others disguise it as a "strategy," and some minimize it as a simple "mistake." However, the reality is that whoever seeks to deceive lies, and whoever lies deceives. The lie's intention to deceive is inherent, as it opposes the veracity of the facts.

If the lie, like the truth, had a unique face, life would be simpler, as we could easily discern the truth from the false. Unfortunately, the lie has countless faces and an unlimited field of action. Living with deceitful and treacherous people is like living on a constant battlefield, where telling the truth becomes a revolutionary act of great value.

The most dangerous lie is the one we tell ourselves. Adjusting the lie to our convenience increases the likelihood of falling into our deception. However, by recognizing and confronting lies, we can experience personal growth and empowerment as we take control of our lives and relationships.

I observed the contrast between bright and dark, peace and war, security and doubt, straightforward and complex, and black and white. In the same way, there is a contrast between being faithful and inaccurate between truth and deceit. The most severe types of lies are slander and gossip. The stakes are high because an innocent person is a cause of a fault; he did not commit to the malicious advantage of another.

This causes problems, fights, divisions, frustration, hatred, and, in extreme cases, even death can occur. Deception originates in the malice of the heart, where some men engage in actions to harm their home and be unhappy. We do not accept that the pleasures that fill the senses with betrayal and lies only manufacture tons of anguish reflected in reality.

Those who live deceived in the lives of business, sex, and pleasures squander their fortune, lose their pride, and erode their faith. Over time, the habit of deceiving can make us insensitive to the voice of our conscience. The result is loneliness and confusion, where one finds oneself sick and trapped in an environment of deceit, shame, and desolation. On the other hand, embracing honesty is not just a moral choice but a path to personal well-being and ethical living.

Just as trees produce fruits according to their nature, we, too, must strive to bear good fruit in the fertile land where the Creator planted us. Lies foster distrust, doubt, and disbelief and undermine the trust placed in us. Those who lie often try to cover up their faults with more lies, creating a vicious cycle that only perpetuates vain defects. The easiest way to deceive oneself is to believe that others are idiots, feeling more intelligent than anyone else. But we have the power to choose honesty to break this cycle and cultivate trust and respect.

When a liar is discovered, they often adopt the position of a victim or become enraged, seeking escape routes. Arguing with someone who clings to their lies can be exhausting, a draining battle that often leads nowhere. The truth is preferable, even if it doesn't always bring a smile to a smile deceived by falsehoods. A liar lacks shine and light, like a dull sun or a lamp without a wick. The word of slanderer has no value, like tasteless salt or an extinguished lamp. The bad reputation sown by lies brings distrust, shame, contempt, and loneliness.

The quality of a liar's life will never exceed the quantity of their fakes. Know yourself and ask about your past, where they originate, and why they exist. Be honest with yourself, change your thoughts, and you will change your life.

Practice honesty, and you will notice that not being around certain people is not painful but healthy. Life is easier when we move away from lying, aggressive, and hostile people. Do not forget that whoever cultivates deceit and lies creates evil and misfortune; you will only reap unhappiness, bitterness, and loneliness.

The habit of lying becomes a lifestyle that wraps you in a false package, always giving the appearance of what you are not and what you do not feel. Deceiving is an act that slowly alienates you from others, God, and your purpose in life. If you want to know how closed your reasoning is, it is not difficult to understand; observe how harshly you judge others. Some people think they can get away with lying; they invent a thousand excuses and swear even for their loved ones. With this attitude, they could save something of their present, but they condemn their future, and the most severe thing is that they cannot return to repair. This is because he who sows lies loses opportunities.

"You can fool everybody some of the time. You can fool some of them, all the time. But you can't fool everybody all the time." (Abraham Lincoln).

- How many times has he deceived and lied?

- Have you ever thought about changing that attitude?
- Do you know how to rectify and repair the damage caused?

I invite you to analyze the habit of lying by writing it down so you can find the reasons and motives. This way, you can see the necessary tools to stop this habit. Remember that only those who admit they are sick can have a cure.

I lie and cheat for the following reasons.

_____

_____

_____

The following people have also misled me.

_____,

by_____

_____,

by_____

_____,

by_____

_____,

by_____

Suppose you want to change your habit of lying and cheating sincerely. I recommend the following seven steps to commit yourself.

1. I promise not to accept disorientation or lies anymore.
2. I admit that I have wounds to heal
3. I admit that I need help to overcome my shortcomings and move forward.

4. I admit that deceit and lies have only brought me problems, insecurity, and hostility.
5. I promise to learn where prudence, faith, strength, and intelligence are, eliminating pain from my life.
6. I promise that I will not invent with my mouth what I do not see with my eyes.
7. I promise that today, I will be reborn and be a new me, full of strength to fight and move forward. I will leave confusion behind, trusting more in God and myself, leaving behind everything that harms me.

Many people are not loyal and are only dedicated to what they need from you; once their need is satisfied, they also change their loyalty. If you are one of those people, you should know that your attitude affects you and others. You should also know that you can't fix it by yourself. You will need help from your parents, family, or a professional.

If you have faith, you can turn to God; if you have not been able to do much on your part, now you can heal. God's love is like many things. It is as big as the ocean, and we do not know where it begins and where it ends, but we know that it is always there. You can go to retreats, workshops, and seminars with the confidence that you can heal your inner self.

To kick the habit of cheating and lying, I will start by.

_____

_____

_____

_____

_____

_____

_____

_____

I am willing to make the following changes

_____

_____

_____

_____

Remember that you are responsible for what happens to you and what may happen to you. Therefore, take your destiny in your hands, fall in love with a project or a life plan, and honestly bring it to reality. Live in the fact that you exist; it is accurate that life has much to give you. Be passionate about the truth, what is just, moral, and ethical, and why not fall in love with God because He has already fallen in love with you.

"With a lie, he usually goes far away, but with no hope of returning." (*Jewish proverb*).

THE CIRCLE OF EMOTIONS

At a seminar, two old friends, Aldo and Laura, who hadn't seen each other in a long time, finally crossed paths. Aldo, a 45 years old man, was apprehensive about his daughter Ariana's upcoming surgery. Laura, a kind and empathetic woman, was Aldo's companion at the seminar. After a brief greeting, they began to talk.

Aldo (looking severe and concerned): *"Laura, how have you been? It's been a while since we last met."*

Laura (smiling warmly): *"Hi Aldo, it's great to see you! But what's going on? You seem troubled."*

Aldo (sighing deeply): *"Honestly, I'm overwhelmed. In two days, Ariana will undergo knee surgery, and I can't help but feel uneasy."*

Laura (understanding his concern): *"I completely understand, Aldo. It's only natural to feel this way when your daughter is about to go through something so significant. Anxiety is a normal reaction."*

Aldo (nodding): *"Yes, you're right. But I had a similar surgery six years ago, and I still deal with the aftereffects. That brings up all sorts of fears."*

Laura (looking at Aldo with compassion): *"It makes sense that those memories would cause you some anxiety. But remember, every case is different, and medical advances have come a long way since your surgery."*

Aldo (with a hint of resignation): *"I know you're right, Laura. But it's hard not to be afraid when it's your own child's health on the line."*

Laura (gently taking his hand): *"Aldo, let me share something I learned today in class."*

Aldo (intrigued): *"What did you learn?"*

Laura (smiling enthusiastically): *"We talked about the 'circle of emotions,' a tool to help manage our feelings more effectively."*

Aldo (raising an eyebrow with curiosity): *"Circle of emotions? How does that work?"*

Laura (explaining in detail): *"The idea is that when we're overwhelmed by a negative emotion like fear or sadness, we can counter it with a positive action that brings about an opposing emotion."*

Aldo (reflecting on this): *"That sounds interesting. What kind of actions are recommended?"*

Laura smiled and explained:

"If I feel depressed, I'll sing.

If sadness creeps in, I'll laugh.

If I feel tired, I'll work a bit more.

If I'm scared, I'll take one more step forward.

If I run out of money, I'll think of abundance.

If I feel insignificant, I'll revisit my goals.

And if I succeed and feel overly important, I'll look at a cemetery."

Aldo (curious): *"And what's the purpose of all that?"*

Laura (smiling): *"To remind myself that destiny and faith require a good dose of humility and trust in God, which helps improve my emotions."*

*"And if ever in doubt," she added, *"ask God for guidance."*

Aldo: *"I'll keep that in mind, Laura. You're a great friend."*

Our lives have no meaning or purpose without emotions, and our emotional history begins before birth. Emotions establish the nuances of experience and give vitality to our existence. All the feelings received from our mother's womb are engraved in our unconscious.

We continue to grow, learn, and develop our presence, and together, we form our emotional system with all we have lived and learned. Looking at our planet from another perspective, it seems like a laboratory of emotions. This has happened for thousands or millions of years, and we still need to find the formula well. However, emotions, whether good or bad, are a fundamental part of our existence.

Humans, with our innate intelligence, creativity, and transformative potential, are capable of significant change. However, this complexity can sometimes lead to a loss of emotional control, triggering unnecessary existential crises. Impatience, impulsivity, harmful behaviors, shortsightedness, and destructive potential are all examples of how uncontrolled emotions can negatively impact our lives.

The dire consequences of poor emotion management, such as conflicts, wars, and environmental destruction, underscore the urgent need for better emotional regulation.

From the moment we enter the world to our journey through childhood and beyond, we experience many emotions that define our humanity. However, a traumatic event often shatters our idyllic view of the world. Before such an event, we may believe in justice, the inherent meaning of things, and the goodness of God.

But after a deep emotional wound, this optimistic vision can crack. We may feel we've lost control over our lives and the world and even feel betrayed by God. Vulnerability, disappointment, anger, depression, and resentment can then take over, completely reshaping our worldview.

The impact of accumulated pain is profound. The sum of all the painful experiences we collect throughout our lives can create internal conflict. This accumulation gives rise to a hidden pain composed of trauma, incomprehension, fear, hatred, complexes, and stress, which can lead to confusion and illness. However, this pain also presents an opportunity for growth. It allows us to experience the various anxieties and stages of emotional pain firsthand, and in doing so, it can clarify our relationship with ourselves and others, leading to personal growth and understanding.

Humans' natural responses to certain emotions depend on specific circumstances. They arise and are controlled according to the situation, knowledge, lifestyle, and people around us. Emotions are immediate responses of our interior to the actions and facts of the exterior, making us react to our thoughts, attitudes, and countenance according to what we receive.

Human beings express emotions, generating various states depending on the situation. These can include joy, optimism, sadness, will-go, fear, disgust, confusion, empathic pain, horror, anxiety, envy, and insecurities. Emotions also imprison our soul and understanding without us realizing it. Consequently, they slowly destroy our lives, minds, faith, and confidence, blocking our full potential.

Note. The number of emotions, which most of us believe to be six: happiness, sadness, will go, surprise, fear, and disgust, has changed. The newspaper (Berkeley News) of the University of California in the USA, in its publication of September 6, 2017, published research conducted by the same university that identified 27 different categories of human emotions.

Distorted Instincts: In the whirlwind of modern life, our survival instincts have become skewed. We prioritize instant gratification, such as indulging in unhealthy habits or making impulsive decisions, disregarding long-term consequences like health issues or financial instability. In doing so, we lose the ability to recognize the weight of our words and actions. This emotional shortsightedness turns us into desensitized beings, unable to distinguish between right and wrong.

While the heart plays a crucial role in shaping our emotional experiences, the brain processes them and translates them into actions. Unfortunately, harmful and toxic emotions often dominate our behavior. They cloud our judgment, driving us to act in destructive ways, usually hurting those we love most.

The deep emotional scars we carry—born from experiences like abuse, abandonment, aggression, disappointment, and injustice— pull us into a spiral of doubt, insecurity, and uncertainty. Fear, anxiety, disillusionment, terror, anger, and resentment become our constant companions, drastically and unpredictably affecting our mood.

The Emotional Rollercoaster: Our emotions are like a wild ride, swinging between peaks of joy and valleys of despair. Our moods rise and fall, drifting aimlessly like a feather in the wind, lacking control and direction. This unpredictability can leave us feeling unsettled and in need of stability. Anxiety grips our hearts, blurring our perspective and generating deep distress, which often brings to the surface hidden desires lurking within us.

It's a stark reality that toxic emotions don't just harm us on an individual level—they have a broader negative impact on society. Confusion, violence, arrogance, deceit, and lack of authenticity are consequences we see in our surroundings. Speaking the truth has become an act of courage, as it risks alienating friends and relationships. Hypocrisy and superficiality prevail, while authenticity and honesty become ever rarer values.

Do not allow negative and badly channeled emotions to imprison your logic and reasoning, nor fantasy to dull your understanding. The man who acts wisely is more profitable than money and more profitable than gold; nothing can compare to him. In his right hand is a long life. In his left hand, wealth and glory; in his heart, forgiveness and love. He makes his ways a delight because he controls his emotions consciously, transforming them into the advantage of life.

Whoever loses control loses himself and becomes a self-hijacker. Emotional that sometimes is difficult to recover. Because when we offend or do a wrong action, it is difficult to correct it, and, in some way, someone has been hurt. If we do not rectify this, it becomes a lifestyle, generating habits of a hateful and annoying person in what he says and does.

Likewise, we fall into intense emotional states that cause us to lose control. Consequently, we react violently and senselessly, resulting in disastrous results. We do not measure the long-term consequences of our actions and words. We cause irreversible spiritual, mental, and physical damage, affecting our health, inner peace, and the way we perceive and live life.

The internet and social media are invading our privacy daily thanks to new platforms and services. They make us live in a society that analyzes and judges our every word and action, although it seems increasingly permissive and liberal. However, they study and judge our every word and deed.

It is okay to be competitive, but the struggle to be the most popular makes us do stupid things. They also limit our way of being and acting and force us to appear to be what we are not. As a result, we change how we think and do things in life. As a result, confusion and desolation remain in our emotional life, losing control of ourselves.

We seek something with eagerness and genuine desire, and after much wandering and searching, I have found it: it is called *"calm,"* which brings *"peace."* It took me many storms to obtain it. Thank you for understanding that I should not expect others to understand my path. I learned to make demands on myself without expecting someone else to do it for me because, in the end, I am not a product of what others say about me but of my vision and my own decisions. So, think about what hurts you today, whether physical or emotional, and ask yourself the following questions.

- What are the ingredients that compose it?
- How can I overcome it differently and effectively?

Human beings have personal plans and dreams. So, to analyze and make the right decisions, we must first learn to know and master the emotions that block and limit us. It is an invitation to reflect on the ignorance, selfishness, and pride that confuse us, on the arrogance that invades us. To learn that sometimes, to truly love means to break with everything that blurs and blocks us. We must understand that sometimes the best becomes the enemy of the good due to our misunderstanding of the purpose of our existence and our ignorance of our mission on this planet.

If you are a person who easily loses control of emotions, I invite you to write down the causes. Use a separate piece of paper if necessary. I easily lose control when.

_____

_____

_____

_____

_____

_____

I get furious when.

_____

_____

_____

_____

_____

I get very depressed. Why?

_____

_____

_____

_____

_____

I feel fear when.

_____

_____

_____

I sense insecurity because.

_____

_____

_____

_____

It is impossible to list all our emotions in a few lines, but we know what to do and how to start. Attending workshops, seminars, and retreats for emotional and spiritual healing is advisable. Also, read books, and if you have faith, get closer to God. Whatever your emotions are, good, toxic, and harmful, you can practice the following.

- Before you judge, examine yourself
- Do not miss big or small things
- Learn to wait; you must have awareness and patience
- I expressed their emotions and feelings
- Think and analyze before you act
- Do not act on impulse alone
- Don't take things too personally

And within his being, he says the following. --- I promise to be more in control of my emotions and actions. --- I will think twice before I act; I will never forget my achievements and virtues. ---

- I will reflect on my future, write down my plans, and remember that emotions are useless in my relationship with God.

---I will not remain in inertia waiting for things to change on their own; it is decisions and actions that make the difference. --- For we are the measure of our results and, to say with strength and faith, "It wasn't easy, but I did it. --- It *was* not ***easy, but I did it***!

"The best things in life are not things; they are moments, emotions, memories [illusions, love, and faith]."

THE CIRCLE OF ENEMIES

We are born without enemies and destined for happiness; this is God's vision for us. Yet, as we go through life, we encounter challenges and barriers that hinder our aspirations. In this vast universe, the existence of hostile enemies is an unavoidable reality: they are tangible, dangerous, and sometimes devastating. The presence of enemies even reminds us that the Creator of the universe Himself faces opposition.

People may hate us simply for being who we are—for being tall or short, thin or robust, attractive or not. We may be rejected for our strengths or our flaws: if we are wise, we are seen as a threat; if we are naive, we are ridiculed. We may be judged for the wealth we possess or the poverty we carry. Ultimately, it doesn't matter what we do or how we are—there will always be those who see us as a discomfort or a nuisance, regardless of our noble intentions, pure hearts, or enlightened minds.

The true friend is not known in prosperity, nor is the enemy hidden in adversity because, in trouble and difficulties, even those who claim to be our best friends abandon us. On the contrary, when we prosper and succeed, our enemies become sad and angry.

However, when we prosper and succeed, the enemies are saddened and gnash their teeth angrily. Failures will hate us if we succeed. And, when we do well, someone will hate us because our brilliance overshadows their losses. For this reason, it is better not to shout too loudly about your achievements because envy is a light sleeper and wakes up quickly. For this reason, we should be as sly, stealthy, and secretive as possible.

They will always talk about you; they will say that you are not what you say you are. That your successes are fleeting, trying to hurt you as much as possible. If they can't be with you, they will do it with your image or one of your loved ones. Never trust an enemy, for his wickedness is like bronze rusting because he has a sore soul, and even if he takes a humble attitude, be wary and careful. Treat him as one who polishes and carries a mirror, nor sit him beside you. Because if you do, he will surely take your place.

Enemies always speak with honeyed lips, but in their hearts, they are digging your grave. Even tears may come out of their eyes with the illusion of seeing you bleed. He will find you in whatever misfortune you have, and when you try to get up, he will trip you up, and you will be hurt. Many of us have enemies because of what we express. Imagine what it would be like if they knew what we think.

For this reason, please do not give the enemy a truce or bring him into your house, for he is cunning and dangerous. Please stay away from him and avoid him as much as possible, lest he hurt you. My advice will be remembered; it is better to prevent it than regret it. We must accept that we are not a **_"taste bone"_** for many and were not born to please everyone.

Beware of who is next to you; liars will always lie, gossipers will always get you into gossip, and those who are resentful are specialists in disuniting others. Those who hate to need to make you hate; those who suffer need to make you suffer; those who are frustrated need to make you see that you will not achieve your goals; those who mock need to make fun of others. Malicious criticisms will never be lacking; someone will always try to annoy us and make our lives bitter, regardless of the reason.

Geniuses and ignorant, millionaires, and the underprivileged alike all have enemies. These enemies could be external forces, such as societal norms, personal challenges, or internal struggles like self-doubt or fear. Even notable figures such as prophets, philosophers, and sages throughout history have had their adversaries. Jesus Christ, not even God the Father, managed to win everyone's favor. In short, human beings, regardless of who they are, face hostility at some point.

However, we all possess the ability, talent, charisma, gifts, and passion to perform meaningful actions. But above all, it's our will that reigns supreme. It's a force that surpasses electrical energy and is more potent than an atomic bomb. This power lies within each of us, waiting to be unleashed.

We must act according to our abilities, moving forward without needing external approval. Ultimately, the only approval that truly matters is the one we give ourselves. This self-approval liberates us from the shackles of seeking validation from others, allowing us to live authentically and express our true feelings without fear of judgment.

"To have enemies, you don't have to declare war; you just have to speak your mind." (_Martin Luther King,_ US civil rights leader).

HIDDEN ENEMIES

We face various battles to preserve our spiritual being on life's journey. Our soul traverses this journey, experiencing suffering, joy, challenges, and skepticism. However, we must contend with the hidden enemies obstructing our path to elevating intelligence, consciousness, and the soul to higher levels.

These enemies darken our perception, cloud our understanding, and fog our minds. They can even deceive our thoughts and influence our hearts in despair when we seek solace in them. The hidden enemies can be divided into two categories: internal and external.

External enemies. These come from outside, are the most evident, and are always part of your closest circle. They are hidden among **friends** and within our **family**. Their attacks and wounds are deadly because they always take us by surprise. They are even worse than declared enemies, as you never know where or why they will attack.

When they attack and insult you to defend yourself, the best thing you can do is assume the attitude of a wall. This means not letting their insults affect you. Just like a wall, you remain unmoved and unaffected by their words. To do this, imagine a wall and ask yourself: What do they gain by insulting a wall that cannot hear anything?

Well, imitate the wall, and you will not hear the insults of your close enemies. That is to say, do not hear, see, or feel; after all, when an insult is not returned, it still belongs to the one who says it. Tolerating those you consider enemies, or aggressive people does not make you false or hypocritical; it shows you possess the maturity and character to cope with such situations. It's not about being passive or weak but about having the strength and wisdom to rise above their negativity.

There is a profound truth in the idea that the only way to avoid having enemies is to do nothing, say nothing, excel at nothing, and disappear as soon as possible. However, this choice can lead to a deeper understanding of our actions and motivations.

Internal enemies. All enemies are dangerous, but these are lethal if not handled cautiously. The main objective of this enemy is not to let you live in peace. It begins by invading your mind and reasoning. It envelops you very subtly with different facets and masks. For instance, it might manifest as self-doubt, fear, or negative self-talk. It makes you believe that it is necessary. It harasses and corners you. Its purpose is to destroy you miserably.

You may wonder what your internal enemies are. They are the ones you do not consider as such. They are quiet and subtle. They envelop you slowly and slowly. Their names are ***"the self-destructive past"*** with bad memories. We also have grudges, hatred, resentments, deceit, lies, greed, arrogance, lack of forgiveness, vanity, and an uncontrolled mouth. These destroy your values and morals, hurting your thinking and perception of life.

We have already met the enemies within. Now, we can visit the ***hidden anteroom of human horror***. The place where the real and the unreal, logic and illogic are confused. A site where reasoning and conscience are numbed. Where a partner, family, and even children are lost, and it is in ***the spiral of vices***. We have created their emotional wounds, weak character, and lack of self-love. Sadly, almost every human has vices and habits that affect our minds, souls, and lives. It is something that can subtly and slowly destroy us. However, we continue to tempt our benefit without resisting self-destruction, and, in the end, we cannot resist it. What a pity, *how hurt we are!*

These enemies plan their ruin very subtly. It starts with the mask of fulfilling a need or a self-reward or gratification, which is how they begin *the gambler, the alcoholic, and the drug addict* with *sex* and *food*. They make us want to acquire things to the point of bowing down to the superficial happiness of materialism. It distracts us by completing our eyes desire more and more things. It can also come as a consolation when it begins its nefarious habit, affecting the work, the dignity, the family, the economy, and finally, it ends up with nothing. His enemy imprisons his soul, plunges him into misery with a disease, possibly abandoned in the street or hospital waiting to give him his end.

The same happens with drugs; it starts as a curiosity or a need to release tension, problems, and stress, then becomes a habit. Very subtly, it slowly and softly involves them, leading them to economic and mental misery, destroying their identity and family, and miserably destroying his physique and ending his life. This is your *enemy's ultimate purpose*, which is to unhealed emotional and inner wounds. That is to say, the enemy is yourself, your way of seeing and perceiving life due to a lack of awareness, forgiveness, love, and understanding.

Just look and analyze the streets, hospitals, prisons, and places of recovery; the only thing you can perceive and see is *human misery*. In that circle, the foremost being that can help you and get you out of there is the one you have forgotten and even ignored: the eternal God. Now that you know your inner enemy and his mode of operation, when he appears and attacks, you know what to do; you can ask for help or let yourself be seduced; *it's your choice*!

- Do you already know who your enemies are?
- Do you think they are stronger than you?
- How would you defeat your internal enemies?
- Do you know how to prepare for them?

I invite you to describe your internal and external enemies. My internal enemies are.

_____

_____

_____

_____

My external enemies are.

_____

_____

_____

_____

The way I'm going to beat them is.

_____

_____

_____

_____

How to Quit an Addiction. Overcoming addiction is a complex process that requires both determination and professional guidance. While developing an addiction can be relatively quick, breaking free from its grip is a challenging and often lengthy endeavor. With its intricate neural pathways, the brain can struggle to recognize and respond to self-imposed limitations, blurring the lines between reality and fantasy. Before embarking on a recovery journey, assessing your readiness to quit is crucial. According to the National Institute on Drug Abuse (NIH), effective addiction treatment often involves a combination of strategies, including:

- **Be honest** with yourself.
- **Professional Help:** Seeking guidance from a qualified healthcare provider or addiction specialist is essential for developing a personalized treatment plan.
- **Therapy and Counseling:** Cognitive-behavioral therapy (CBT) and other therapeutic approaches can help individuals identify triggers, develop coping mechanisms, and address underlying emotional issues.
- **Medication-Assisted Treatment (MAT):** In some cases, medications can aid in withdrawal symptoms and reduce cravings.
- **Support Groups:** Connecting with others who have experienced addiction can provide valuable support and encouragement.
- **Healthy Lifestyle Changes:** Healthy habits, such as regular exercise, a balanced diet, and sufficient sleep, can contribute to overall well-being and reduce the risk of relapse.

If a habit is the starting point of an addiction, the challenge is to break it in the same way: ***as a habit.*** If this addiction began because you believed you needed it, and your mind reinforced that belief until it became routine, you can now apply that same technique in your journey to freedom.

Train your brain: tell yourself repeatedly that you don't need it, that you were born whole, free from this dependency, and turn that affirmation into a new mental habit. ***Explain clearly to your***

brain the harmful consequences of holding onto this habit. Gradually, you'll notice the need fading until it disappears completely. Remember, the power of transformation lies within your mind.

Additionally, enriching your process through reading books on healing and personal growth and cultivating an active spiritual life can be tremendously supportive. Turning to God and prayer with genuine faith strengthens your willpower and renews your awareness. My book, *Emotional and Inner Healing Workshop*, can be valuable for inner healing and spiritual freedom. Remember, faith, willpower, understanding and acceptation work together to help you overcome addiction and reclaim your life.

"He who lives among delights and vices must later spy them with humiliation and misery." (Friedrich Schiller, *German Poet and Playwright).*

THE CIRCLE OF ENVY

Envy is a devastating emotional evil for human beings; it is an affliction that blinds a person little by little. It is to feel sadness, anger, discomfort, or pain for the triumph of others. It arises in the personal and social context and is related to the lack of acceptance. And, if you are doing poorly, you want someone else to do the same or worse, ! *How ugly it is to feel that way*!

Unfortunately, envy in human beings is more frequent than commonly believed; it is a negative feeling, a toxic and destructive emotion. It is frustration and anger for what others have achieved. It also brings other plagues, such as hatred, greed, frustration, criticism, rejection, slander, revenge, and the special guest, violence, and even death can make its appearance. The first case of envy in the bible is when Cain killed his brother Abel.

Likewise, the case of Joseph and his brothers shows that envy is also in the family.

The negative attitude of envy awakens the dark side of the person who feels it. They may not recognize it because it presents itself in two ways: unconsciously and consciously. It is a secret emotion because opening entirely from the heart is impossible. He can feel joy for the success of others. Still, he compares himself with their life, feeling inferior or superior.

That is to say, the one who feels envy carries a two-edged knife because the truth makes it look like a lie, and the lie makes it look like the truth. This resentment occurs in people of the same sex and profession or trade; for example, a doctor will not envy a butcher, and a footballer will not be jealous of a writer. The popular term "*healthy envy*" is a mask to make oneself and others look good. In fact, this rivalry exists in people who do not accept the happiness and success of others, for example.

- Feel anger, rage, or frustration, creating a general discomfort with the success of others.
- When someone else does poorly, you feel satisfaction because you are not the only person who has failed.
- Fear of feeling lesser than others
- You block someone else's joy and blessings by arranging other events or situations to overshadow others.
- Disqualifies, criticizes, and gossips about another person's accomplishments or goals achieved
- Falsely praising
- Minimizes the achievements of others

Envy is a harmful sentiment that can corrupt the soul and conscience of anyone who experiences it. This feeling can lead to various illnesses, and those who feel and live it often do nothing more than try to dim the success and image of other people. For no apparent reason, they actively seek ways to harm others without imagining the curse they place upon themselves. Whoever returns evil for envy will never be free from evil in their life and home.

The key to freeing oneself from the shackles of envy lies in redirecting attention and energy toward personal growth. It is essential to let go of the obsession with the lives of others and, instead, focus on overcoming one's weaknesses and pursuing life's goals. By changing one's focus and attitude, one can experience a profound transformation in how one perceives others, bringing hope and optimism into one's life.

Envy is a mental deficiency, a sign of ignorance and error. Remember that whoever does not cling to anything possesses everything. Envy is exploited for the benefit of companies and large corporations, generating all kinds of competition. For instance, in the marketing world, companies often use envy to create a desire for their products by showcasing the possessions or lifestyles of others. For example:

- Sexual envy is the fuel of morbid curiosity and pornography.
- Beauty envy fuels the beauty and fashion business
- Economic envy is shown in the consumerist frenzy in our society.

They manipulate us, and we allow ourselves to be controlled without realizing it. If someone wishes you evil out of envy, you can expect them to be good because each person offers what he has in his heart.

When you know others are successful or doing well, I invite you to analyze your reactions and emotions.

_____

_____

_____

_____

Analice, why or what are you envious of? What triggers that feeling in you?

_____

_____

_____

_____

To avoid that feeling and emotion, I will go to

Ask yourself what that person has done to get what you want but has been unable to do. Now, carefully analyze the following questions.

- Have you already put yourself in their shoes?
- Have you already traveled your way?
- *Do you think you can have the same and achieve a better goal?*

In other words, you should put yourself in the other's place, see how you would feel if they did the same to you, and see if that pleases you. This is what every envious person lacks; suddenly, they become aware and look for a solution as inner healing.

«*Envy is like a poison that we drink, hoping the other person will die.* »

CONSEQUENCES OF ENVY ON HEALTH

People who suffer from envy usually have low self-esteem and fear of feeling inferior. This, in turn, causes loneliness, as they cannot share their experiences with the rest of the world. None of the emotional symptoms of envy we described above bring anything positive. None of them contribute anything constructive. They prevent them from growing and advancing, putting them in a hole of emotional and personal stagnation, clouding even their common sense. However, these are not the only consequences of envy. That is, its effects also end up triggering various ailments and physical conditions such as.

- The most frequent sign is stomach pain, which could quickly become a stomach ulcer.
- Envy causes the immune system to weaken, which can lead to infections such as respiratory tract infections.
- Constant thoughts of envy lead to constipation, appetite or sleep disorders, and even chronic fatigue.
- The resulting stress prompts the body to produce more cortisol and adrenaline.
- In a study, the University of Helsinki linked envy to bruxism, "the unconscious habit of clenching or grinding the teeth," which causes dental damage.
- Other consequences of the frustration caused by envy are headaches, fatigue, tremors, dizziness, poor circulation, and the inability to concentrate.

With your current information, you can make a life plan, knowing that every goal requires discipline, work, risk, dedication, and effort. In other words, if you are stuck, it is because you want to be that is your choice because you decide not to do anything. Possibly, you are in your comfort zone, waiting to benefit from the efforts of others. You must learn to trust yourself and God if you want to change and improve. Seek professional help (*therapies, workshops, retreats, conferences*). Talk to your spiritual leader, and get closer to God, who will help you heal the wounds, strengthening your soul, spirit, thoughts, and mind.

If you are envious, it is because you have no faith and feel no love for yourself or others. You must learn not to compare yourself with anyone and to feel gratitude for what you have. Learn to live with what you do not have and discover the reason since only those destined for God's great purposes pass through the desert. Learn to know yourself and ask the creator to strengthen your heart to know him. To avoid feeling envious, I will do the following:

_____

_____

_____

_____

_____

I will stop competing out of envy and start.

_____

_____

_____

_____

_____

"Envy numbs the mind, corners the spirit, and rots the reasoning. Therefore, wisdom overcomes it as light overcomes darkness."

THE CIRCLE OF FAILURE AND NEGATIVITY

Failures, undeniable teachers because very few get it right without making mistakes first, is when life teaches, and few learn. If we do not fail, we lose the opportunity to know how to do well. A failure is a bad achievement, an adverse result, or a pitiful fact resulting from a project or an action a person did or was doing. The number of people who fail is more significant than those who succeed. Not all failures, however, are assumed in different ways. The leading causes of most failures are due to one or more of the following reasons.

- Lack of aspiration
- Lack of a life plan
- Lack of self-discipline
- Procrastination
- Lack of persistence
- Lack of self-belief

Understanding the consequences of failure is crucial. It often occurs when what was attempted did not achieve the expected results, did not fulfill its purpose, or did not reach its goal. Another common cause of failure is the influence of negative people whose advice or comments are followed without question. These situations are not limited to projects but can also apply to personal relationships, such as marriages, relationships with children, or friendships. You can avoid these causes and pave your path to success by understanding them.

Excessive ambition, greed, pride, and selfishness often lead to short-term or long-term failure. Some achieve their goals with effort and perseverance, while others, unfortunately, never succeed. Understanding that the path to success is rarely easy or quick is essential. The more challenging the path, the more rewarding the reward, ultimately improving the quality of life. By 'quality of life ', we mean not just material wealth but also mental peace, emotional stability, and a sense of fulfillment. If you are a person who constantly complains, complains, and asks themselves questions such as:

- Why is this happening to me?
- Why does everything go wrong for me?

If you act this way, it is already wrong, and *self-pity* and *self-blame* lead to *self-sabotage* and *self-abuse*. The victim syndrome will not allow you to move forward. You cannot find inner peace, enjoy life, or be happy about escaping failure and negativity. The reason is that you like to live with it, thanks to the fact that you always mention loss, which is where you live. His life purpose is stagnant, and he has a negative mental attitude and lacks faith. They prove that people who do not advance or achieve success in their lives is because they are trapped in negative thoughts that do not let them grow. It's lucky for us that we can demonstrate that we can change and modify our thoughts. Thanks to the fact that the brain has the elasticity to reinvent itself.

We must evaluate who is next to us because many failures do not want us to succeed. They will use it as a pretext to show that they are not the only ones who fail. One of the disadvantages of arguing with a failure is that it will bring you down to their level, and you could beat them by experience. When you do not fit in where you are, and they look at you as an outsider, look for another place more conducive to your plans.

We don't all fail or cry similarly because we are different. For you, something is a failure; for other people, it is a minor obstacle. Some triumphs show defeats and smiles that hide tears. You should know that failure is also an opportunity to start over with more intelligence, patience, and knowledge than before. We are formed from those mistakes because they leave teachings and life lessons.

Leveraging Failures. Every achiever has been a beginner, and every master started as an apprentice. It can be said that he has not failed but that he did things differently. We must know how to handle frustration (which confuses reason) and eliminate pride and arrogance (which bring misfortune). We must also be optimistic, love ourselves more, and have confidence in God.

We need to learn to love our neighbor and be aware that loving and serving others is better than doing oneself, thanks to this, transcending joy and sadness. One of the causes of failure is performing poorly and helping others. We must assimilate that rivers do not drink water, trees do not eat fruit, the sun does not shine, and flowers do not spread their fragrance for themselves. True triumph will come when we know how to live with and for others.

Sometimes, it is easier to deny reality than to accept and face it. No human power can change a second of the past, so *learn to admit your mistakes*. Failure is a lesson, not a destiny; know how to eliminate the negative, your wounded ego, and *most importantly, do not try to deny or make up reality*. You must investigate your history instead of running away from it. Blaming others does not solve anything; instead, you must travel to the source of failures instead of living, hiding, and regretting them so that you will find the origins and their causes. Analyze well, and you will realize that now, you have more knowledge and awareness about failure. That is, you are now ready to try again with knowledge.

Failure can be emotionally draining, so you must change your mindset. Our brain is the beginning of everything we are. Getting out of self-blame and feelings of failure is not easy, but it is also not impossible. You should keep in mind that a boxer will never become a champion if they don't take a few punches to get to success.

Don't cloud your mind with failures through self-denial and self-blame. Strengthen your plans by eliminating the fear of failure. Start by dreaming big, asking for help, and being resourceful. You have gifts and God with you. Have confidence, and you will discover that when your dreams are born from the heart and faith, no obstacle or fear can stop you. More importantly, don't contradict yourself; be consistent with your actions.

We sometimes get what we want. Right now, you are not what you want to be but what you are. But with your intuition, courage, and faith, you can keep your mind focused on your purpose. Discipline, intelligence, and knowing how to work are evolving, an internal and perpetual transmutation to live purposefully.

It is a universal and continuous law. If you want to overcome failure and become successful, you must have an ideal and be sure of what you want.

That is, you must have and follow your ideals of what you want to be shortly. Likewise, it would help to improve your self-image, which is how you see yourself and think of yourself. It is your internal mirror of how you perceive yourself. To have the desired success, you must see yourself as a winner.

Make a list of the failures and what you think may have been the origin and cause of these failures.

_____

_____

_____

_____

_____

Now, write down how to prevent them from starting over.

_____

_____

_____

_____

_____

Some people take everything personally and become police officers, jailers, accusers, judges, and executioners. This is due to the tendency to highlight only the negative and the failures of others; why? Because they are also failures and negatives, they are the so-called *"black holes"* that do not allow progress. Who are they, where are they?

They are close to you; they surround you and have access to your world and life. It would be best to avoid these people because being close to the wrong people can ruin you. You must let go of attachments even if they hurt because continuing with attachments means remaining in the same zone of stagnation and failure.

I invite you to make a list of the "*black hole*" people in your life that you want to get out of your life

_____

_____

_____

_____

_____

The world is full of people who want to pick fruit from a tree they never sowed. Some people go through life without living, making their lives empty and becoming a nuisance to themselves and others. Some live lost in nothingness, without helping themselves or anyone else.

To this life, we must give value and meaning; plant a tree, and you will feel proud to see it grow. Give importance to your existence; the meaning of life is in life itself. The negative and the rigged *who live in their comfort zone* do not like dedication, sacrifice, or working with intelligence. They want everything easy, fast, and effortless. This is why most of the projects of a "rigged" person fail. They give up quickly and stagnate without realizing that to succeed is to live.

Successful people and great achievers have integrity and unity. They succeed and fulfill their dream because there is no difference between what they think and what they say; they coordinate their emotions, thoughts, and actions well. If you think you can do everything yourself, you are finished and will get nowhere. Please don't pretend to do it all by yourself; we will always need other people's influence, ideas, and help.

No matter how often you try, keep trying with renewed confidence in God and yourself. He will not do things for you but give you the strength, ideas, and abilities to keep going. Remember that bad and difficult days appear in our lives to teach us a lesson. So, man should not be ashamed of his failures and should not be embarrassed to admit that he has made a mistake. In doing so, it corresponds to saying today you have more experience and know more than he knew yesterday.

Living in failure, negativity, and sadness are traces of attitudes of repression and decaying emotional life. Reset your internal chip; the only one who can destroy or reprogram it is you, with your thoughts. You are not afraid of the darkness since you live in it; you fear your brightness since you do not know it.

The best thing you can do is to let yourself be loved by God and act with true faith and positivity. Your will is the mouth of your soul, the engine of your life. A golden rule for success is to help others, a precious gift from God. For this reason, you should strive to awaken, discover, and use the engine that moves your will.

In addition, he already has the most important thing, "knowledge," because he has a broader and more precise vision. The money, the merchandise, and the input can be obtained more efficiently with a loan, savings, or the support of a third party. But no one can lend knowledge, nor is it easy to have it.

Remember that no one has died because you must start again from scratch; remember that you have the strength to reinvent yourself a thousand times. "Act with great patience and gentleness with yourself. Distractions or failures should not bother you, but only in starting over without a second thought." (St. Francis de Sales).

"If you want to start over, don't think you are starting from scratch or the ashes; you are starting with "experience" which is invaluable."

THE CIRCLE OF HAPPINESS

Happiness is an elusive, arid, and complicated subject, and each person has a different concept. It also depends on the experiences, emotions, ideas, education received, beliefs, and the social and cultural environment surrounding us. It is a great mystery that has not yet been revealed with an answer that satisfies everyone because we still have a voracious appetite for happiness.

It seems that the natural state of human beings is sadness. From the moment we are born, we seek to be happy, and some people believe that being happy means not having problems or having a lot of money. Being happy is living with meaning, well-being, and inner peace, a state that frees us from our pessimistic nature, the constant creation of needs, and the habit of complaining about everything. Problems and difficulties are the teachers who give us life lessons to overcome them with wisdom and coherence between what is said and what is done.

We must learn to enjoy life internally. Giving and receiving genuine love and cultivating meaningful relationships are vital to achieving happiness. Pursuing happiness is not a destination but a journey in which everyone finds their path based on their values, experiences, and understanding.

Happiness is subjective and influenced by various reasons, conditions, and circumstances. However, at its core, happiness is intrinsically related to appreciating what one has, the desire to learn, and, most importantly, self-knowledge and knowledge of God. These elements enlighten our path to happiness, inspiring us to live a more fulfilling life.

Valuing oneself as an individual and appreciating others are fundamental steps towards happiness. These simple acts, such as smiling, greeting, and enjoying kindness, open us to an inner world of peace and freedom. The true essence of happiness lies in life itself and in adopting values rather than pursuing material possessions.

The true essence of happiness lies in life itself, not in the relentless pursuit of material possessions. We err in associating happiness with money, pleasure, or power over others. These superficial goals, far from satisfying us, can lead to a profound crisis of mental and spiritual understanding. Genuine happiness is found in being in tune with our inner selves, understanding our values, and pursuing inner peace. This path requires self-knowledge, honesty, and the willingness to navigate the ups and downs of life.

Moreover, we cannot be happy or make any progress in health, love, and the evolution of spiritual consciousness if we do not heal negative and toxic emotions and insist on denying and maintaining them. To be happy, we must first love ourselves. Indeed, how can I love someone if I don't feel love for myself?

How do I progress if I don't let go of the blockages that blind me? For this reason, we must recognize that emotional wounds are an obstacle to life's evolution.

When seeking happiness, it is essential to appropriately address the healing of our internal wounds beyond emotional moments. Healing our inner self is a delicate process that involves learning to forgive and ask for forgiveness, recognizing that we have been hurt and hurt by others, sometimes unintentionally. The key is not to surpass others but to strive each day to be a better version of oneself without hiding reality.

Human beings seek happiness in a multitude of ways. Some find it in the serenity of inner peace, family comfort, or the joy of well-being. Others, in the allure of wealth or the excitement of fleeting pleasures. Some believe they've discovered it in vices like drugs and alcohol or in actions that harm others—such as theft, envy, or destruction. Some even seek happiness through manipulation or deceit, regardless of the toll it takes on others' well-being. In the most extreme cases, the thirst for power or control leads some to the unthinkable act of taking another's life, losing sight of themselves, others, and God. These harmful methods of seeking happiness should give us pause and prompt us to reflect on our own pursuits.

These behaviors are masks used to hide a declining emotional life. Fulfilling the needs of the senses, such as quenching thirst, feeling cold, or satisfying hunger, cannot achieve true happiness. People find true happiness in created needs, such as getting a new car, undergoing surgery, pursuing another career, feeling the urge to dance, traveling, relocating, liking pants, wanting a blouse, needing new shoes, exercising, etc.

Genuine happiness also lies in cultivating authentic relationships and connecting with oneself and God. It is not about satisfying impulsive desires or superficial needs but about finding well-being, lasting inner peace, and a deep meaning in our daily lives.

If you analyze deeply, you will notice that many decisions only bring occasional happiness. They work like a cream, like when you suffer from peeling, and apply it for temporary relief. However, if you enjoy eating, drinking good wine, traveling, and dancing, this satisfies but does not bring happiness. Happiness is a state of being that fills the heart, love, faith, and inner peace and does not require a special place to feel it. Suppose you have time to help the poor and needy. In that case, you may experience an emotional benefit that will bring you closer in the search for elusive happiness.

From now on, dedicate yourself to being as happy as possible because life is borrowed, and you never know when it will be asking for. If you learn to be comfortable being alone, it is good because you can seek happiness by choice, meaning that you have found one of the best ways to achieve it.

Every day has its drama and meaning; we must learn to live them with intensity. Happy people are indeed more grateful, which tells us that ungrateful people are not as happy as they say. Let's analyze the following metaphor to give us a more precise idea of how we look for happiness and what we think about it.

Don Carlos was sitting in his rocking chair when his granddaughter Isabela approached him and asked him the following question.

--- Grandfather, *what does happiness mean to you?* Don Carlos answers.

--- My daughter, everything is an expectation; when you are a child, you believe you will be happy when you leave school.

--- But the first few years pass very quickly, and you find out that you still must graduate from college.

---Tell me something, Isabela, do you think that when you graduate from college, you will be happy?

--- I don't know, Grandpa, but I guess so! Isabella replied.

--- When I married your grandmother, I thought I had found happiness, but it was like raindrops. --- It was partially because later, we planned to buy our own house to be happy and to complement our plans.

--- Later, we planned to have our children; 18 months later, your father was born, and two years later, your aunt Sandra was born.

--- Excellent grandfather, and what happened? Did you find happiness?

--- Yes, partially, because I thought I would be happy when our children were born, but responsibilities make you work hard.

---- Mmmm, Grandpa, and didn't work bring you happiness?

--- No, daughter, there are sometimes satisfactions in work, but not the happiness I expected to find.

--- Then I thought, I will be happy when my children grow up, study, become professionals, and get a good job.

---- And well, my children grew up. They became professionals; your father married your aunt Sandra the following year, and I was getting older.

--- Therefore, I thought I would be happier when I received my retirement.

--- So, Grandpa, what is happiness? How do I find it?

--- Daughter, you spend your time searching and waiting for happiness that never comes. It is like a search that has no end.

--- So, to speak, some people sum up happiness in a wait.

---It is not that I have not been happy, but rather that I stopped being happy in many moments because happiness is a journey, not a destination.

--- So, Grandpa, what should I do to be happy? In your words, should I wait for happiness to come to me?

--- No, my daughter, if you ***want to be happy, listen to and apply the following advice and keep it in your heart!***

---Love as if you had never been hurt and dance as if no one was watching.

--- This life goes fast; don't fight with people, don't criticize, let others live in peace, and learn to enjoy the sunlight.

--- Don't complain too much about what you don't have or can't achieve; learn to enjoy what you have right now.

--- Don't torment yourself with bills; take care of today; tomorrow comes with its own dream and drama.

--- If you have the wrong partner, don't regret it; don't make your life bitter or make someone else bitter; look for another partner who will make you happy.

--- If you have children, remember they will follow your example, not your advice.

--- Never forget your children; always try to be your best and raise them to be happy.

---Do not strive for what you can leave them, for each must earn what he needs.

--- Don't take things and offenses too personally; keep moving on.

--- Don't worry too much about luxuries and comforts; none of that you can take with you when you die.

--- Better travel, enjoy, visit new places, and indulge yourself by eating the food you like the most.

--- Don't keep that delicate perfume too long; wear it like your favorite clothes. The special day is today!

--- Call the person you resent, talk to them, invite them to reconcile, forgive, or ask for forgiveness. Then, you will feel the best of God's goodness.

--- My daughter, life is too short to live angry with someone or, even worse, to live bitter, so it better not get so angry and live more.

--- Grab your cell phone, go on, make that call, and tell that person you have in your head that you want to see her and that an actual kiss is worth a thousand imaginary ones.

--- If something bothers you, say it at that moment and not when you get annoyed so that you can say it with their best words and not with their worst offenses.

--- To be happy is not to have a perfect life but to know that life is worth living despite all the difficulties.

--- To love and bring happiness, you must first love yourself.

--- To be happy is to recognize that life is worth living despite all the challenges, misunderstandings, and dark periods of our existence.

--- Love, forgive, and embrace more, worry less, live more intensely, and emphasize the significant things, one of which is to be with God.

--- My daughter, I hope you have learned a little about this subject, but, above all, you must keep the following in mind.

--- When it is your turn to die, no one will die in your place, so live without listening to criticism because no one will live for you.

--- And what could that be, grandfather? Isabela asked, a little puzzled and curious at the same time.

---- Your life, my daughter, you must know how to live it because no one will live it for you; stop being a victim of problems and become the protagonist of your own story. --- actress of your movie.

---Live for yourself and not for the opinion of others, for people are not as happy as they appear to be, nor are they in love as they say they are, nor are they sincere in the way they express it.

--- Also, remember that at this moment, you are not what you want, but what you are, with your capabilities and what you achieve.

--- And especially remember this: when nothing is hidden, we can live with more smiles, joy, and peace in our hearts!

--- May your life become a garden of opportunities. The best time to be happy is now, so treasure the moment you live!

--- Likewise, a person is happiest when God is in their heart!

As Aristotle said: "the most coveted pursuit of life is the pursuit of happiness, for to be happy is the main purpose and essence of life."

"The best way to be happy with someone is to learn to be happy alone so that company is a matter of choice, not necessity." Mario Benedetti, Uruguayan writer, poet, and playwright (1920-2009).

He invited you to express in your own words: What is happiness for you?

_____

_____

_____

_____

Happiness is intrinsically linked to love and fully manifests when we learn to love ourselves and accept ourselves as we are. This journey of self-acceptance is not just a process but a transformative experience that leads to self-discovery, both personal and spiritual. It's a journey where faith, hope, and freedom become our guides, filling us with hope and optimism for the future.

In this state of self-love and connection with the divine, we find elusive happiness. In this moment and state, everything flows harmoniously in our lives because, with the presence of God, everything is possible. Like a faithful companion, happiness becomes a constant presence on our journey, reassuring and comforting us with its illuminating light.

«Happiness is a choice, an enjoyment, an adventure to share in the present, with the person and place of your choice. »

POEM TO HAPPINESS

Happiness, where are you, my beloved? Why are you running away? Where are you? Where are you hiding if I long for you so much? My soul and my whole being thirst for you. Please don't run away, don't hide, let me reach you, let me embrace you.

Come, my beloved, without you, there are no horizons. Without you, there is not yesterday, today, or tomorrow. I've been looking for you since before I was born; I've been looking for you since the very beginning of time, where and when I lost you.

Come, my beloved, feed my hunger and thirst for you; let me possess you, fill me with your charms and dawning delight. Let me taste the sweetness of your honey; let me lose my mind in you. I know you are the reason to have love and faith; you are the force that makes me live and grow.

Elusive, my beloved, I get lost between reality and fantasy when I think I have you. When you go to bed with me, I wake up, and you're gone. Without you, I feel like a clock without time, like a sea without water, like a sky without clouds, like a poet without inspiration or strength.

Oh, beloved happiness, they say you are in my midst, like a victorious warrior, and I can delight in you with joy. Happiness, you renew with love and anger. When in me anguish increases, your presence encourages me and nourishes me. My beloved, who could believe it? Your company alone makes me grow.

Fleeting happiness, where art thou? In what secret place does your essence reside? Are you a mirage dancing in the air? Or are you an illusion, fading at dawn? In your absence, my soul dissolves into tears.

They say you dwell in a pure heart, in goodness and selfless love, in giving without expecting anything in return, in inner peace, and in a liberated soul. They say you dwell in the very essence of God.

I will keep looking for you, my beloved, to possess you and make you mine. It will all be wonderful because I feel strong in this mad struggle to have you by my side. To love is to have and possess you.

When you are finally mine, I will open my soul inside you; the expected answer will come from your joy. My illusion would be that having you is not a dream, thus enjoying my fantasy of possessing you. I will discover God's wonders in me, your mysteries, your delights, your love, and your sweet blossoming.

Come, my beloved, with you, I want to walk the paths of life, and even if the olive harvest fails and the fields do not yield their crop, just by touching a veil of yours, I feel alive.

Bernardo A. Arango.

« Happiness can be found in the simplest moments, often with the person and place we ignore. »

THE CIRCLE OF IGNORANCE

Ignorance brings blindness, foolishness, clumsiness, and a staggering absence of knowledge and reasoning. It denies life's lessons and is the root of most evils, a source of reckless audacity. In their mental laziness and absurdity, the ignorant neither question nor doubt, lacking the necessary tools to reflect on any matter. Their lack of knowledge keeps them in the darkness of their ignorance, a fact that is almost unbelievable.

The ignorant often begin by pretending to know everything, a facade that quickly crumbles to reveal their true lack of knowledge. Their only recourse is to act impulsively from their prejudices, a lack of control evident in their actions. The naive is revealed through indifference, excessive insults, and offenses when they lack valid arguments to support their position.

The ignorant's shouts denote their weakness, slander reflects envy, and aggressiveness is a sign of insecurity. Anger and arrogance carry them away, taking refuge in the senseless ignorance within them. They descend to unknown levels, carried away by the wind of ignorant stupidity, without understanding that they are one of the cruelest killers that exist.

We make many mistakes because of ignorance. It is worth quoting the words of the French writer François de La Rochefoucauld on ignorance.

- Not knowing what you really should know
- Knowing what you know poorly
- Knowing what you shouldn't know

Ignorant people are easy to manipulate and cause their misfortune. It is difficult to know if they are ignorant because of genetic or mental inheritance or their own or someone else's cause. Some people study to get out of ignorance, but they confuse study with education because, despite studying, they are still idiots.

We know that above the clouds, it never rains; for this reason, if your understanding is cloudy and your world is gray, you have not risen high enough. Let us not imitate people who know nothing and are not interested in learning more than they need daily. These people do nothing and still form hordes to defend any idea they think is right, believing themselves wise.

What is the point of having eyes if one refuses to see or ears if one refuses to listen? What good is studying if one cannot comprehend? Such a person is as blind as someone who chooses not to see and deafer than someone who refuses to hear. They stumble around in broad daylight as if it were night. Ignorance is a form of blindness, the most severe kind, for it enslaves the mind. In contrast, knowledge is a beacon of light, illuminating the path to faithful living.

An ignorant person is their own worst enemy. They study the material but do not truly learn from it; they read the text but do not deeply understand it. They receive teachings but cannot actively engage with them. This lack of active understanding leads to suffering and a sense of weariness. In reality, they are not living but merely existing.

Ignorance is the night of the mind without the moon or stars, the storm of understanding as if the truth did not exist. It is as if intelligence is blocked by closing the windows of knowledge and does not let it in. It dwells between the living and the healthy as if it were dead. He trusts nothingness and speaks falsehood; he mocks everything because the ignorant use this means to feel more than others.

That is to say, he is sick because he ignores his ignorance, forgetting that every matter has its when and how. Through ignorance, man commits absurdities; for example, when the wise man points at the moon, the fool looks at the finger. There are honest people treated according to the conduct of the corrupt, and corrupt people are treated according to the conduct of the righteous. There are honest people treated according to the conduct of the corrupt, and corrupt people are treated according to the conduct of the righteous. All this is thanks to the bribery of the evil that causes damage and the collaboration of the ignorant who accept it.

The bad thing about ignorance is that it acquires more confidence with time, originating failures. Ignorance is combating with studying and gaining wisdom, conscience, and nourishing knowledge. Wretched is the person who despises education and learning; vain will be his hope, his efforts will have no results, and his works will be useless. Ignorance can be overcome by first recognizing that we are ignorant and that what we think we know is nothing more than opinions. Reality is often brutal to accept, but what other alternative is there?

Life's lessons are like going to school; the higher you level up, the more complex and demanding the classes will be. The truth is like a surgery that hurts but heals. Likewise, a lie is like an ointment that, when applied, gives instant relief, but the root of the pain is still there. Believing to know too much and doing things from the protagonist and arrogance is an act of ignorance.

We can understand that the greatest enemy of ignorance is knowledge, which invites us to expand our horizons of life. Understanding our ignorance is the best part of knowledge, asking us to recognize that it is better to criticize the wise than to hear the praises of the fool. It is like the difference between a wise man and an ignorant man, the exact difference between a living man and a corpse.

I bring you some phrases of ignorance, which are linked to names of philosophers, writers, and thinkers throughout history who, in their time, analyzed them very well.

- Learned ignorance (unrivaled in its field)
- Guilty ignorance
- Excusing ignorance
- Rational ignorance
- Dear ignorance
- Inevitable ignorance
- Conjectural ignorance

Ignorance has no excuse, especially that which is neither total nor presumptuous, resulting from self-deception. It is a morally objectionable way of evading one's responsibility, demonstrating deep inner wounds. Lying, falsehood, envy, pride, and arrogance work together; their chief is ignorance. For this reason, you must make a complete connection and reflect on life.

Each person must try to question and understand the environment that surrounds them, the world where they live, and what they believe in. It originates paths as we walk to find meaning in existence and what to do with it. We have a responsibility to ourselves and others because we are not alone on this planet. Some people should not consider study as an obligation or imposition, for it is an excellent opportunity to get out of the circle of ignorance.

Now, I invite you to write your conclusions. Ignorance for me is.

_____

_____

_____

_____

The best way to overcome ignorance is.

_____

_____

_____

_____

"The Ignorant considers false everything that he is unable to understand. [Because he is unable to explain it]."

Some books and personalities claim that many human beings inhabit the planet. The worst thing is that out of ignorance, they want us to believe that the earth is overpopulated. The virus was necessary to balance the population. This, apart from being exaggerated, is irresponsible.

The planet's entire land mass consists of 36.8 billion acres of habitable land (when, in fact, all of humanity could fit on the Canary Island of Tenerife, which measures only 502,700 acres, one square meter per person). This indicates that the world's population distribution is highly unequal. Some areas need to be more populated, and others are sparsely populated, not to mention profit and wealth.

According to World Meter's most recent United Nations estimates, the world population is 8,175,081,794 as of Sunday, September 8, 2024. The entire world population would fit in the state of Texas in the United States of America and the island of Tenerife. In conclusion, we are not overpopulated, but out of ignorance, they pull the wool over our eyes. Humans occupy a large portion of the earth's surface, about 55%, but we need less than 1%. And the planet's wealth belongs to only 1.1% of the population.

As a species, we recklessly discard precious resources like water and food at an alarming pace. The annual loss of a staggering $763 billion worth of food, equivalent to 20% of the world's meat production, is a stark reminder of our wasteful habits. This sacrifice, the equivalent of 75 million cows, is not just a statistic. It's a call to action. While some revel in excess, others struggle to survive. The urgency of this issue cannot be overstated.

Food waste is not just a distant problem—it's personal. On average, each of us wastes approximately 121 kilos of food yearly, and more than half of this waste occurs in our homes. Fruits and vegetables, the foods that nourish us, top the list with a staggering 42% of the total wasted. This is not just a statistic—it's a reflection of our choices and habits. But it also means we have the power to change.

Our insatiable consumption affects more than just us. It impacts the lives of mammals, fish, and birds struggling to survive in an unbalanced world. We hunt and fish excessively, often beyond what we need. This not only disrupts nature's delicate balance but also threatens the very existence of these species. It's a stark reminder of the interconnectedness of all life on our planet.

One way to reduce food waste in our homes is to plan meals and shopping lists and store food properly to prolong its freshness. Using leftovers creatively and composting food scraps can also help minimize waste. We can all contribute to a more sustainable future by taking these simple steps.

Some governments, multinationals, and prominent figures, blinded by insatiable greed, cannot find satisfaction in what they already possess. Fortune and business success are not synonymous with wisdom or a commitment to social and environmental well-being. The ability to influence public opinion through economic power does not guarantee the truthfulness of words.

Meanwhile, most humanity is trapped in a cycle of ignorance that limits its ability to act in the face of the impending environmental, economic, and moral crisis. This ignorance, fueled by misinformation and lack of access to education, threatens our existence and the future of our home, the Earth. Therefore, it is crucial to spread awareness about the impact of food waste and the steps we can take to reduce it, as education is a powerful tool in the fight against waste.

"The Ignorant considers false everything that he is incapable of understanding. [Because he cannot explain it]".

THE CIRCLE OF INTELLIGENCE

The two most innate qualities of the human mind, intuition, and logic are the essence of our mental existence. Intuition leads us to experience and analytical reasoning, making us mental beings. This sets us apart in the universe; everything else obeys the mind.

Our brain resembles a more enigmatic, mysterious abyss than the ocean. Within our minds, infinite dimensions unfold, hiding God's secrets, which could be interpreted as the ultimate truth or the fundamental principles of existence, humanity, creation, and the universe's evolution. We are guardians of this mystery, endowed with the ability to explore and understand the very fabric of existence.

Human intelligence operates according to laws as intricate as those governing electricity, physics, and nature. These laws include learning, memory, problem-solving, and decision-making principles. The evolution of intelligence likely had its roots in the primordial need of the human being: communication, first with oneself and then with God and one's environment. This need has driven the development of our communication and intelligence capacities.

This evolutionary process is fascinating because of its endless and infinite nature. In general terms, our intelligence encompasses the ability to learn, plan, and act. It is a constantly developing force that allows us to understand and shape the world.

Intelligence can be defined as using the capacities and abilities to solve problems, make life projects, and achieve goals. It originates in the brain and includes the ability to reason, learn, think, and manage thoughts and emotions. To solve problems and face life, we act with logic and rationality.

Intelligence is formed from a combination of factors, including genetic predispositions and lifelong learning. Genetic factors determine an innate aptitude for a particular type of intelligence. It also develops through study, analysis, and experience. Its residence is the brain, where humans process, plan, and execute actions with the ability to do things correctly about their needs and ambitions.

In simple terms, most humans are born with the same brain capacity and intelligence. However, intelligence development is an exclusive matter for the individual, who must learn to develop, apply, and take advantage of it. If there is no intelligence, reasoning, or mind, there is no God because he is our intimate intelligence.

Humans are highly sophisticated and mentally complex, which sets us apart from animals. Intelligence manifests in the satisfaction of the senses and in knowing how to do things, applying it to study, life projects, and acquiring material goods.

Apply it to study, life projects, and material things; for example, I want to study architecture, or I want to study medicine; when I work, I will buy the car, build the house of my dreams, take the trip I aspire to, I have an idea to make an invention, etc. Intelligence offers us these opportunities, but it is essential to remember that being intelligent does not necessarily mean being wise. This distinction is crucial, as many smart people may need to be wiser.

Wisdom is forged in the crucible of failures, where fire sculpts pain and tears. Until recently, intelligence was a univocal concept, a magic wand that measured human potential. However, in 1983, Howard Gardner, psychologist, researcher, and professor at Harvard University, challenged this paradigm with his theory of multiple intelligences. Gardner revealed that human beings are kaleidoscopes of cognitive abilities, each with its light and hue.

A universe of intelligences. This new paradigm expanded our horizon, revealing a universe of intelligence beyond logic and language. Among them, we find:

- Logical-mathematical intelligence
- Linguistic intelligence
- Spatial intelligence
- Musical intelligence
- Kinesthetic-bodily intelligence
- Intrapersonal intelligence
- Interpersonal intelligence
- Naturalistic intelligence

Gardner and his Harvard team warned us that academic intelligence, that collection of titles and educational merits, does not define an individual's intelligence. A clear example can be found in those who, despite shining in the classroom, stumble in the complex world of interpersonal relationships. Education is not synonymous with intelligence. A doctorate does not guarantee wisdom or conscience.

Intelligence without wisdom; the paradox of power. Adolf Hitler, a terrifying example of this imbalance, rose to power in Germany relatively quickly. His strategic intelligence allowed him to seize territories and unleash the Second World War. However, his lack of wisdom and conscience turned him into a ruthless tyrant, leaving a legacy of pain and destruction. This highlights the crucial role of wisdom in guiding the use of intelligence, as without it, power can be easily misused.

Intelligence in the service of good. In contrast, the pioneers of technology, the inventors of the radio, the automobile, television, the telephone, the computer, and the cell phone, have given us tools that have transformed our lives unimaginably. When used for good, their intelligence has not just improved but also revolutionized the world, filling us with optimism and encouragement for the future.

Even without a high level of intelligence, we can all benefit from the fruits of collective intelligence. We fly in airplanes, use cell phones and computers, and enjoy music and technology without having in-depth knowledge of their operation or history. This collective intelligence has bequeathed a world of possibilities, making us all part of a larger community of progress and innovation.

We also have emotional intelligence; according to Dr. Goleman, it recognizes our feelings. The feelings of others motivate us and adequately manage our relationships with others and ourselves. The objective is to know how to handle situations where uncontrollable emotions appear, using techniques and strategies that allow us to reflect and think about the best option. According to Dr. Goleman and other specialists in this field, it is complex to establish an ideal categorization of the types of emotional intelligence. This depends on how the person was raised, his experiences, and his way of seeing reality. However, emotional intelligence can be classified as follows:

- Personal Intelligence
- Intrapersonal Intelligence
- Interpersonal Intelligence
- Social Intelligence

H Intelligence involves more than just intellectual knowledge; it also encompasses the ability to apply it and adapt to change. For example, knowing a lot is different from being intelligent. Intelligence goes beyond the mere accumulation of facts. A knowledgeable person possesses a vast intellectual repertoire and can apply this knowledge practically and effectively in various situations. Moreover, intelligence is characterized by the capacity to adapt to the changes and challenges presented by the environment. This adaptability makes us feel resilient and capable, even in novel situations. In this sense, some individuals may have a wealth of theoretical knowledge yet struggle to put it into practice or confront novel situations.

Intelligence and wisdom: What is the difference? While intelligence and knowledge are closely related, they are not synonymous. Intelligence refers to the capacity to learn, understand, and reason. In contrast, wisdom involves applying this knowledge and experience reflectively and judiciously to make sound decisions and live fulfilling lives. By understanding the role of wisdom in decision-making, we can feel empowered and in control of our lives. A classic example of this distinction is the saying: "The intelligent person knows what to say; the wise person knows when to say it.

- The intelligent is not wise, but he can become wise
- The wise man, in fact, already possesses intelligence
- To have wisdom is also the knowledge of the Creator of the universe.

Now, I invite you to participate a little more in the subject; I invite you to make your analysis and write it in the following lines.

For me, being smart is.

_____

_____

_____

_____

_____

People I consider intelligent are.

_____

_____

_____

_____

_____

To me, an emotionally intelligent person is.

_____

_____

_____

_____

_____

Carefully analyze the message in ([Proverbs 15: 33](#)). The fear of the Lord is instruction in wisdom, and before glory, there is humility.

"Too high an ego separates us from others and our creative source, eternal God."

THE CIRCLE OF LEADERSHIP

Leadership: A multifaceted potential that unfolds in diverse domains, from the religious and military to the political, business, technological, and many more. The essence of genuine leadership lies in guiding and motivating a group of people, an organization, a company, a political party, or even a country to transform a vision into a tangible reality. An Authentic leader leverages their innate skill set to achieve a set of predetermined goals designed to generate benefits and satisfy the genuine needs of their followers.

IS A LEADER BORN OR MADE?

The answer is both. The nature of leadership lies in a dynamic combination of innate characteristics and skills acquired over time. While some people are born with leadership predispositions, such as charisma or the ability to self-influence, these qualities can be enhanced and perfected through study, the development of intellect, and emotional intelligence. An effective leader can generate enthusiasm and admiration among followers, inspiring them to achieve common goals. Additionally, they can make sound decisions with minimal risk, always seeking personal excellence daily.

In the current context, marked by high competitiveness, globalization, technological advances, new marketing trends, changing investments, government reforms, and the evolution of the workforce, leadership has become a challenging task that demands constant adaptation and the development of new skills. This constant need for adaptation and skill development should engage the audience and challenge them in their leadership roles.

Those aspiring influential leaders in this dynamic environment must be prepared to face rapid changes and successfully lead companies, institutions, or countries. In this sense, a new generation of achievers emerges with a transformative power, ready to respond to the demands of the modern world. This transformative power is inspiring and should motivate the audience to step up and lead in their respective fields.

Leadership has become even more challenging post-pandemic. This is due to the intensification of competition and accelerated changes in globalization, technology, marketing, and investments. Government reforms, the new workforce, and other demands of the modern world necessitate rapid adaptation on the part of companies. This rapid adaptation demands new skills and abilities from leaders, highlighting the importance of adaptability in the post-pandemic era.

In this context, those who aspire to be leaders and guide a team, company, institution, or country must be increasingly prepared. This is forming a new generation of achievers with transformative power. These leaders adapt to the changes and shape the future, capable of leading their teams and organizations to success in an ever-changing world.

Leadership is a role of great responsibility involving the guidance and inspiration of a group toward common goals. Influential leaders, whether born with innate predispositions or developed through study and experience, share a key characteristic- the ability to set ambitious goals. They navigate both short-term and long-term objectives and possess the skill to overcome the challenges that inevitably arise on the path to success.

The qualities of a leader are forged in the crucible of adversity. These qualities are honed and strengthened through adversity, constant study, the accumulation of experience, and the increasingly demanding demands of the modern world. A true leader is forged, like iron at high temperatures, amid difficulties and challenges. For these exceptional leaders, the more significant the challenges, the more outstanding the achievements.

A true leader does not give up in the face of difficulties or become discouraged by obstacles. Instead, they demonstrate remarkable resilience, seeing challenges as opportunities to grow, learn, and strengthen. These exceptional leaders understand that the path to success is often paved with obstacles, and they confidently repeat the phrase: "The greater the obstacles, the greater the achievements." Difficulties are the crucible that forges true leaders, preparing them to achieve extraordinary purposes.

An exceptional leader is a beacon that guides their team, showing adaptability in the face of change. These outstanding leaders can perceive the needs of others from afar, recognize the paths that lead to success, and learn to earn the loyalty and respect of those they guide. They know how to tolerate mistakes, which they turn into lessons to set goals and expectations, showing authenticity and confidence in their ability to adapt.

The qualities of a solid leader: A deep analysis.

- A leader first leads him/herself, knowing his/her strengths and limitations.
- Strategic thinking always puts a step ahead and decides for the future. Carefully evaluates current work methods and systems.
- He is always ready to collaborate
- Emotional intelligence: a leader who shows optimism, self-confidence, and empathy is recognized for the emotional strength that is key to leadership and motivate
- Has the personality to exercise and inspire authority
- Leaders do not need attachments because they need more leaders.
- Leaders are not envious because they inspire success.
- A true leader can communicate by clearly expressing his ideas and building trust and confidence.
- Critical thinking and analytical questioning accelerate the best decisions and do not cause "paralysis by analysis."
- He knows how to listen to others with judgment and conscience; he makes his interlocutor feel accepted and respected.
- As a coach, the leader does not do his followers' work but worries that each one does his job. He teaches to improve the work and that his team makes the right decisions.
- He is visionary, reliable, courageous, a driving force, an integrator, and a discoverer.
- Generating a positive climate and conditions for development

- Selecting and promoting talented supporters
- Prepare successors by delegating tasks and sharing responsibilities.
- Leaders don't need to shine because they carry their light.

These qualities are necessary for a leader, but they should stand out the most for solid leadership.

- Humility (admitting mistakes, leaving pride and ego aside).
- It has values and virtues.

Consequently, this makes their work a priority.

- Protecting the dignity of the individual
- Protecting the dignity of the family
- Protecting human dignity
- Protecting the dignity of the company

A leader's lack of humility and human values will inevitably lead to failure. Without these qualities, a leader will lack the legitimacy and respect necessary to inspire and guide others. History is full of examples of leaders who never achieved the true essence of leadership despite holding positions of power.

The qualities outlined in this analysis are necessary for a leader striving to establish solid and effective leadership. Humility stands out as the cornerstone of authentic leadership. This humility earns the respect and appreciation of others, inspiring, motivating, and guiding them toward achieving shared goals and collective success.

An Authentic leader is not only defined by their skills and achievements but also by their unwavering commitment to learning and continuous improvement. They are a driving force that encourages their team to realize their potential and reach ambitious goals. This commitment to growth and development is contagious, inspiring the team to strive for excellence.

It is easy for anyone to maintain calm and composure in tranquility. However, it is in difficult times, when life's storms rage with force, that the true character of a leader is tested. An exceptional leader remains unshakeable in the face of adversity, maintaining composure and the ability to make sound decisions. The economic crisis triggered by COVID-19 has radically transformed the global landscape, reconfiguring how to do business and work.

In this challenging context, an effective leader not only adapts to new circumstances but also uses them as an opportunity to grow and strengthen their team. A true leader can build an oasis of prosperity even amid the most arid desert, facing thirst and the sun's harshness with courage and determination. Amid crises, they tirelessly seek excellence in knowledge, trust, integrity, and the security of their team. An authentic leader understands that true leadership lies in serving others, an attitude that makes them an inspiring and captivating figure.

WILL ALL LEADERS ARE GOOD?

Every leader excels by influence and procedure with people. Being a leader does not mean being good; a leader is not good if he lacks humility and values. Many do not have a concrete idea of humility and respect because they have too much pride, a high ego, and greed. However, they easily influence and manipulate others; they are usually tyrants, with authoritarian leadership, for example.

Drug traffickers have leaders; thugs have leaders; gangs have leaders, and white slavery has its leader. Osama bin Laden was a leader, as were Adolf Hitler, Muammar Gaddafi, and Saddam

Hussein. All of them were leaders but bad leaders in man's evolutionary chain.

The person who makes mistakes can change, but the one who never changes will always live wrong. We know from experience that no leadership is eternal. The characters mentioned above knew they were terrible, but they had the diabolical need to continue the destructive chain of creation. No matter the power, they ended up in the same place where all living things end up.

After carefully analyzing, we can conclude that the formation of leaders begins at home. From the example and influence of their parents, he studied and disciplined. For this reason, parents do not worry so much about what they will leave their children; instead, they worry about what kind of children they go to in the world. Because we already have enough tyrants, exploiters, murderers, and traumatizers.

Today, we need more coherent leaders who understand the reality of our lives as human beings and are rational shapers of society. We do not need leaders with bought votes, personal favors, cronyism, or those elected with the tip of the finger.

Many political leaders confuse leadership with rank, privilege, or money and ignore the personal and family situation of the society they claim to govern. What should we say about the laws they pass to lead a culture or a country? Many of these laws lack moderation, sobriety, and even common logic. Some are so out of the ordinary that they border on the ridiculous.

Any group of people, company, or society that chooses its leaders without knowing who they are, evaluating their principles and morals, examining them in depth or their history, and only choosing them for cronyism, popularity, and favors will not be able to have good leadership with principles, justice, and social progress.

For this reason, to elect, we must inform ourselves, study them well, and know for whom we will vote. We must learn to elect those who aspire to lead a group, a city, or a nation. We must learn to elect judges and all the people who aspire to hold public office and positions of general power. It would be best to remember that when you give your vote, you give control over yourself. When you do not exercise your right to vote to elect, someone else will elect for you.

I invite you to describe your conclusion, for example, *who is a true leader for you*? For me, a true leader is the one who.

_____

_____

_____

_____

In my opinion, a true leader must have the following qualities.

_____

_____

_____

_____

"The most powerful person who has ever known on the planet, with the strongest leadership, is Jesus of Nazareth."

THE CIRCLE OF GOALS AND ACHIEVEMENT

In the daily whirlwind, we pursue goals, from the simplest to the most ambitious, encompassing various aspects of our existence. However, in this constant struggle, we often question the *'why'* of events without pausing to reflect on the *'what for.'* In these moments of reflection, we truly understand the purpose and significance of our pursuits. Here, the crucial question arises: How much time have we wasted in vain? How many years, months, and days have we let slip by aimlessly? This reflection compels us to break the cycle of monotony and embark on a conscious journey toward new goals.

Achieving our goals often requires risking everything to gain everything. However, before savoring success, it is essential to identify and cultivate the values necessary to build lasting goals. Remember that a significant challenge implies a great risk, and a patient wait.

Solid success is not harvested overnight or by chance. Once achieved, the next challenge is to sustain and manage it wisely, as it carries considerable risks. While people appreciate it when we do things well, they rarely tolerate our surpassing them. Similarly, they will value our intelligence and achievements if they do not eclipse their own. Therefore, we must forge our path, avoiding following in the footsteps of others.

Following in the footsteps of others will only lead us to where they have been, not where we aspire to go. The possibility of achieving our goals lies in the extent to which we believe in their viability. The impossible only resides in our minds. No one can harm us more than ourselves with our thoughts and emotions.

Patience, the nutrient of tolerance, is the art of understanding and the sustenance of love. Love, in turn, nourishes forgiveness, and forgiveness is the seed of peace, which nourishes the spirit. These ingredients fuel our goals and achievements, guiding us towards personal and professional success. Patience is not just a virtue; it's a powerful tool that can help us navigate the challenges to personal and professional success.

From a certain angle, a book has six sides, but for some, it will always have only two because their minds are limited in perceiving them. This is due to the preconceived ideas that bind them without daring to broaden their horizons. Similarly, it happens with the paths to achieve our goals. Discarding the accumulated 'mental garbage' (discovering all the sides of the book), renewing ideas to break paradigms, and opening ourselves to new possibilities is necessary. Let's not limit ourselves to what we think we know, but instead, let's embrace the unknown and the unexplored.

It depends on the angle you look at it. A book has six sides, but it will always have only two for some people because that is all their minds can grasp. This is due to your preconceived ideas without daring to change. Likewise, they are the paths to achieving goals and reaching objectives. It would be best to throw away the accumulated mental garbage (discovering all the faces of the book), renewed ideas, and broken paradigms.

To achieve this, you must consolidate the projects with study and advice. Plan with strategy, and you will win. Learn to see that within the difficulties, permanently hide opportunities. These have the power to make us grow in our abilities. In this way, the soul's eyes teach what it desires, reaching the traced goals with success and firmness.

To achieve this, you must solidify projects with study and advice. Plan strategically, and you will conquer. Learn to see that opportunities always hide within difficulties. They have the power to make us grow in our abilities. This way, the eyes will show what the soul desires, arriving accurately and firmly at the goals. Strategic planning is the key to unlocking your potential and achieving your goals.

The enemies of success live within us, limiting our potential and preventing us from achieving it. These enemies are often invisible, but with self-awareness, we can recognize and overcome them:

- Lack of strategy.
- Insecurity.
- Complacency.
- Inconsistency.
- Procrastination or postponement is a powerful enemy of goals and success. Postponement is the false belief that there will be a better time shortly to take the action we need today.

- Doubts are undoubtedly the worst enemy to defeat. The biggest problem is when doubt paralyzes us and neutralizes action.
- Fear is the most terrifying of all. It paralyzes ideas and creativity, limits, distracts, and ultimately leads to total failure.
- Pride is failing to recognize that one is doing something wrong and refusing to admit it.
- Lack of knowledge.

We can overcome these attitudes by assimilating that it will not be easy, but neither will it be impossible. Achieving success and triumph hurts, as it involves making difficult decisions, such as leaving people who do not add value to your life, changing habits, giving up your comfort zone, and other expectations that you thought made you happy. Growing hurts, but it is necessary.

YOU HAVE THE POWER TO ACHIEVE YOUR DREAMS

Learning to project and visualize is essential for achieving our goals and succeeding in any area of our lives. This means creating a clear and detailed mental image of what we want to achieve with determination and courage. By preparing our minds this way, we strengthen our determination and focus all our potential on the goal.

WHAT IS VISUALIZATION? Visualization is like drawing a map to success. We create a clear mental image of our goals by visualizing ourselves receiving a diploma, in a large office with a panoramic city view, or closing a big deal, seeing us happy and successful. This program helps our brain find the best routes and overcome obstacles. With determination and focus, we can turn our visualizations into reality.

Beyond having our goals clear, we must also cultivate an attitude of strength and greatness and awaken intuitive power. The sixth sense allows us to detect opportunities where others only see obstacles. As athletes train their bodies, we must train our minds with powerful affirmations. Saying and repeating positive affirmations to ourselves daily, such as the following:

I am love, I am intelligence, I am power, I am well-being, I am health, I am happiness. I am wealth; I am strength, and my future is bright by the glory of God. It is important to personalize these affirmations so that they resonate with you on a personal level. These affirmations are like seeds that we plant in our subconscious. We will reap the fruits of our desires by cultivating them with faith and action.

Remember, visualization is like sowing a seed; more than dreaming, it creates your reality. By planting the seed of our dreams in our minds, we create conditions for it to flourish. But for this seed to become a solid and leafy tree, we need to nourish it with consistent actions. Perseverance is your best ally on this journey.

Keep in mind that the true transformation to achieve success occurs when we move from visualization to action. Every step we take, no matter how small, brings us closer to our dreams.

Thanks to your growth in achieving great goals, you have the power and ability to turn something simple into an outstanding achievement. I invite you to describe the goals you want to achieve.

My plans and goals are as follows.

_____

_____

_____

_____

_____

I know there are difficulties or obstacles, and I will overcome them,

_____

_____

_____

_____

"The most profound and dynamic beings in history who have achieved their goals have struggled with difficulties and with themselves."

THE MARRIAGE CIRCLE

Before marriage, two people who are on different paths meet and decide to marry. At that moment, they become one, beginning a joint journey with shared goals. However, it is essential to understand that marriage does not involve finding the perfect person but the 'perfect opposite help,' a travel companion who complements us, challenges us, and helps us evolve in ways we couldn't on our own.

If we analyze carefully, the love of our lives is not the one who fell in love with us and left, nor the one who promises always to be there but never is. True love resides in the one who accepts us as we are, is always there for us, and never abandons us. This love accepts our past with its scars without trying to blackmail us. This love embraces our strengths and weaknesses, inviting us to share a journey on the same train.

Love is not a calculation of quantities nor a comparison of who loves more or less. It transcends mere emotion. Love is forgiveness, understanding, acceptance, tolerance, and reciprocity. It is being together in good times and bad, waiting, tolerating, listening, being silent, speaking, helping, and accompanying. These qualities are the pillars of a solid and enduring relationship.

This person deserves our company and love. They treat us as they would themselves with their sincere words and actions, giving us all their attention, love, and protection in any circumstance and accompanying us to the end.

It is the one with whom we share the worst joke, yet they laugh with us. It is the one who says, "I don't want you to leave; I want you to stay with me." The one who expresses, "I want to kiss you in the rain, dance in the kitchen, cry, laugh. I want to have a million adventures with you, have pillow fights." It is the one who gives us all their attention and says, "When I look at the sky, I ask God for you." This person who cherishes shared experiences is the one who deserves to accompany us on the most important journey of our lives.

If we have already achieved the most challenging thing, which is finding each other among millions of people, now we can focus on the most straightforward thing: not losing each other and fighting to keep love in the first place. Marriage is a commitment that demands dedication and constant effort to nurture love and overcome together the obstacles that arise along the way. It's a journey that requires perseverance and a shared commitment to keep the flame of love burning.

Marriage was born out of love, companionship, and moments of happiness, procreation, succession, and being the basis of the family and society. But painfully, it is a custom in the process of extinction. Although it is the ideal circle for the realization of people, as human beings, we could compare it to a tree that is planted in the ground to grow and bear good fruit. There is no doubt that the best way to have a successful marriage is to understand what your goal is. The question is, *do you know what love is?* How do you know you are loved if you cannot define love*? How do you know you are in love?*

Likewise, it is impossible to love someone if we do not love ourselves. Do not allow mistakes to become more significant, and do not allow the past to put pressure on the present; if you let it, you are screwed. In a stable marriage, coordinates must be directed to the same goal to find the ideal state. This is because married life is the perfect way to reach perfection. A man or a woman separately will not be able to achieve a perfect balance because the couple is the ideal support for personal, family, and social development.

Therefore, before getting married, don't marry solely for sexual fulfillment, money, to fill the void of loneliness, or to seek happiness so that you don't regret it. You should marry for and with love or feel its arrival as a beautiful illusion for life. We must seek fundamental values in a partner, such as ethics, gratitude, empathy, sexual understanding, patience, humility, responsibility, faith, tolerance, honesty, family values, and trust.

No marriage or couple remains without trust. Among other things, that woman should become your weakness and your security. Just as water serves as a mirror to see your face, moral values, ethics, trust, respect, and faith are the mirrors of marriage. These elements are the foundation of a strong and healthy marriage. Moral values and ethics guide our actions and decisions, trust and respect build a strong bond between partners, and faith provides a sense of security and comfort in the relationship.

In living together as a couple, the individual time and space to which each person is entitled as an individual is respected. When we love our spouse, we love them with all their mood swings. We do not reject or criticize their flaws with other people but rather try to understand them and have tolerance, even if, at the worst moments, they reach a point of maximum annoyance for us. This understanding and tolerance are not just virtues, but they can also cultivate empathy and patience in your relationship.

In marriage, we must accept disagreements, gray hair, wrinkles, and weight gain that come with age. This acceptance is a vital part of a successful marriage. Disagreements are inevitable, and aging is a natural process. Accepting these changes and challenges as part of the journey is essential. We must also take the physical, hormonal, and character changes that time brings. If you notice that your spouse changes over time, you have also changed. You may not realize it, but it is expected when the years pass, and adulthood arrives, so we must accept it.

Marriage with love is like the tree and the fruit, resembling a single body. When you mistreat your partner, it is like mistreating your own body. When you talk behind your partner's back, it is like criticizing yourself. In marriage, spouses unite to love each other as themselves, so no one hates or curses themselves. This love is not just a feeling but a powerful force that can make you feel cherished and valued in your relationship.

Instead, one takes care of and nourishes oneself with care and affection, treating one's partner like the apple of one's eye, like one's own face and skin. With gossip and complaints, whoever talks and criticizes their spouse demonstrates disunity, lack of love, and traces of unhealed emotional and inner wounds. Living in marriage even highlights a person's most minor imperfections.

It is the only way to repair our imperfections at their highest level. A joint life plan is essential; for this reason, you should know how to choose. In marriage, in addition to love and companionship, the couple unites to grow and enrich themselves, seeing common goals and telling each other. This mutual growth is not just a possibility but a beautiful reality that can inspire and motivate you in your relationship.

--- my love, all that I have lived, all that I have spent at your side, the happiness and the difficulties if I were born again, with you, I would go through it all over again.

An airplane can fly, thanks to its engines. In marriage, "*love, fidelity, respect, and tolerance,*" among others, are the main turbines that drive this union and its dreams. Being a couple does not mean having difficulties or problems; it means being together, fighting to overcome them, and seeing a promising horizon. To define in total form what the love of a couple is complicated since it is a personal concept thanks to the critical mind, the free choice, the freedom of thought, and the lived experiences. However, we can define what love can do in marriage and the person, for example.

- Love does nothing wrong, does not seek its own, is not irritated, and does not bear grudges.
- For love, everything is suffered, everything is believed, everything is expected, everything is tolerated, and the partner is cared for with delicacy.
- Love does not enjoy suffering or injustice but enjoys what is beautiful, just, and true.
- Love does not envy; love is not boastful and knows how to be supportive.

145

- Out of love, that person becomes addicted to you, loves you, how you are, and your past, history, defects, and qualities.

True love is not about giving up one's identity or tolerating disrespectful behavior. It's about accepting your partner with their virtues and flaws and growing together. A lasting marriage is built on teamwork, respect, open communication, and shared faith, not on the unrealistic expectation of perfection.

Remember that whoever loves does not abuse, does not use, or emotionally blackmail. If you want to see a person's actual state, it is not enough to see how they act in front of the world; the most important thing is to see how they behave in their most intimate environment, which is day-to-day. That is, at home, where things will always happen that will make the person show who they are.

Just as a metal is sharpened with another, showing that both are needed to make each other practical, each fulfilling with perfect harmony and coordination, so is a lasting marriage. This is built with teamwork, respect, mutual admiration that makes each partner feel appreciated, and tolerance with an inexhaustible dose of love, humility, gratitude, forgiveness, understanding, coordination, and God in their lives.

Infidelity and adultery are akin to poison for a marriage, corroding trust, respect, and love. These self-serving actions inflict profound pain on the partner and the family, leaving emotional wounds that can be hard to heal. It's crucial to remember that fidelity is not just an outward commitment but a manifestation of the love and loyalty in the relationship. Spiritual fortitude and fidelity to values are crucial for sustaining a healthy marriage and resisting temptations.

When confronted with the trials and tribulations of married life, spiritual strength and fidelity to values are the bedrock for a healthy marriage. Seeking spiritual guidance and upholding values such as honesty, responsibility, and commitment can fortify the relationship and offer the necessary resilience to surmount obstacles.

Do not be absent from home for too long, nor from your spouse or children; it is not mentally or spiritually healthy to be absent for extended periods (months away from your home). Before doing so, I invite you to observe how a bird wanders away from its nest carefully. You will notice that it flits from place to place. Just as the bird wanders away from its nest, so does the man far from his home.

"When a marriage works, nothing in the world can replace it." (Helen Gahagan).

SOME HABITS TO BE A HAPPY COUPLE

Develop and cultivate Common Interests. Have several activities to share as a couple, such as walking to the park, going to the movies, choosing meals, practicing a sport or activity, dancing, or listening to music.

Walking and holding hands is comforting, energetic, communicative, and flattering. It physically coordinates the heart rate and reinforces emotional closeness by allowing one to feel the balance of giving and receiving, symbolizing a stable relationship.

Trust and forgive. Arguments, disagreements, shouting, and misunderstandings take an emotional toll. The best way is to focus calmly on what matters, avoid the opinion of third parties, and forgive each other, with no winner or loser.

Highlight what your partner has done well. In a relationship, highlighting accomplishments and what the other does well is essential. Highlighting (*complimenting, applauding, celebrating*) what the other does well, making him/her feel special and that he/she is not ignored.

To embrace, to feel the presence of the Other. Almost all of us are unaware of the dimension of fullness that hugs provide us; they are given and received. They help to reduce stress, regulate the heartbeat, feel protection and love, and help us forget our problems.

Be tolerant and say, "I love you." *If you always live defensively and do not express your feelings, you undoubtedly have emotional problems that you need to heal to learn to live as a* *couple, to be tolerant, and to* say "I *love you*" without shyness. That is achieved with love, the best and most effective medicine.

Saying good morning / good evening. Affection, understanding, and love are cultivated and cared for like a flower. With affectionate, loving words, letting the partner know that "I care about you, and I think of you."

Try to go to bed at the same time. It seems to be the main reason couples in established relationships have better health and live longer. It contributes to mental well-being, reduced heart disease, health, happiness, and couple satisfaction.

Be children from time to time. Play with your partner like you were a child, talk like a child, play like a child, and get angry like a child, i.e., don't take anger seriously. It is easier to forgive and more satisfying than when we were children. It is fun and allows you to be more original.

Reconquering your partner. Flirting in a couple is a habit that should never end and is essential in a relationship. Most importantly, we should never make comparisons; each person is unique on this planet. Your partner is exceptional; you must fall in love with your spouse several times to keep it.

Return to the first encounter. Return periodically to the first time you liked your partner, repeating that first look, the moments of pleasure and enchantment. Because for a marriage to be lasting and happy, we must fall in love with that person often.

Laughing at each other is therapeutic. It allows one to disclose defects without offense, make jokes, "tease" each other occasionally, and laugh at the other's attitude. It brings closeness and sympathy.

Dedicate time to be alone and respect that space. Human beings are a tumult of emotions; we need company, and at the same time, we need solitude. In marriage as in relationships, being alone is important for an encounter with oneself. Liad Uziel, a Jewish professor in the psychology department at Bar-Ilan University in Tel Aviv, Israel, says that time alone "shapes our character from different perspectives.

For some, love is a heavy burden, a bittersweet and unavoidable pain. This is because they do not know how to and cannot live in a more healthy, intelligent, and heartfelt way. Being faithful does not mean being foolish; it means maturity and knowing how to appreciate and value your partner because love and happiness grow with life. I give these in fact and cause; from personal experience, I have practiced them, and they work. However, having God in our lives has helped us the most.

Remember, only those who love and give love because they have learned that to love fully, we must first love ourselves, just as those who know how to be happy give happiness. If you have lost some loving habits with your partner, I invite you to write down the ones you want to start having again.

For example, I would like my partner and I to have the following habits.

_____

_____

_____

_____

To begin with, I will go to

_____

_____

_____

May your purpose always be to preserve fidelity and trust because when trust is lost in a couple, it is like when a mirror is broken. No matter how much you pick up the pieces, it will never be the same. You can pick up the larger pieces and put them together. Let's say you can see your image again, but only you can see it. Because your partner, no matter how hard you try, will see the distorted image because adultery is never forgotten; it will always be with you like a shadow. The differences that we have, I think, can be solved in the following way.

_____

_____

_____

_____

I can forgive and ask for forgiveness.

_____

_____

_____

_____

_____

_____

If you are ideal for your spouse or partner, this person will become your best friend, the person you trust, the person you want to be with the most, and with whom there is more sincerity and openness. Because the best friend is not chosen, it comes naturally because no one is forced to be a best friend. So before listening to gossip, applying Socrates' three sieves is healthy.

Tamis means *(to examine or select conscientiously)*. Accordingly, before listening and judging, ask the following questions.

- Have you checked if what you will tell me is true?
- What do you want to tell me about my friend? Is it a good thing?
- Is knowing what you will tell me about this friend helpful?

By asking and applying these questions, you will avoid many problems, especially if it is your spouse, partner, or friend.

"Likewise, *the husband ought to love his wife as his own body. He who loves his wife loves himself.*" (Ephesians 5:^{28}).

THE CIRCLE OF SEPARATION AND DIVORCE

A marital separation or breakup is a tough time in any household in the world and for everyone involved. Problems and disagreements between spouses are included in the package you chose. All couples know it is undeniable that it takes love and maturity to overcome them. If you are separating and plan to divorce your spouse because you disagree, you can't talk effectively, creating frustration. You have problems, and you have realized that you think differently and have different points of view. Well, you should know that you are about to make yet another mistake in your life.

I analyzed the following well: if you had no conflicts with your partner, would you consider separating or not? This indicates that the reason is not your partner but the conflicts. It is like when many people leave their marriages, claiming love is over. The next question is, ***when your vehicle runs out of gas, do you abandon it or refuel it again***? So *why do you want to separate*? What is the cause, *lack of commitment, conflicts, and arguments*? You want to run away and not know anything. It is possible that with this attitude, you will not solve anything; you will only hurt those who love you the most. To your spouse, your children, and, in fact, to yourself, when separating, the problems may get bigger.

The relationship can be healed in a marital crisis if both people are committed. Problems and disagreements are solved as a couple with love, tolerance, and patience. If you choose between other people and fight hard to conquer the love of your life, now do not change it for another love or another life. Do not try to be unhappy if you find someone who gives you love and understanding. Human beings are strange; we do not know how to be happy; it seems that our specialty is to make problems to be disappointed. We seem satisfied walking in darkness, running away from the light and the people who love us the most.

If they got married, it was because they loved each other; they conquered each other. They have domesticated each other, accepting each other's past and defects and not because they are equal. If your spouse is the person who tells you that life is mine, but my heart is yours, and the smile is mine, but the reason for it is always you, that person deserves your company and your love. It is not worth separating because you do not think alike, because of a disagreement or because you do not have the same tastes.

Don't think you are wrong; all human beings are different. If your spouse does not accept your impositions and does not allow himself to be dominated as you wish, it is because he has life, will, voice, and vote, and we must respect that. Moreover, even God respects free will and free expression, both in individuals (remember Mary of Nazareth) and couples.

It is not about being the perfect couple but a shared partnership. We are all different in our thoughts, plans, and actions because we have free will and choice. The Creator made man and woman different to be a perfect complement and the ideal opposite companion in their union. They became one to perpetuate the species, helping God in the perfection of creation. This means that we work with God; we are co-creators with Him.

In marriage, there must be a "***stable balance***"; for this reason, we think and understand things differently. Imagine a balance scale (of pans or crosses). To reach a perfect balance, there must be the same weight; if there is an imbalance, it is because there is overweight on the other side. Well, the ***same happens in*** *marriage*. A balance is necessary to maintain the union even if we think differently or agree on everything. Consider the following: if your spouse were to feel as you want, then he/she would not be a person; he/she would be your puppet, a being that you could manage at will and as you please. Today, if you live with a person who only "wants to impose his will," where there is no opinion, respect, and trust, there is simply nothing.

To be aware, analyze the following: We have two hands that seem the same size but are not. One is longer than the other and is placed in opposite directions. Each on its side fulfills its function; what the right hand does is not done by the left. Even one hand cannot do much, but the two work together in wonders, with the power and ability to transform the world. *The same is true in marriage.*

We have two feet; although similar, they are different. The right one is generally longer than the left one. Just as the arms are placed in the opposite direction, and each one fulfills its mission, the two complement each other and need each other. For example, with only one foot, you can not go very far, but with both, you can run at a speed of 34.74 km / h, and walking can reach infinity. *The same is true for marriage.*

Although similar, our eyes are not equal. One sees farther than the other. Each fulfills its mission: One sees objects up close, and the other sees them far away. This indicates that both are needed to see objects well. With only one eye, we see with difficulty, but both can see a better horizon with great ease. *So is marriage.*

In conclusion, each thing is necessary for life; similar, they have different functions, and both, with care and coordination, fulfill their function: build, walk, and see. The *same is true of marriage*. What one spouse cannot do, the other will do; we have eyes and a critical mind, which is the logic of the human being. So, if you do not separate yet, be patient; as time passes, you will see how wonderful it is to live with the one you love.

If you have different points of view, you must be supportive and understanding and have a good dose of tolerance. In this way and step by step, you will be able to reach fulfillment because marriage, thanks to the Creator, is like that. I invite you to write your problems and disagreements with your spouse in the following lines. The problems I have with my spouse are the following.

_____

_____

_____

_____

_____

The causes of the problems and disagreements are as follows:

_____

_____

_____

_____

_____

I understand that all human beings, in one way or another, suffer from abandonment, abuse, aggression, and disappointment at some stage of their lives. If my spouse has them, I will lovingly help. The best way to solve our problems and disagreements is as follows.

_____

Seek information and solutions, go to therapy, overcome inequality, and divide responsibilities. Learn to distribute income and share responsibility for the children. Express your emotional, physical, and psychological needs. Also, learn to overcome routine with creativity. Do not allow the interference of third parties (*mothers-in-law, siblings, relatives, and friends*). Above all, strengthen trust and never disrespect each other.

If you are bothered by your partner's mistakes and defects but live happily with yours, it is an indication that you are emotionally ill. I invite you to reflect on the ignorance, pride, and selfishness that confuse the arrogance that invades us. We must learn that sometimes, genuinely loving means breaking with everything and understanding that sometimes the best becomes the enemy of the good due to our misunderstanding of life's purpose.

All humans have existential crises; let us not make life an existential drama. It would help if you made a chronological analysis of life to learn that living together in marriage is to learn and grow; it is not a tragedy as you want to believe. Problems are to overcome, for God gave us intelligence and wisdom.

Think about it: do not undo your marriage; technically, we could say that he who destroys marriage destroys civilization. Meditate deeply, detaching yourself from ego, pride, and your false self. And, if you find that your love is genuine if you are married in love, don't fall for the mental errors and wrong advice of others. Save your marriage because if you cannot live with the one you love, *who do you think you can live with?* If you can't fix the problems with the one you love, how will you fix the issues with people who have no attachment or affection for you? Don't *fool yourself*!

Infidelity is like a malicious spirit that wants to destroy your relationship and your happiness. It is more bitter than death, for it brings desolation, betrayal, confusion, jealous torment, insecurity, and low self-esteem. It traps your reflections, stuns your judgment, shackles your heart, and confuses your feelings by overcoming your will. All unfaithful passion ends, as it begins, in one blow. The defeated ends up being a slave to the one who defeats him, so do not let yourself be defeated. It is worth repeating it; nowadays, for many people, it is easier to disrupt a marriage than to cook rice.

After pandemic seclusion, we have all experienced some changes. Likewise, the way we view relationships has changed. During this time, marriages and couples have spent more time together than usual. They have had to occupy different roles and obligations that they used to occupy with other people, for example, with friends and work. So, what is in the usual routine a perfect opportunity for a restart, to learn from that period of inactivity together? Marriages and couples can emerge from confinement and routine stronger than ever if they are willing to learn from the past and look to the future with confidence and renewed love.

If there is true love, there will always be solutions, one of them being to turn to God, who is the number one protector of your marriage. "*Proverbs 3:^{5-6} : Trust in Yahweh with all your heart and lean not on your understanding; acknowledge him in all your ways, and he will make your paths straight*". You must have more faith and trust because whoever lacks God lacks everything, and whoever has God lacks nothing. Where there is faith, there is love; where there is love, there is peace, and where there is peace, there God is, and where God is, there is union, understanding, happiness, and prosperity. In this way, you will be able to say: my love, in my heart and my life, there will always be a special place for you, not because I say so, but because you have earned it; I want to grow old, because, with your love and God in our lives, nothing can defeat us.

However, for a spouse with a tendency to infidelity and to commit adultery, no one can put up with that. There are always opportunities to change and repair, but persisting with that attitude indicates that each one must follow his or her path separately. No one likes to live with permanent **"horns,"** and those who live like that do not live but agonize. Because **"fleeting loves"** is what they offer in the market of artificial happiness.

They are like fireworks that make noise and dazzle for a moment. But moments later, they are extinguished; they disappear, and only silence, emptiness, and infinite loneliness remain. The only thing left is the guilt of the mistake and its consequences.

"Roses lose their petals but bloom again with more strength."

THE CIRCLE OF FAMILY AND CHILDREN

Just as grass and trees bear fruit with their seeds according to their kind, and birds and animals reproduce according to their type, man also produces fruit according to his kind. They are his sons and daughters, thus forming a family and perpetuating humanity. It is the most extraordinary thing a human being can give and the most beautiful task the Creator gives us.

We were created for this most significant purpose. They come through us, but they are not ours; they are the sons and daughters of tomorrow because they have their own thinking and decisions; just like you, they will be God's collaborators in creation, our species' evolution, and the universe's expansion. Thanks to the joy of being able to have children, and with this, the Creator of the universe is inviting us to collaborate in his creative work with all our love and strength. You and your family are the foundation of society.

The greatest gift you can receive in this existence is to be able to procreate, so revel in the joy of parenting and the potential of your children as much as possible. In childhood, it's essential to pamper your child, give them abundant care and love, and teach them that they cannot have everything they want on a whim. They must learn that there are duties, rules, and obligations to fulfill, and that depends on you. Children learn from their parents' example, so we must do our homework well. Setting boundaries is not about restricting them but about preparing them for the responsibilities of life.

Remember that your children will follow your example, not your advice. Try to be your best and raise them to be happy, not useless and insecure. Please don't kill yourself for what you can leave them, since each one must earn what he/she needs, because they will grow up and by natural law will have other interests. Do not worry about how much you can leave to your children; worry more about what kind of children you will go to the world.

That is to say, the planet is full of people with complexes, unhappy, irresponsible, petulant, thieves, greedy, swindlers, profiteers, prostitutes, proud, envious, and murderers. You must know how to educate them. Otherwise, you will be to blame for what they are and what happens to them because children are the portrait of their parents and the mirror of their family.

There is no manual for parenting, neither do they have one for being children. You must be aware that one day, you will not be there to give him what he needs when he falls; teach him to get up on his own. Teach him to fend for himself and live independently, prepare him for life, and not be a lazy whiner. We are in the age of electronic and technological evolution, with a torrent of hardly tolerable information.

Philosophy, faith, theology, and understanding are unimportant or meaningful for children and teenagers. For them, having a fashionable cell phone or an electronic game is more important than listening to suggestions and advice. They are even incapable of making their bed, tidying their room, or serving themselves food. They idolize their friends and live faulting their parents, whom they blame for all their traumas and misunderstandings of life.

In other words, in many homes, they raise sons and daughters who are lazy, uncomprehending, and incapable of coping with life on their own.

Those of us who are parents know that at some point in our lives, we experience crises in our children's behavior, especially in times of rebellion. In this situation, we are overcome with emotion, desperation, and the desire to solve the problems at home. However, problems may arise when we embark on the journey of parenthood. It is a duty to raise emotionally healthy children who can face life's challenges.

If a child in his childhood and adolescence experiences problems and conflicts in a highly emotional situation (parents, families in conflict, problems at school), this fact can generate emotional wounds. A child may react to these conflicts with despair, rage, anger, arrogance, hostility, rebellion, mockery, resentment, repudiation, frustration, criticism, or sarcasm. According to their interpretation, they can be affected differently and are unprepared to face these situations appropriately.

It is not advisable to give your children everything they want; give them rewards for fulfilling their responsibilities (which do not merit them since they are a duty). If you do this, it is a big mistake; tomorrow, you may regret it. It may be difficult and painful, but it is the best thing you can do for them.

Limiting them with likes is to love them, educate them, prepare them for the future, and teach them the value of things. A parent who loves his or her children is responsible for reprimanding them. It is better to teach them to fish than to give them a fish, and rather than giving them material things and making them interested, it is better to provide them with the quality of love.

For this reason, you must accustom him to controlling his desires and emotions and supplying his needs as much as possible without altering his learning or nature. Remember that everything has its place and time, its when and how. Teach him to respect and say no when it is no and, more importantly, to recognize his mistakes. You may think they are small, but today's children understand everything quickly and flawlessly when you explain it well.

Teach them hunger, injustice, pain, sickness, and death exist. If you do not do it, let yourself be carried away by love, ignoring the reason for being. You are doing him a great wrong, making him ignorant of the reality in which we live. You are teaching him to walk as if he were blind, and he will not know how to defend himself against the hurricanes of the vine. For this reason, he should not avoid life's difficulties but rather teach him to overcome them with creativity and intelligence.

Children are taught to live, not agonizing; they should learn that life has difficulties, stumbles, and struggles. They should remember that they can fall into a hole, not a grave, that life should not be dramatized, but that they should know how to live it, enjoying what is beautiful and just. That is his most beautiful task, a precious gift from the Creator. Teach him gratitude, and there is nothing better than a grateful child. When he comes home, his smile lifts his parents' spirits. Moreover, when it is known that he fixed a problem or achieved something new, pride comes to the chest, and one says to them.

--- What a fine son you are; I am proud of you.

--- What a joy to see him like this.

When a child has a problem and reflects sadness, don't ask yourself what is wrong; remember that we all carry our drama. We are their co-pilots in the program of this life; we must show them the map and warn them of the obstacles along the way. But they are the ones who take their route; we are their companions on the journey, but they are the pilots, the ones behind the wheel. We are their parents, not dictators; we are the bow, and they are the arrow.

Son, learn, enjoy, and enjoy as much as possible because we are not eternal on this planet. Enjoy the beautiful things in life, your parents, when they are alive. Spend quality time with them when they are alive and not whole nights when they die. It is better to hug a living parent and squeeze that tired body from working and not hug a coffin when they die. Tell them you love them and that you need them when they are alive, and do not scream the same in silence when they die. Learn to enjoy a weekend or holiday and take a short walk with your parents when they are alive, so you don't long for those moments when they die.

G It's more meaningful to give a rose, a flower, or a small prayer now, while we're alive and can appreciate it, than to dedicate long prayers or poems to our graves when we're gone. Let's share our time and love now rather than make long trips to visit our graves later.

We must value the time and effort we've dedicated to each other while we're alive, so we don't regret it when we're gone. Let's express our love and appreciation now so we don't regret not doing so when it's too late. Remember, you are the greatest gift in my life, now and always.

Children, I advise you to learn to live, enjoy, value, and improve yourselves. Choose what is beautiful, just, and reasonable. It's important to express your love when you feel it, help those in need, and give food to the hungry and clothes to the naked. But above all, respect your classmates at school, university, and work. Remember, bullying is never acceptable, as it can cause irreparable harm.

Learn to give quality time, enjoy the people who love you, and respect them like God loves and respects us. By doing so, you're preparing for the future with a conscience and ready to be citizens of a country and the planet Earth, universal citizens.

CITIZENS OF PLANET EARTH

Children are the foundation of the family, which is essential for society. Society, in turn, is crucial for a nation, and nations are integral parts of the planet. After the COVID-19 pandemic, the world changed significantly, moving towards a global or planetary community. We are experiencing large-scale changes, and the idea of being citizens of planet Earth is gaining ground.

- Communication has undergone a significant change in the way we communicate.
- Space Exploration and Cooperation: International cooperation in space is increasingly common.
- Globally, migration and education are becoming increasingly interconnected.
- Humanitarian Aid: The global response to natural disasters is more coordinated.
- Military and Economic Assistance: In cases of conflict, international aid is crucial.

- International Hiring: Hiring personnel from other countries is increasingly common.
- Racial and Social Prejudice: There are significant changes in the perception of diversity.
- **Digital Nomad Visas:** Facilitate remote work from anywhere in the world.
- **Global Education:** Educational institutions promote the study of international affairs and global citizenship.
- **Migration and Diversity:** Visa-free travel and ethnic and cultural diversity foster understanding and mutual respect.

These signs show clear progress towards global citizenship. We must prepare and educate our children to be citizens of this new world. They are not just the future but the architects of the future. In a broad sense, being a citizen establishes rights, obligations, an identity, and a sense of belonging. However, being a global citizen also implies taking care of the place where we live. The question is, where do we live? On planet Earth, right?

Global Responsibilities. As we have seen, a pandemic does not only affect one race, ethnic group, or country but spreads throughout the world. The butterfly effect demonstrates that actions in one place have global repercussions. This is valid for political, economic, technological, environmental, and military actions, highlighting the interconnectedness of international issues and the urgency of our involvement.

Considering Evolution, AI, and Technological Changes

Global citizenship has never been more relevant in an era of rapid technological advancements, artificial intelligence, and global interconnectedness. As we stand on the precipice of new frontiers, such as space exploration and AI-driven societies, we must raise a generation of citizens who understand their role in shaping a sustainable and equitable future for our planet.

The digital revolution has facilitated unprecedented levels of communication and collaboration, breaking down geographical barriers and fostering a sense of global community. The COVID-19 pandemic has underscored our world's interconnectedness and highlighted the crucial need for international cooperation to address shared challenges. It's not about individual efforts but about coming together as a global community.

To thrive in this evolving landscape, we must cultivate in our children a deep understanding of global issues and a commitment to social responsibility. Education is crucial, equipping them with the knowledge and skills to navigate a complex and interconnected world and empowering them to become active agents of positive change. By instilling in them a sense of global citizenship and its values, we can inspire them to promote sustainability, foster intercultural understanding, support human rights, and embrace technological advancements.

As global citizens, our responsibilities extend beyond national borders. We must strive to:

- **Promote sustainability:** Protect our planet's resources and combat climate change.
- **Foster intercultural understanding:** Celebrate diversity and challenge prejudice.
- **Support human rights:** Advocate for justice and equality for all.
- **Embrace technological advancements:** Utilize technology to solve global problems and improve lives.

By fostering these qualities, we can empower our children to become active participants in building a more just, equitable, and sustainable future for themselves and future generations.

This shift towards a global mindset is a future possibility and a pressing need. It's happening not only at the governmental level but also at the corporate, community, and individual levels. The idea of being global citizens is already underway, with examples as mentioned previously. The UN and UNESCO promote Global Citizenship Education (GCED), which is beginning to dominate movements like multicultural education.

Social networks, communications, the economy, free trade agreements, imports and exports, and hiring are becoming increasingly global. This means individuals are not just gaining social and global responsibilities but becoming an inevitable part of the benefit of all societies. However, to become planetary citizens, governments, businesses, and individuals must make profound changes for universal adaptation.

Future generations, such as our children's children, could be a reality for everyone in two or three decades. We are not just leaving a legacy when we learn to develop a universal mindset, responsibility, and consciousness in all aspects. Still, we are shaping the best legacy we can teach our children. It's about teaching them to love God, their brothers, and their neighbors and to respect the laws, which will be the foundation of their global citizenship.

What can we do to educate the new generations for global citizenship?

For our children to become planetary citizens with a promising future, they must receive an education that is not just adequate but exceptional. This is not the same education that governments have been providing for years, but one that is at the forefront of technology. If they are not educated and adapted appropriately, they will be replaced by humanoid robots, already programmed to perform human tasks.

We must learn to develop our brains more, increase our intelligence levels, and be worthy planetary citizens. This is not just a choice but a necessity in a world where the robotics industry is evolving daily, and many human jobs are being replaced. This is a reality that cannot be stopped but one that we must adapt to.

Concrete Actions. How should we educate our children properly so they can face the technological future and be planetary citizens? Here are some suggestions:

- Teach about Cultural Diversity: Foster tolerance and mutual respect.
- Promote Critical Thinking: Develop problem-solving skills.
- Encourage volunteering and community service.
- Please provide them with the tools to become agents of change.

The future of humanity is in our hands. We can create a better world for all. It is time to step forward and assume our responsibility as citizens of planet Earth.

Enhanced Translation Incorporating AI and Technological Advancements

This shift towards a global mindset occurs not only at the governmental level but also at the corporate, community, and individual levels. The idea of being global citizens is already underway, with examples such as technological advancements, AI, and international cooperation.

The UN and UNESCO promote Global Citizenship Education (GCED), which is beginning to dominate movements like multicultural education.

Global citizenship has never been more relevant in an era of rapid technological advancements and increasing globalization.

The rise of artificial intelligence, automation, and interconnectedness is reshaping our world and demanding a new generation of citizens equipped to navigate these complex challenges.

To prepare our children for this future, we must foster a global mindset that encompasses:

- Digital literacy: Equipping them with the skills to use technology responsibly and ethically.
- AI literacy: Understanding the implications of AI on society and the economy.
- Environmental stewardship: Promoting sustainability and conservation.
- Global perspective: Cultivating empathy, tolerance, and respect for diverse cultures.

By fostering these qualities, we can empower our children to become active participants in shaping a more just, equitable, and sustainable future for all.

What is your opinion about being a universal citizen?

_____

_____

_____

_____

My view on this project is as follows.

_____

_____

_____

_____

Yes, I agree because.

_____

_____

_____

_____

_____

_____

I'm afraid I must disagree because.

_____

_____

_____

_____

"Above every child, there should be a sign that says, treat with love, because he contains the future."

THE CIRCLE OF FEAR

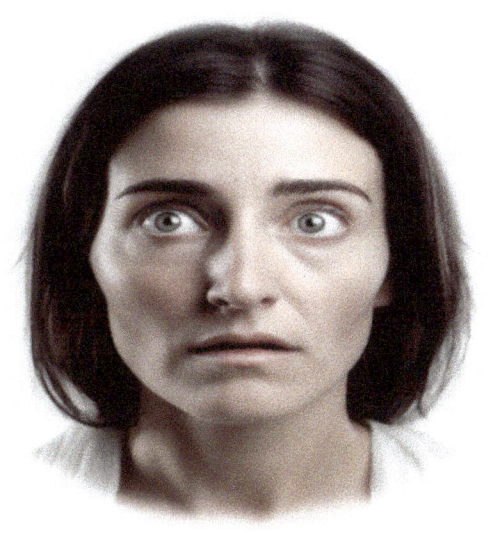

Fear paralyzes and limits; it manifests itself differently in each person. It is a disturbance, anguish, and panic; in fact, it is the most difficult emotion to handle, and for those who are afraid, all noises frighten. Pain cries it, anger screams it, and in fact, fear serves to lose everything. Some things make a dream impossible, and it is the fear of failure, just as the one who fears to suffer already fears fear.

All fear originates in the brain, creating a chain reaction and physical inability to do or say anything. It is an alteration of emotional mood that produces fright, terror, body rigidity, and paralyzes before a natural or imaginary threat prevents you from reaching your goals. Fear is one of the most lethal killers that the human being has. It can kill your goals, dreams, love, friendship, and joy. And, as a final blow, it makes you feel impotent before a decision or situation, isolating you and generating a sense of defeat.

Fear affects your mentality, how you see things, and creative, intuitive, and reactive potential. It makes you sick by causing stress, ulcers, colon irritation, and anxiety. It is the most subtle and destructive disease you can have. It is one of the worst miseries that human beings have. Feeling panic is like feeling a bomb exploding inside you, making you fall to pieces, because fear always makes you see things worse than they are. Whoever lives in fear is the same as living as a slave; he is not accessible because the mind and heart that live in panic are empty of hope.

Fear, regardless of its origin, can invade us at any age and in any situation, forcing the mind and body to undergo unexpected changes. It exhausts the resources of reason, the heart beats faster, and the pupils dilate; it reaches the amygdala through the thalamus, which causes an immediate reaction in most of the body. In other words, it is biologically impossible for a person to develop his full potential if he lives in fear. In reality, he does not live but rather martyrs himself and even agonizes.

Fear originates in the amygdala, located in the brain's limbic system. For many people, it functions as a "stop" signal, i.e., stop, analyze, plan, and act, as a survival method. This works in both humans and animals. However, animals use panic much better than humans because most develop their instincts 100% more than humans.

FROM TERROR TO HOPE
OVERCOMING FEAR IN TIMES OF CRISIS

The fear, horror, anxiety, and stress caused by COVID-19 brought significant challenges to humans, scientists, and public health worldwide. The fear and horror of the virus made us give up many things and habits that, before the pandemic, we would never have changed. As noted above, fear understood as a cognitive response to a threat, favors human adaptation to certain dangers. But if this fear is maintained over time, it can predispose to the emergence of physical illnesses and psychological disorders, such as horror, anxiety, stress, etc. According to the scientific journal "*La Psychiatry Research*," During the pandemic, fear and horror harmed us in different ways and spheres in our personal lives, particularly in mental health.

During the pandemic, fear was characterized by being infected, suffering, and meeting death. We have witnessed millions of deaths around the planet. Some doctors and nurses even committed suicide because of the helplessness of seeing hundreds of their patients die and not being able to do anything about it. In one way or another, many of us were affected by the death of a loved one, a family member, a friend, or an acquaintance. However, what can we do with or without a virus *when it is our turn*? The world is different, but we must adapt and know how to move forward.

Moreover, thanks to God and science, the vaccine was discovered after the crisis calmed down. The horror we feel passes to fear and then only to a slight fear. After the vaccination, we feel safer. In the same way, it changes our mental state, which consequently raises the body's defenses. As a result, both the vaccine and the body's defenses work together, evacuating the fear.

Vaccines make us feel safer, as well as concepts such as resilience, hope, knowing how to resist, and faith. Fear is the product of feeling helpless in the face of imminent danger, not knowing what to do, and not having anything to face it with. But once overcome, there are only those who invent their fears, raising their anxiety, depression, and stress, afraid to live.

Now, ask yourself the following question.

- What benefit does fear bring you?
- What is afraid achieved?
- What is the benefit of giving up your dreams?
- What is the benefit of not taking charge of your life?
- Are you happy with your fears?

Ask yourself, how much have you lost because of your fears?

- Did you know that fear is a friend of stagnation and poverty?
- Did you know fear sometimes prevents you from enjoying life's small and big pleasures?
- Do you live satisfied with your fears? No, you don't!

I invite you to overcome them and give yourself better opportunities because God and life have better things for you.

"Fear neither prison nor poverty nor death, you must fear." *(Giacomo Leopardi, 1798-1837 Italian Poet).*

In the following lines, inventory your fears, things, situations, and places that cause you to panic.

_____

_____

_____

_____

Now, try to identify the origin of those fears. Go back to your childhood, adolescence, and school, and ask yourself when, where, and why those fears were born. Why are they there?

The origin of my fears is.

_____

_____

_____

_____

Make a personal and silent retreat, penetrating your inner self. Isolate yourself from everything: people, noises, TV, cell phones, and distractions. Try to find the spirit that dwells within you. Avoid all the usual mental activities, such as feelings, images, reflections, and memories.

In an inner silence that goes beyond the senses until you feel that peace that transcends feeling joy and sadness. If you manage to analyze well within yourself, you will notice that most of your fears are unfounded by others; others were created in your mind by you.

If I fail at something, I try again. Confidence and love are the best antidote to panic because where there is love, there is no fear. True love takes away fear, and he who loves God has nothing to fear. If you love yourself enough, you will leave the slavery of fear and face it with all you have: strength and heart. Master the sensations of fear and control your thoughts; dare to do what you have never done because there is a risk advantage.

You can devise a plan such as attending therapies, conferences, workshops, and retreats, commit, and start a transformation at a conscious level. Without making up the reality, with your level of responsibility, the main objective is to control your thoughts, which are the ones that feed the emotions. These, in turn, control the feelings that lead you to act and act in real life. And, if you go somewhere, ensure it is without fear and trepidation.

Fears are feelings that come from thoughts as an emotional reaction to a situation, where memory is also involved. I know this; therefore, I commit myself to changing my thoughts. Today, I decided to stop being a puppet of fears, bad experiences, and memories.

Today, I commit to having faith and trust in my abilities, talents, and virtues that the Creator has given me. I ask God to help, teach, and accompany me to make quantum leaps in my life, thoughts, and actions. I have the disposition to make drastic changes in my existence and to get out of the mental and spiritual ballast because I was born to be something more significant. I will eliminate my fears and apprehensions with faith and confidence to start.

_____

_____

_____

_____

I will overcome the obstacles in the following way.

_____

_____

_____

_____

Fear is the sting of logical reasoning and self-confidence. It blinds our minds, robs us of sleep, makes us lie, and is cruel to ourselves. It demonstrates the lack of God in your life because he who has God fears nothing.

"Fear is the sting of the mind and reasoning; it blinds logic and self-confidence."

THE CIRCLE OF PROBLEMS

Each of us is a unique individual with unique qualities. Problems are an inevitable part of life and are essential for our growth. However, remember that we can overcome any challenge that comes our way. Problems may be uncomfortable, but they are also opportunities for learning and development. Many see them as "*obstacles and complaints*," but life would be stagnant without challenges. These challenges are not just hurdles but stepping stones for our personal growth, empowering us to become the best version of ourselves.

For example, we wouldn't have a cell phone, TVs, computers, vehicles, airplanes, medicines, hospitals, public transportation, electricity, etc. We have all these things thanks to the people who, in their time, considered that not having these comforts was a problem for them and others. Likewise, we have more economic, environmental, health, and daily life problems. If life were only about eating, sleeping, and doing whatever we want, then we would be nothing and have no purpose. The best way to have no problems would be to be an animal. For example, a cow, a horse, or we could also die because the dead have no problems. However, if we live on this planet, we must know how to deal with problems.

Life itself is a problem, so it is better to try to understand it than to lament it. Difficulties make us grow and teach us to correct our mistakes so that we do not repeat them. Difficulties are more than that; they are teachers of life who do not choose religion, social or economic position, or intellectual level.

We must know how to act in the face of problems, so the optimist sees an opportunity in every situation, and the pessimist only sees an obstacle. For instance, a job loss can be an opportunity to explore an alternative career path, or a failed relationship can be a chance to learn more about oneself. For this reason, leaders and people with fixed goals find themselves when they measure and intelligently overcome their problems.

Likewise, worries about problems never solve anything, but they do make our lives miserable. We must reconcile ourselves and be the best we can with ourselves. Trying to live without problems is like catching the wind with our hands; even when we are not looking for them, someone brings them. Not all issues can be avoided, but we can prevent some by practicing the following habits.

- Do not reveal anyone's secrets. In truth, nobody knows how to keep secrets, and in the end, they always find out, and your discredit has no solution. You cannot ask for discretion when you do not have it yourself. A secret can be kept between two people, but it becomes gossip when a third party intervenes.

- Don't meddle too much in your neighbor's house. If you don't want to know about other people's lives, you annoy your neighbor and call for trouble.

- Do not make false statements against your brothers, relatives, friends, neighbors, and neighbors. It is something like playing with a hot iron as if it were water. It will burn your tongue, mind, and soul.

- Never trust a betrayer. You can forgive, but do not fall back into their game. It is a stubbed tooth and a wavering foot who trusts a traitor or gossip in times of trouble.

- Do not think you are too big, and do not presume to know everything. It is better to be invited to the first place than to suffer humiliation when told to retire because that is not your place.

- Respect your neighbor's partner. Do not covet her company. A big problem is a woman jealous of another; nothing good will happen. Just as when a man is betrayed by his wife, cold winds will come from the north, and he will act like a wounded lion.

- Respect the property of others. Do not take what does not belong to you or what you have not earned. It always brings disgrace, dishonor, and jail, and whoever does it always brings curses to his life.

- Don't take everything too personally, better work on your self-esteem.

- Do not make your plans known, nor shout too loudly about your triumphs, for envy is a light sleeper whose ears are open.

- Learn to control your emotions, especially anger, fear, and emotional wounds. Retreats, seminars, and workshops help you overcome these inner problems.

The best way to solve problems is to face them so you will have the opportunity to demonstrate your abilities and skills. You will notice that they also contain some secrets for the development and knowledge of life, full of experience and wisdom. Likewise, you will realize that you would not know life if you had no problems on this planet.

God does not send us problems if we do not have the strength to cope with them or the wisdom to overcome them. If your problems are too big and you feel that despite everything, you cannot cope with them, give them to God, and he will help you. If you don't, in a way, you are letting him down, so talk to God; he is waiting for you always and forever, acting at the right time. In the following lines, I identified your problems; I used a separate sheet of paper if necessary. My problems are.

_____

_____

_____

_____

Now, write down *the causes* of these problems.

_____

_____

_____

_____

It would be best if you were bigger than your problems, gained awareness, and determined to solve them.

_____

_____

_____

_____

There are people (*friends, relatives, acquaintances*) who are natural carriers of problems, for this reason I should stay away from

_____

_____

_____

_____

Try this practice often, and you will notice positive changes in your life. You will help yourself solve unnecessary problems, expanding your understanding of your life's horizons.

"He who has not faced adversity does not know his strength."
(Benjamin Johnson).

THE CIRCLE OF NEEDS AND VANITY

In this vicious circle, out of vanity, we will always need something newer, more modern, bigger, and faster. We need a new job, a house, and a tighter dress. I need a partner who is more in line with our lifestyle. We need to earn more money and a new car; in other words, we create multiple and varied needs without cause. Some have no scruples or satisfaction.

Others have enough resources to satisfy their needs and follies. But most of them are limited because the needs we generate are infinite. In other words, when we are so disenchanted with life, much is little, and little is nothing, starting with vanity, arrogance, and pride. Faced with this emotional crisis, we must prioritize our needs. Decide which are necessary, which ones we can satisfy, and which ones we must renounce.

When we manage to satisfy the needs we create, we assume that we are happy, satisfied, and complete. But after some time, we think we need a newer car, and we notice that the ideal partner has many defects. The profession we studied is incorrect, and the dress we dreamed of is not as elegant as we thought. In this way, we fabricate a disenchantment that has no end, thus creating a vicious circle of dissatisfaction, needs, and unnecessary whims.

The circle of "*I always need*" and vanity is one of the most daring, unsatisfactory, and unnecessary human emotions. This is because, most of the time, it is accompanied by arrogance, pride, and an overly high ego. We always create needs for ourselves because we never have enough. In this way, we remain like a tree without leaves because of unfulfilled whims. We even feel a sense of repression, dissatisfaction, and reluctance for not being able to obtain what we do not need.

The needs have a classification that perfectly fits the whims of every human being, for example:

- The need to exploit man for man,
- The need for money for greed and
- The need to enslave the needy.

In other words, slavery and abuse have not changed their philosophy, only their name. The greedy only trusts in money, just as a hungry lion only trusts in meat.

As a species, we have yet to fully comprehend the insignificance of material possessions in the grand scheme of life. I encourage you to converse with a surgeon or a funeral home administrator and inquire about what the deceased may have taken with them. The surgeon will undoubtedly affirm that none of those who have passed on have been able to take anything with them. Similarly, the funeral director will share that of all the people he has laid to rest, none of them took anything with them.

If you still have doubts, you can go to a cemetery and look for a corpse that has taken a house, a car, money, or fame. You will notice that no one has been able to take anything; rest assured that you will not find anyone who can give you information! Because the dead, of nothing under the sun, can take anything with them. In fact, they are more alone than ever, for as the years go by, they are forgotten among the living.

In 1943, humanistic psychologist Abraham Maslow formulated Maslow's pyramid theory in his *"A Theory of Human Motivation."* In it, he explains what drives human needs and behavior. The pyramid consists of five levels that are hierarchically ordered according to needs. It starts from the level of basic needs such as food and breathing.

When we satisfy the primary needs, we fill the base of the pyramid, and when we cover those needs, we can move to the next level. At this level, there are the secondary needs and, further up, the tertiary needs, and when we fulfill all of them, we move to the next level, which is to invent more needs.

That is to say, we human beings make a misfortune out of lack, with so much lamentation and inconformity that we turn it into a tragedy. We must understand that life does not consist exclusively of the material, nor should it be the axis of what man must satisfy his senses. It is not what is on the outside that fills us, but what we have in our hearts to enjoy what the Creator and life have allowed us to have.

Between the years 764-800 of our era, Charles the Great, who was also called "Imperator Augustus," enjoyed an exceptional destiny, was a great emperor, and said the following: --- "When I die, and I am to be buried, I wish you to show my hands open and empty."

--- And for what purpose, my lord? Asked one of his servants. Carlo Magno answered him.

--- So, mankind will understand that I arrived empty-handed and will leave empty-handed. ***What a demonstration of coherence***, isn't it!

Dissatisfaction, like a persistent shadow, distances us from happiness and personal growth. It keeps us stuck in a cycle of frustration and selfishness, preventing us from moving towards a more fulfilling life. It's time to break free from this negative pattern and open our minds to the abundance surrounding us. Let us pay close attention to the warmth of human connection that envelops us, the beauty of nature, and our abilities and talents. We are children of God, jewels of creation worthy of love and value.

Gratitude is not just a practice; it's a source of joy. Instead of dwelling on what we lack, let's celebrate the blessings we already have. Let's thank God for the gift of life, the opportunities that come our way, and the ability to savor every moment.

Don't let yourself feel needy or miserable. Look around you and bask in the warmth of those who love you. Consider the grandeur of creation, the earth's kindness, the sun's warmth, the flow of water, and the simple ability to breathe. Reflect on your skills and abilities, and nurture and develop them. Recognize the greatness within you as a child of God the Father, as a jewel of creation. The actual value of your worth comes from within, not from others. Give yourself the respect and appreciation you deserve.

Let's pause and consider: are our needs truly our own, or are they merely vanity? Are we feeding our arrogance, ego, and pride with our desires? We often go to great lengths to satisfy our whims, such as taking on debt for cosmetic surgery or personal care. The beauty industry is booming, with more and more people spending significant amounts on beauty products. But are these expenses essential, or are they a product of our vanity?

Let's make a conscious effort to distinguish between our genuine needs and the ones we create out of vanity and arrogance. By doing so, we can redirect our resources towards what truly matters and bring us joy and fulfillment.

I invite you to make a list of the things you think you need. I need next.

_____

_____

_____

_____

_____

_____

Now, in a deep inner encounter, ask yourself. What I need is.

_____

_____

_____

_____

_____

To use in the following way.

_____

_____

_____

_____

_____

_____

You may need extra sheets of paper or a notebook. If you resort to this practice, many headaches can be avoided. So, when you want to buy something, ask yourself the following questions.

- Why am I buying it?
- Do I need it?
- Why do I need it?

You will notice that there are things you should never buy because they do not make sense. Let us remember a famous phrase of Cicero: (*He works very severely and tries to obtain with money what he should receive with virtue*).

"Human beings are full of needs, but once fulfilled, none satisfy us."

THE CIRCLE OF FORGIVENESS

The first logical reason for forgiveness is to want to forgive and be forgiven. I invite you to ask specific questions about your problems with your partner, parents, family, friends, work, and people you do not like. Those people that when you see them, your stomach turns, and you don't even want to mention them. Also, think about the effects of emotional wounds caused since childhood and adolescence by abuse, abandonment, aggression, disappointment, and injustice. If so, ask yourself the following questions. Forgiveness has a healing power, offering hope and optimism on your emotional journey.

- Do I feel hatred or resentment for someone or something?
- Do I live with resentment towards someone?
- Do I live with bitterness?
- Do I live with anger? Will you go and pride?
- Why do I feel disgusted with a specific situation?

- Do I complain daily about everyone and everything?
- Do you feel that your life and your plans have no meaning?
- Believes that there is nothing wrong with badmouthing or taking dirty laundry from people he doesn't like
- He believes that half the world criticizes him behind his back.
- Memories of his childhood do not leave him alone.
- The scenes of abuse, aggression, abandonment, and disappointment that he experienced in the past are constantly replayed in his memory.
- Is it difficult for you to find a partner? Are you not living well with the one you have? Do you not see any plans or a near future?
- Think of beating, torturing, and making someone suffer for the sufferings they went through.
- He thinks that he could attack or even attempt against someone's life because of the bad memories, bitterness, and bitterness he feels.

When someone you love hurts you and hurts you, you can either hold on to your anger, resentment, and ideas of revenge or choose forgiveness and move on. The emotional symptoms of resentment, abandonment, abuse, aggression, disappointment, injustice, and hatred are more. If you live with constant anger and resentment, everything irritates you, you shout at everything, everything bothers you, and you live with frustration and bitterness. It is because you allow negative and toxic emotions to affect you, dominating your life.

It is a sign that you do not live in peace and have emotional wounds to heal. These wounds are real, and their healing is crucial to your well-being. There are people you need to forgive and others you need to ask for forgiveness. If we want to live well but with hatred and resentment without forgiving or asking for forgiveness, it is like taking poison and waiting for someone else to die.

WHY WE DO NOT FORGIVE

Forgiveness is not necessarily a detailed and emotional act but an act of the heart and will. Forgiving fully is a process that takes time. We commonly do not forgive because we consider it an act of injustice and an outrage to our feelings. An unjust forgetfulness of the mistreatment, abuse, outrages, loneliness, abandonment, and violence to which we were subjected. Internally, we cry out for justice but must examine our hearts because we rightly remember and do not forgive. You may not forgive because you identify more with the feeling of justice and have been denied reparation, which you are crying out for within yourself.

- It does not forgive because you think it is a matter of weakness and lack of character.
- It does not forgive because it does not accept that it has already happened and considers it still happening today.
- It does not forgive because it has imprisoned its understanding and spirit and needs to add pain details to the misfortunes of its personal history.
- It does not forgive because deep inside, it cries out for an explanation and reparation.
- He does not forgive because neither life nor anyone else has done him justice.
- It does not forgive because it has disappointment, will go, resentment, and resentment.
- It does not forgive because it needs emotional and inner sanction.

- Consequently, he does not forgive because he is far from God.

In a deep analysis and inner encounter, I invite you to describe why you cannot forgive. I do not forgive because

_____

_____

_____

_____

The memories and emotional wounds that haunt me the most are.

_____

_____

_____

_____

To live with attachments of hatred, bitterness, and resentment is to live in low levels of consciousness, turning it into agony. It imprisons the soul and damages the mind, feeding it with self-destructive thoughts. You do not live and enjoy fully what surrounds you; that is, if you live with resentments and constant grievances, you will end up in a spiritual prison full of bitterness.

You will live with resentment that limits you, putting a wall to your potential, achievements, and goals. Having your understanding and spirit imprisoned will not allow you to realize your projects. Feeling that your opportunities are slipping away, just as your life is slipping away, you are allowing inner hurts, confusion, and hate to dominate your life. If you allow it, you sink into spiritual and experiential misery without being able to move forward.

Stop living with the problems and hurts that bind you because you are paying a very high price for carrying them. Instead, think of the solutions that are available to you. It would be best to forgive the people who hurt you, not because they deserve it, but because you deserve to be free of everything that hurts you. Hatred is not cured with more hatred, nor offense with another offense.

Whoever thinks this way lacks heart, understanding, love, and God. The loneliness caused by resentment hurts, as do the wounds that do not stop bleeding. How can they not bleed if you do not let them heal? It hurts the lack of asking for forgiveness from the one who hurt and mistreated him so much. But his attitude hurts more because he lacks conscience, inner humility, and knowledge of how to ask for or give forgiveness.

Arrogance, pride, and high pride are enemies of forgiveness. To forgive others, you must first forgive yourself. You cannot truly forgive if you have anger, envy, arrogance, and pride, continuing with bad memories, feeding your wounds. To forgive is to transmit love and peace; you cannot forgive by being an accuser, judge, and jailer simultaneously. You must forgive with heart, will, conscience, and soul because action and heart define forgiveness, not emotions.

Forgiveness frees the soul and mind, the bad memories and experiences that have marked our lives. By doing so, we also free others because the person not at peace with himself is constantly at war with the world. Forgiveness is the sterilization of the soul, the cleansing of the mind, and inner liberation, transforming it into a place of forgiveness, not guilt. A being of life and not of death, forgiveness brings joy, where bitterness produces sadness and healing, where bitterness causes illness.

In times of plenty, remember misery; in times of wealth, think of poverty; and in times of faults and failures, think of forgiveness, for as birds nest with their kind, so forgiveness nests with those who practice it. Pride, resentment, and anger must be overcome to do good. Hatred is a lack of mind and heart. To forgive is a personal decision; it is to look with new eyes at a person and life. It is to give yourself inner peace; you deserve it because you have a spirit of faith and courage that knows and feels the value of forgiveness. A vile spirit never forgives because it is not in its nature. Forgiveness is not feeling anger or rage against a person. A life lesson accompanies every act of forgiveness.

"Inscribe grievances in the dust; words of good inscribe them in marble." (*Benjamin* Franklin).

It is not enough just to read books, to be conscious for a few minutes, and that's it, it's over. Returning to the usual spiritual inertia, going back to being a puppet of resentment, bad memories, and toxic emotions. With this, you will not achieve anything; you will remain the same, and the purpose to change and grow will fall on deaf ears. You need to act consciously, forgiving and asking for forgiveness; a heart that acts this way is a just and grateful heart with God and life.

So, I invite you to act. If you want to free yourself and not go to the grave with those feelings, the best option is to forgive and ask for forgiveness. Consider yourself; it is the best thing to do since you don't know when you are going to die, and you can't leave with those bills unpaid. List the people who hurt you and caused you pain and sadness.

The people who have hurt me are.

_____

_____

_____

_____

_____

_____

_____

Look carefully at your reactions. Do you think you can forgive those people who hurt you, causing you pain and sadness? You should be aware that true forgiveness is not weakness but rather a matter of understanding, level of consciousness, and spiritual courage. To forgive, we must feel empathy, the offense, the pain, and the humiliation the other person received. If you are ready to leave the emotional void, fill yourself with courage, and with God's help, forgive with all your heart.

I need to forgive, , from my heart, and in the name of Christ, I forgive him for the mistakes he made with me.

I forgive in the name of God, too. for all that he made me suffer, I forgive him because I deserve a better life far from hatred and resentment.

I forgive in the name of God. for all that made me suffer. I forgive him and myself, overcoming the mistakes and faults. A forgiving heart is a grateful, just, and sincere heart. Forgiving others for their offenses will raise my self-esteem because I will receive forgiveness.

If the person disappears and you don't know where he/she is or if he/she passed away. The best thing to do is to visualize (imagine) it in your mind, sit face to face and look into his eyes, mention one by one the offenses, and claim each of the insults and contempt. Not all the offenses together, but *one by one*, without omitting any. Tell him if that was what you wanted for yourself; tell him how much it hurts and still hurts, carrying bitter chains

195

you don't have to drag. If you feel you can't talk to him, you can write him a letter explaining how you think, how much he hurt you, and how it has affected how you live and perceive life.

Tell her you deserve a better life and to live free of attachments. Cry, cry as much as you want, scream if you want, tell him that you want a change, and leave all that bitterness and resentment. Tell him that you want to be reborn, that in the name of God, you forgive, and in the name of God, you free him. Tell him/her you decided to love because God is with you now. You feel a great love that you can share with those who need it, and you are one of those people.

Now, in deep inner silence, I burned that letter while observing how the fire consumed the paper. He also felt his bitterness, hatred, bad memories, and traumas disappearing. Afterward, I sought a space to meditate and find myself. He can feel that he has found the missing link in his life, coming out of a dark void that did not allow him to see a promising future.

EXERCISES TO ASK FOR FORGIVENESS

Forgiveness is not only forgiving those who have hurt us. It also recognizes our mistakes and the damage we have caused to ourselves, our parents, spouses, children, friends, colleagues, and others. To forgive is to be sincere and to look for ways to correct our mistakes, regaining trust. Forgiveness also consists in seeing the other as oneself, as God's favorite child, not as a cursed and unpleasant being. Humans have committed offenses and harmed others throughout our lives; no one is spared. Life gives us hard blows and sometimes unfair, but it is with all humans.

At this moment, you should be aware that you have committed mistakes and injustices. It is not only about forgiving; you must also ask for forgiveness from anyone who has offended or

196

offended you. Now, you can practice asking for forgiveness for the offenses and faults committed. Also, if it is your case and it comes from your heart, seek reconciliation with that person.

I need to ask for forgiveness from you. _____From my heart and in the name of God, I ask your forgiveness for the mistakes and wrongs I have done to you.

In the name of God, I ask forgiveness, too. _____for what I made him suffer, sorry for my pride, ignorance and arrogance.

From the bottom of my heart, I apologize to _____for the offenses and bad moments. I ask that we overcome offenses and faults, for a forgiving heart is a grateful, just, and sincere heart. Let us raise our conscience, and if we all forgive each other, our world and lives will be better.

If the person has passed away, you may write to him or her using the following lines or a sheet of paper. In all sincerity, open your heart and conscience.

_____

_____

_____

_____

_____

_____

_____

"Whoever conceals his sin never prospers; whoever confesses and forsakes it finds forgiveness." (Proverbs 28:[13]).

This reminds me that I admired enterprising people when I was young. Now that I have grown older, I admire caring and understanding people. Understandably, we don't all speak the same language, but we can share the same sentiment. The one who forgives redeems himself because living with guilt and resentment is not emotionally healthy, and I know that the truth hurts once, but torture hurts every time you remember it.

For this reason, we must forgive without differences in religion, language, race, or customs. This attitude is the way of life that brings peace to the world. You must remember that receiving forgiveness is not a license to continue making mistakes. Forgiveness is not a matter of weakness but instead of character, redemption, and self-love for God and others.

We cannot leave this life without forgiving and asking for forgiveness. The pressure of the past must be removed from the present since forgiveness heals the wounds of the soul, the spirit, and the body. I say of the body because living with resentments causes traumas and sickness, numbs the reason, and causes illnesses. Forgiveness and love are the most significant therapy that God gives us. Let us imitate that goodness, and in his name, let us learn to forgive and remember what he tells us.

"Rather, be kind and compassionate to one another, and forgive one another, just as God forgave you in Christ." (Ephesians 4:[32]).

It is difficult for you to forgive if you do not want to forgive. It is a sign of a hurting heart with deep inner wounds. To avoid going too far, let's apply logic based on reason, intellect, the ability to argue, and, in fact, common logic itself, and we will be able to notice that.

- Who judges will be judged
- Who seduces will be seduced

- He who steals will be stolen
- He who deceives will be deceived
- He who swindles will be tricked and
- ➤ He who **does not** forgive will **not** be forgiven

We rarely place ourselves in a position where others see us but on our own. However, we always seek forgiveness, and God's love is forgiveness itself, so if he forgives us, we must also forgive. **Are we greater than God** *for not to forgive?*

It is worth repeating that forgiveness is an act of will that means different things to different people. But in general, it implies a decision to leave behind hatred, resentment, trauma, bitterness, and thoughts of revenge that blind the heart and reason. Forgiveness brings physical, mental, and spiritual benefits.

- Healthier relationships with those around you
- Better peace of mind
- Less stress, anxiety, and hostility
- Lower blood pressure
- Fewer symptoms of depression
- A healthier and more robust immune system
- Better heart health
- Better self-esteem
- A higher state of consciousness
- Relieves heavy emotional and mental burdens
- Forgiveness frees both the giver and the receiver of forgiveness from bondage
- More spiritual peace and closeness to God
- Better understanding and tolerance with spouse, family, and those around him/her

Remember a famous phrase by Desmond Tutu, a South African theologian, professor, and pacifist (*Forgiveness is an absolute necessity to continue human existence*). We will not have peace and total evolution until we all see each other as equal children of God and love each other as one. Because in nature, there is no meanness; it is in our way of thinking and interpreting things. Something we learn when we accept the lessons that life gives us.

"*Forgiveness redeems us, love completes us, and grace transcends us.*"

THE CIRCLE OF DEBTS

David and his family walked through the mall, and his two children asked him for ice cream. David smiled and said yes, but when he looked to his left, he saw his neighbor Alex. He became upset, as he had owed him money for nine months and defaulted on his payments several times. So, to avoid this, he quickly left the mall.

--- Let's go, children, I have something urgent to do. David answered them.

--- But Dad, why are you ruining this moment? What happened?

Elsewhere, Adrian parked his car in the residential complex where he lived and went to his apartment to rest. Ten minutes later, there was an insistent knock on the door, and he was told that his car was being taken away, so he rushed out to see what was going on.

---Wait, what's going on, why are you taking my car? Adrian asked.

--- Easy, sir; I called your dealership. I work for a repo company, and they ordered me to retrieve this vehicle.

On the other hand, Lily came home from work, went to pick up her mail, and opened two envelopes notifying her of two consecutive lawsuits for not paying her debts for eight months.

--- You see what happens to you for getting into so much debt, I warned you. --- Ask your uncle Christian for help; he can help you, his mother replied.

--- Mom, I can't; I owe him money and haven't paid him. Lily answered.

In Colombia, 42-year-old Diego, a family man, was driving his motorcycle fast. He needed to get to a pawnshop because he had to pay two million pesos to his local pawnbroker that afternoon.

--- Hello, tell me how much you lend me on the bike, it's new. Said Diego.

--- I can only lend you 1.5 million, interest at 36%. They answer

---I need two million. Replied Diego.

--- It's easy, bring more stuff. They replied.

--- You can lend me what I need if I bring you a refrigerator. ---- Of course, they replied.

--- All right, I'll pawn the bike and the cooler.

On the other hand, BBC News, in its edition of February 7, 2019, says that a 32-year-old woman threw herself from a bridge with her 10-year-old son. The motive for the suicide was the desperation for the debts she had. She had made a "***drop by drop loan***" with an interest of 50%. Unable to pay, she chose to commit suicide, and in her desperation and madness, she took her son with her.

Debt makes you sick, destroys friendships, tears families apart, generates conflicts, and can even cause death. It is like a demon, a destructive force that takes hold of you. People get into a lot of debt on this side of the planet. This is due to how we have been brought up, our consumer society, and the peculiarities of where we live. While there are many types of debt, not all are considered equal or beneficial. They do so according to their income and lifestyle, but this is not the case for everyone. The types of debts that people commonly use are.

- Mortgage loan (*home purchase*)
- School or student loans
- Vehicle purchase loan
- Loan to build or strengthen a business (*investment*)
- Credit card (*consumer*) debts
- Subsistence debts (*mid-term or end-of-month loans*)
- The loans are known as "gota a gota" (drop by drop).

There are powerful reasons to take out a loan. After all, mortgage debt is the only way a middle or low-income person can afford a home. Likewise, it is the only way to purchase a vehicle for many people. Likewise, approximately 75% of students take out loans to finish university studies.

These debts are obligations that can accompany us for 15 to 30 years if it is a mortgage loan. Nevertheless, credit is a tool that can help us achieve our goals. However, it can be detrimental if you don't know how to manage it. On this side of the planet, paying a mortgage, making car payments, or taking out student loans are typical debts.

So, maintaining a healthy discipline and an excellent financial culture to stay under control is utopian for many people. This is because, similarly, they are gradually acquiring more and more loans. They borrow on one side to pay on the other, and most of these debts are to invest in almost nothing, becoming a hefty financial burden. Some become compulsive debtors, acquiring the syndrome of economic disorder.

Compulsive Shoppers. These people have no impulse control when shopping, so they buy things they do not need, especially on the Internet. Likewise, those who like luxury items want to be fashionable and be the envy of their social circle. They spend more than they earn because they find financing that allows them to use the money, they don't even have but hope to earn in the future. Some lose control and do not even realize it. They ignore their reality and go beyond their financial possibilities and ability to pay.

Consequently, when they review their accounts, they realize they have become over-indebted, and frustration sets in, destabilizing their emotional state. Their desperation is so great that they take their belongings to pawnshops, subject to paying higher interest rates. This behavior must be managed so the situation does not get out of control.

We also have a bad credit rating. Lenders lend money even to people who cannot pay because they are already heavily in debt. Similarly, there are specialized companies that deal with these emergencies. They run a high risk but compensate it with usurious interest rates that desperate people are forced to accept because they have no other options.

Addictive Debtors. Disorderly people, without realizing it, get into serious money problems and become compulsive and addictive debtors (*debt vice*). They feel an uncontrollable desire to contract debts, making loans their way of life. They are characterized by stress and anguish due to the urgency of fulfilling their obligations. They take on a new debt to pay the previous ones, generating a vicious cycle from which they cannot escape. Debts become an addiction, believing themselves to be the best solution to their financial problems.

People addicted to debt live paycheck to paycheck. Amid desperation, some take out loans that do not require credit studies. This is the "drop by drop" loan with interest at 6%, the same as 60%, at 10%, equal to 100%, and even at 15%, equal to 150% interest. This drowns the debtor, and he even loses his personal belongings, at the risk of losing even his life.

From experience and common sense, it is known that any excess has adverse results. If we overeat, we can become overweight and obese. If we drink too much liquor, we get drunk, we do and talk stupid things, etc. In the same way, it happens with the excess of getting into debt. It has consequences on physical, mental, and spiritual health.

That is to say, the person who falls into the circle or level of debt has no idea in which circle he/she has lost. It is as harmful as any other vice with its consequences. Compulsive debtors and addicts generally buy credit cards and ask for things that do not make any sense, and the most severe thing is that they fall into total contradiction, for example.

- Buying brand-name clothes and traveling by public transportation
- Have a new vehicle but rent a house
- Buying expensive items in installments or in installments
- Buy the latest trendy cell phone with a lowered plan or don't even have to buy minutes

- Buy books you never read and programs you don't know how to use
- Going on vacation with a debt
- Investing in unknown businesses
- Buying unnecessarily with debt to indulge oneself
- Getting into debt while in debt, exceeding payment limits

You can see the lack of coherence and common logic in whoever acts this way. You are the one who must change, not others. Do not burn your head trying to understand others' attitudes. And, if debts make you sick before getting cured, ask yourself if you renounce the things that made you ill and if you are willing to pay and not get into debt again.

DEBTS AND HEALTH CONSEQUENCES

Because we do not calculate the consequences of long-term debts, we become pessimistic and have low self-esteem, feeling defeated. When we see ourselves cornered and with no way out, our heartbeat speeds up, our blood pressure rises, and our psychological state is altered, falling into sadness. Some people are frustrated with their plans, whether marriage or studies, and changing their life plans.

On the other hand, a study conducted by anthropologist Elizabeth Sweet, who studies the relationship between debt and health at the University of Massachusetts in 2015, found that the burden of debt could contribute to poor health. Most of the existing studies in this regard link diseases such as stress, anxiety, and depression with difficult economic situations. Similarly, some experts, such as clinical psychologist Jonathan Irreño Sotomonte, say that these mental illnesses can trigger physical problems such as gastrointestinal diseases, lower back pain, or headaches.

Debts, Interest, and Time. To earn money, we must work; to work, you need time—some work eight hours daily, others ten, which equals 40 or 50 hours weekly. Whatever you want to buy will cost you what you earn in one, two, or five days of work. However, other, more expensive things may cost you two weeks, a month, or one or two years of work.

For example, how many days or weeks do you have to work to collect its value if you buy a computer? The same is true if you want to buy a vehicle. In other words, what you buy costs you more than money; it costs you time out of your life.

The same happens when you pay interest on debts; you must work for months and deprive yourself of many things to pay high interest rates. Consequently, you are giving away your time, affecting your health. It is possible that by paying only the interest, you must work half a week; in that order, you would have to give away six months of work of your time in one year. Following this order, you have given away two and a half years in five years; what *about twenty or thirty years*?

The Debtor's losses. Work, household chores, and the pace of life in general leave little time for enjoyment. Debts and high interest rates are stealing time from your life; in reality, you are a ***"slave"*** because you must work to pay. That is, you must spend time to earn money, and technically, nothing is yours; this indicates that, of what you have, almost nothing belongs to you (Proverbs 22:7). Nothing is yours, not even your time, because, in a way, it belongs to your creditor. You decided to become a "slave" of another person, a bank, or any lending institution. Likewise, you lose spiritual authority and respect. Pawnbrokers and pawnshops treat you with disdain and disregard.

Debts and the Spiritual Consequence. *When you do not comply with the conditions agreed in the loan (whether legal or not legal* *before the law),* you unknowingly lose spiritual authority and cause problems for the lender or the debtor. Someone is going to have issues and cause trouble or suffering. Generally, this happens to the debtor; he backs himself into a corner until he sees no way out.

Spiritually, the action of getting into debt or charging interest in an agiotist manner has implications. It also has spiritual roots because God and his supreme court strictly govern this conduct and the relationship with others. Defaulting on a debt and charging usurious interest brings suffering. Starting with failure and disappointment, marital problems, difficulties with children, and the wrong example. Also, issues with relatives, at work, with neighbors and acquaintances, diseases, anguish, hatred, and even death can come.

How often have you asked yourself, "*Why is this happening to me?* What bad luck do *I have,* etc."? The reason is that if you fail to pay the one who charges usurious interest, He is playing with the established rules, causing pain and suffering. Whoever causes suffering by not paying his debt will not be free to suffer the same because life does not keep anything. This can happen to him anytime or at the end of his day. Likewise, whoever accumulates money resulting from usury will lose its value, and its owner, in the end, will not know in whose hands he will end up with all that he has accumulated.

Debts and the State of the Soul. When we contract a debt and do not fulfill the payments as agreed (*if there are no usury interests*). *We "lose twice";* we lose authority and spiritually the divine abundance that the creator assigns us; in some cases, it goes to the person who lent the money. This is because you unknowingly gave up your abundance. Consequently, the debtor is left without the divine abundance assigned by God because instead of waiting for the time, he should wait and trust God, and he decides to trust a person of flesh and blood. Since God does not help or fulfill me, I better go the other way and trust someone else.

For this reason, you do not know how to pay your debts by becoming a slave of your creditor (*explained above*). Being a slave is like being the property of another person, a bank, or a credit institution. There are not many rights, and practically, you do not have much.

Spiritually, you are a slave to your creditor, and in the physical world, for to him, you owe your time since what you earn in your work is part of your life. By working too much, you do not have much time to share and enjoy; your time goes to paying the debt. In other words, you made debt your god to pay debt and interest. All your time, money, and energy are technically for the lender. *How do you think God sees you*?

Living in debt means not being physically, mentally, or spiritually healthy. You will not be accessible until you pay what you owe; your condition will not change. That is your tragedy, a circle you chose because you owe men, not God. Debts to men are different, and you will not be free until you finish paying the last penny you owe (Matthew 5:25). Thus, you will have no one to accuse you before him; remember that in this case, God is a just judge and, consequently, severe. Any debt contracted must be paid, whether a lot or a little. Whether your creditor is poor or rich, you must pay everything in full.

Ask yourself, *is it worth incurring debts, causing yourself all kinds of problems and difficulties that have no end*, even to the point of losing the blessing of abundance? To repent and rectify is to pay what you owe and not get into debt again. We must learn to live appreciating what we have and stop being what we cannot be without appearing what we are not.

He is not happy and possesses a lot but enjoys what he has. You already know that money is only a resource for acquiring things and that what you give is your life. That goes with the time you use to pay debts. Ask yourself this: of the months or years you have been working, producing money to pay debts, *how much time do you dedicate to your spiritual well-being or personal growth?* So, I invite you to rethink your life plan and projects. Make an intelligent plan to become debt-free. Here are some ideas that might be helpful.

- If you are a person who believes in God, pray with confidence and acquire a faith commitment to Him
- If the interest rates are usurious, legal aids are available to help you renegotiate your debt and alleviate the pressure to make payments.
- Make a commitment to yourself in writing and with witnesses, where you agree to pay your debts with judgment and discipline.
- Make a thorough list of your debts and compare interest rates and payment terms. Renegotiate high interest rates
- There are plans to combine all debts into one, possibly with lower interest rates.
- Don't incur more debt by borrowing to pay elsewhere.
- If necessary, get yourself additional income
- Set a time limit for getting out of debt
- Learn to love what little you have; do not pretend to be who you are not.
- Stay away from the *"black holes,"* who are the people who encourage you to spend and get into debt.
- If necessary, become obsessive about paying debts.

Imagine if what you pay in interest only became savings. You would be in different conditions and could have a better standard of living. You can buy where and how you want if you manage your resources. Stop spending like a rich person. Do not lead a lifestyle that is not yours and that you cannot sustain. A new dawn is near, and you can make it shine.

"Debts, just like bad vices, are easy to fall into but difficult to get out of."

THE CIRCLE OF POVERTY

--- I ask fate, the wind, whoever can answer me!

--- Where does poverty come from, who founded it, where are its roots, does misery come out of the ground, does suffering spring from the soil?

--- Does the wind bring desolation? Where does loneliness come from, from loving too much or not loving at all? Is it because I have it by inheritance?

--- No, destiny answered, and pointing to the poverty, with a hard voice, he said.

--- I will answer you, uneducated and daring man, lest you forget, I *remind you of the following*!

--- From the earth springs *life* and wealth. From it, they draw gold and minerals,

If you work, he will benefit from it, just as the first ones lived.

--- Insolent human! All living things walk on the earth, illusion springs, the present is nourished, and the future is forged.

---So, poverty does not spring from the earth, ---- earth, beloved earth, you had better know how to take care of it; otherwise, it will be left with nothing, and you will go hungry.

--- From the earth is hope, *for out of it you were taken, its clay is your flesh, its stones are your bones, and its water is your blood.*

---- Don't ignore who gave him the breath of life and spiritual soul.

--- You have not known how to care for the earth, for do not let it rest!

--- With chemical residues, they poison the water that is their blood!

--- With heavy machinery, they cut down the forests and jungles that are their lungs!

--- Poverty also does not come from the earth or the dust.

--- The wind is a life-sustaining guardian angel; without it, you cannot live; hold your breath for just a few minutes.

---You will see that it does not hold, and if you dare not breathe wrapped in pride and arrogance, you will surely die. --- However, they also poison the air!

---Nor does poverty originate in love, for love is made of sleep and generosity, and out of love the Creator created you.

--- Love makes no dealings with misery or ignorance; love brings wealth and companionship to the heart; it does not bring poverty or loneliness.

---That being so, I ask you, unjust and cruel fate!

--- Will poverty come attached to my parents, relatives or friends?

---One of them had it and transferred it to me to make me miserable, is that it?

--- Answer me, ungrateful destiny! I seek an answer to you who pretend to know everything: where does poverty come from?

---Who made it? Where are its roots? --- I am looking for answers without any confusion!

---- Foolish, the human being is foolish; he only trusts in his pride and arrogance and what he believes to be valid for him alone.

--- You seek outside what you have within; poverty is within you because the Creator has given you and all human beings a breath of life, and He has assigned abundance to each of you.

--- God called us to be the head and not the tail. --- To lend and not to borrow.

--- Most have hands, eyes, ears, talents and abilities, conscience, gifts and soul, and a brain that thinks, analyzes, and concludes.

--- You have the graces and gifts to develop and multiply them - --- So, **use *them*!** Don't fall asleep and stop complaining.

--- you decide to cultivate your intelligence, talents, and gifts, God has given them to you for free; learn to receive them and multiply them, that is, to improve and advance.

--- Foolish man, it's my turn, **now *I ask you*!**

--- Where are your dreams? Did you let them die?

--- Where is your vision? What have you done with your skills and abilities? Why did you build this wall of incapacity and inertia that keeps you from moving forward?

--- Answer me! Where are your charisms? ---What have you done with them?

--- You are free to choose and to make decisions, but you are also responsible for your actions and consequences.

--- You are where you are because of yourself because you have chosen to be there!

---- Look inside yourself and see that you will not find the dimension of your existence nor the maximum motivation to achieve your goals.

--- You must first gain true and actual knowledge within yourself.

---- Poor is he who neither appreciates what he has nor knows how to love it since

---he always gives in expectation of a reward without daring to do more.

---For he is not rich and has much, but he appreciates what he has.

--- The same happens with health because illness is not an enemy but rather an ally that says you should take better care of yourself.

---- Many people are miserable because they do not know how to be happy.

--- It is forgotten that all work brings benefits.

--- Ignorance and charlatanism only bring folly and destitution. --- Some only hope to benefit from the efforts of others.

--- The creator has taught us from the beginning and has given us concepts and instructions to live fully, **so use them!**

--- He should also know that arrogance and pride bring foolishness and to learn --- There are times when an empty wallet and a hungry stomach teach the best life lessons.

Poor poverty, as old as humanity itself, has always existed to differentiate wealth and punish those lacking financial acumen. It afflicts the lazy and the ignorant, those who neglect their responsibilities and disregard advice. We have learned to prioritize material possessions, seek pleasure, and ignore the needs of others.

Yet, the greatest poverty lies not in material deprivation but in the absence of love and compassion. Those who abandon, unloved, and forget may possess a wealth of spirit that transcends material riches. The poverty of heart and love never yields fruitful results. It's time we challenge these societal perceptions and empower those in need.

Next, I invite you to write down why you think you are poor. I am poor because of what.

_____

_____

_____

_____

_____

Visualize your plans, goals, and future; remember that God gave you life to make the ordinary something extraordinary. You were born to help the creator make a better world; God trusts you by giving you life, and I invite you to trust, too. Dare to leave paradigms and inertia behind; taking a step further, you will see the greatness of the unknown.

Pay your debts, start over, and don't hide from challenges. However, people need to hit rock bottom to change. You repeatedly insist that the secret is to be fearless, confident, and humble to learn. The world has been shaped by those who have dared to dream, fight, take the risk, and win. I invite you to express yourself; for me, poverty is.

_____

_____

_____

_____

To break the deadlock, I have the following plans.

_____

_____

_____

_____

Follow your dreams, fight for them, take risks, and, if necessary, die for them. If you are unwilling to give it and risk everything, you have no right to claim anything. Likewise, if you are a person of faith, you must commit to God for economic sustenance. Help the needy and recite with faith the following psalms. Psalm 7; Psalm 14; Psalm 22; Psalm 31; Psalm 36; Psalm 52; Psalm 54; Psalm 57; and Psalm 63. It means that in poverty and abundance, you are the same person.

"Every effort has its reward, but to remain only in words leads to poverty." (Proverbs 14:23).

THE CIRCLE OF WEALTH

MONEY, HOW MANY DESPICABLE THINGS ARE DO IN YOUR NAME

In our relentless quest for contentment, we often fixate on acquiring material wealth, pleasures, and comfort. The allure of fame, success, wealth, well-being, and happiness drives us to don different internal 'masks, 'shaping our personalities to meet our needs and adapt to the socio-cultural landscape. Yet, our society's emphasis on external appearances often overshadows the true essence of a person, leading us astray from pursuing life's genuine purpose.

While it's widely accepted that money can't buy happiness, numerous studies reinforce this belief. For instance, a 2011 study by the University of Victoria in New Zealand concluded that money could contribute to well-being and happiness, but it's incapable of purchasing genuine happiness. The market of superficial happiness offers only transient pleasures. Not everything that shines is gold, and nothing attractive is necessarily correct.

Having wealth is not a sin. Rich and poor have existed since creation began, so it will be until the end. If you have fortune and wealth, this is also a gift from God, a blessing from the Creator that brings abundance, and there is no need to worry. If you provide work without exploitation to working families, men who produce for the common good, blessed be your wealth, and indeed, it will double.

However, the big mistake lies in how we use our wealth, the purpose we assign to it, and how we manage it. *We shouldn't be open-handed regarding receiving and closed-fisted when it's time to give*. Those who hoard wealth with greed, theft, and exploitation do so at the expense of others. Such wealth is bound to be enjoyed by someone else.

What does not a greedy man do for wealth? He sinks in his greed, pride, and selfishness. With petty actions, he buys the conscience of men, corrupts minors and prostitutes, steals, and kills in the name of wealth. He destroys nature, poisons the air, the water, and the earth, and damages the ecosystem.

He who bribes, who exploits the needy and mocks the poor, *what does he gain with many riches, full of demons, torturing his conscience?* He who thus acts abuses and mocks everyone, outraging the Creator and earning their deserved curse.

There is no greater happiness for some than to amass luxury and riches; their days are of joy, enjoyment, and waste. Not noticing that it is only vanity and that all desire for wealth and success is a work that excites the envy of some towards others. And, in a twisted mind, there will be no peace or happiness.

Those who only have eyes for money and luxuries will never find satisfaction and will always feel like they never have enough. They are carried away by madness and greed in their hearts, not realizing that these possessions can only offer them visual entertainment.

If someone loves money so much, how can they truly love another human being? And if they cannot love others, what kind can they offer God? Those who put their love in money, luxuries, and power forget that material possessions are fleeting. They are unaware of their spiritual nature if they cannot understand this. Therefore, fools find amusement in the material, while wise men seek wisdom. The pursuit of wealth is often at odds with the pursuit of wisdom, as the former is focused on the transient and the latter on the eternal.

All material wealth passes like a shadow, like a ship sailing through rough waters, leaving no trace of its passage. It is like a bird flying through the air, leaving no mark on its trajectory. Everything that goes up eventually comes down; everything that is born dies. Such is the human condition compared to eternity: we are born and disappear, just like wealth, vanity, and pride. We die, and everything fades away. Let us always remember that we came into this world empty-handed, and in the same way, we will leave.

Woe to those who amass wealth through exploitation and abuse! They leave stomachs empty and deny the thirsty a drop of water. Economic exploitation is a form of psychological abuse, a cruel mirage for the most vulnerable, akin to searching for water in a desert. True wealth is not about accumulating more daily but about possessing it with a sense of contentment. And true joy lies in helping those in need. What use is it to flaunt wealth on the outside when there is nothing but emptiness within?

Look at the example of the pandemic: how many millionaires died unexpectedly and could not take anything with them. All the wealth they possessed is now enjoyed by someone else. We are in the generation of excuses, justifications, and lies. We live in a society where the pursuit of wealth is often justified by claims of hard work or merit, even at the expense of others. We are in a stage of progress where pride, enjoyment, arrogance, and waste are justified at all costs.

- Excessive greed is called progress
- Tyranny is called discipline
- Exploitation, they call it a business strategy
- Murder, they make it a necessity
- Ignorance was turned into a virtue to subjugate

Let us remember great personalities, geniuses, scientists, and inventors who have died and mysteriously disappeared, such as Jonathan Widon, Andrew Moulden, Tom Ogle, Mark Smith, Troy Reed, Shano Todd, John Searl, Jacobo Grinberg-Zylberman, Frank Saurez, and a thousand more. Nothing can take away this due to the mean and greedy attitude of the power multinationals.

At the time of death, what good has he done with the wealth he boasts? What good is money, property, and luxury? What good is the abundance that fills the senses if he is poor in spirit? Analyze well, and you will see that in the end, you will end up in the same place of the miserable; death does not choose, and we are all the same for her. No one will ask who the cemetery's richest or most famous person is and what the place of the dead is. Wealth is an illusory shadow, and you will not be the exception, believing it will only add more foolishness to your foolishness and more madness to your madness.

In truth, nothing is yours; God and life lend it to you to enjoy, share, and manage while you have it. Do not measure your wealth by the amount you have and what it produces. You should instead measure it by those things you have and would not exchange for money, such as love, peace, and family. Moreover, it has been proven that freedom and free time are above accumulative wealth regarding well-being and health.

To complete your well-being and wealth, share a little with those in need and adjust to life's purpose because we have lessons to learn.

Money is necessary, and having it relaxes, giving an excellent structural and, to some degree, emotional complacency. However, a very high ego and the pride of those who have a lot is not good, as we see wealthy people who have committed suicide because of depression. If wealth originates happiness, the rich should dance in the streets, but only children do it.

There would be no-show businesses, sports, and political personalities lost in drugs and alcohol, and famous models, singers, and actors committing suicide. Wealth and fame do not bring the best marriages or the best partners; they have the worst marriages and countless divorces.

The greedy desire to have money makes many men mean. Foolish, harmful, and greedy desires plunge men into ruin and perdition, block their minds, and harden their hearts. Because in a complex, ambitious, and mean heart, neither peace nor happiness enters. Because he has let enter within him the dark desire of the one who has the most and dominates the most. He mistreats his being, others, the earth, the water, the air, buying consciences. His lack of emotional control is disastrous, wreaking more havoc in the garden that God left us, creating a wrong message of the noble meaning of life.

I invite you to write what you would do with money and wealth.

_____

_____

_____

_____

_____

What would be your priority?

_____

_____

_____

_____

For you, what is the most beautiful thing that exists?

_____

_____

_____

_____

Reflection on True Wealth: Beyond the Material

In a world that constantly bombards us with messages about the importance of financial success and the accumulation of material possessions, it's easy to lose sight of what truly matters. However, as well as reminded in the previous text, true wealth lies in those intangible aspects that nourish our well-being and connect us to what it truly means to live a whole life.

Embracing this truth can bring peace and contentment that material wealth can never provide.

Health: The most precious treasure. Without it, life becomes a complex and challenging journey.

The love of family and friends is a cornerstone in building a happy life. We should surround ourselves with people who love, support, and unconditionally accept us.

Faith and spirituality: A connection with something greater than ourselves, which gives us inner peace, purpose, and guidance in difficult times. 'Whoever loves money never has enough; whoever loves wealth never has enough. This, too, is meaningless (Ecclesiastes 5:[10]).

The security of a home: A refuge where we feel protected, loved, and welcomed in our own space.

A job or business we are passionate about allows us to earn income, realize our talents, contribute to society, and feel fulfilled.

The balance between the material and the spiritual: Finding a balance between pursuing material well-being and developing our inner self. Not allowing greed and the relentless pursuit of wealth, which can lead to neglect of our health, relationships, and personal growth, to dominate our lives, but focusing on cultivating values such as generosity, compassion, and empathy.

Take some time to reflect on your relationship with money and wealth. Identify those areas where you can make changes to focus on the true riches of life. Start cultivating habits that promote your physical, mental, and spiritual well-being.

Remember that true wealth lies within you, waiting to be discovered. This realization empowers you to take control of your life and make the necessary changes to prioritize what truly matters.

. *He who loves riches never has enough. This, too, is absurd!"* (Ecclesiastes 5:[10]).

"Having too much money is as harmful as having nothing at all; both excesses corrupt the conscience.

THE CIRCLE OF FAME AND POPULARITY

Fame and popularity are subjective processes inherent to human beings. No fixed patterns of behavior can delimit their scope and valuation. There is no way to define whether fame is good or bad; this is left to interpretative judgment because fame and popularity are a condition and not an appreciation.

Neither is there any limitation or condition to being famous or popular because being famous or popular defines a situation of something or someone concerning ability and knowledge. For this reason, one can have good or evil fame. Likewise, we must know how famous a person can be, as well as an object, an action, and a place. Let's look at the following examples.

Chris Hemsworth, the Thor star, received $20 million for the movie Love and Thunder.

Johnny Depp wins lawsuit against his ex-wife Amber Heard.

Chris Evans is determined to find the love of his life; who could it be?

Britney Spears surprises with video, singing a cappella.

New love? Johnny Depp walks with a mystery woman in Italy.

Lionel Messi is considered the best and highest-paid player in soccer history.

Tourists most often prefer hamburgers, paella, sushi, bandeja paisa, ceviche, and Chop Suey.

In 2019, Israel welcomed more than 4.55 million tourists. Tourism revenues reached approximately $6.65 billion.

Patrick Mahomes, the NFL player in the United States, has just signed a 12-year, $503 million contract with Kansas City and the Chiefs.

The dream of fame: a path full of challenges. *Who in life has not dreamed of being famous, popular, and with money*? These are dreams that many people set as goals because some of them have them inside them. And others because they have that desire, which is where they want to get to. Many give up and fall by the wayside. Through much effort, hardship, and sacrifice, some achieve their goal of reaching the elusive success.

They gain recognition, fame, popularity, and money. We have always seen this in hundreds of athletes, soccer players, basketball players, singers, composers, actors, intellectual models, certain politicians, some influencers, and others. It is undoubtedly a complicated, competitive world full of a thousand masks. Sometimes, no one knows who is, defining in part what society is regarding fame and spectacle.

Celebrities and their influence on society. The world of endorsements is lucrative, with clothing, shoe, perfume, and sports brands offering substantial sums to the celebrities of the moment. Seeing how much money can be made in just a few minutes of work is often staggering. These collaborations are a win-win for everyone involved: brands gain symbolic value and boost sales, while celebrities enhance their image, popularity, and wealth. All of this is made possible by the support of fans and the public.

The power of fans and followers is immense. The success of famous figures is intricately tied to the presence of their fans and followers. Artists who reach the pinnacle of fame understand that their fans bestow them with power, influence, and the potential for substantial earnings. These fans, numbering in the hundreds, thousands, or even millions, play a pivotal role in the initial success and serve as the bedrock for its continuation.

Among the thousands or millions of fans, it's important to note that most are adolescents and young people aged between 12 and 30. During adolescence and youth, our minds are in a constant process of assimilation, learning, and application. In addition, the emotional system continues to mature at this stage.

It is crucial to note that many young people and adolescents have tended to unthinkingly follow their famous idols in the last two decades, which can potentially harm their personal lives. This blind following can lead to heated arguments and conflicts with their parents, family, and caregivers when the latter disagree with the actions or words of their idols.

It is crucial to recognize that celebrities, in their quest for relatability, often share their most intimate thoughts, chaotic lifestyles, and erratic behaviors with the public. This can inadvertently lead adolescents, young people, and other followers to perceive such behavior as the norm. However, it is hopeful that celebrities are aware of their influence and can wield it responsibly, championing positive values and healthy behaviors among their followers.

The Culture of Imitation. Since ancient times, society has been permeated by fashions, relativism, and hedonism. Today, most fans satisfy their emotional and entertainment needs by imitating what their favorite characters do and speak. Many fans, *regardless of age*, imitate the words and actions of their idols. Songs, whether they have good or bad messages, are a source of inspiration for fans.

A celebrity's lifestyle, words, hairstyle, gait, tattoos, and clothes become the way thousands of fans want to imitate. Everyone wants to clone how they walk, dress, talk, and act like idols. This is known as the "copycat culture." For this reason, celebrities and characters who have fame and success and are recognized by a large majority must care about what they offer their fans, such as words, songs, and lifestyle.

Imitating my Star. Teenagers, young adults, and fans think it's normal when their idols get arrested because of drugs, alcohol, prostitution, and abuse. And, since my idol does it, I can do it too. That's how they start trying to do the same with disastrous endings. An ordinary person has no economic power to pay for big bail or expensive lawyers or rehabilitation centers. Consequently, they stay in addiction or jail, apart from carrying the emotional trauma.

It is severe to think that teenagers and young adults may believe that it is right to self-destruct. They do so by imitating vices such as alcohol, drugs, sexual promiscuity, and domestic violence, following the example of their favorite idol, be it in sports, show business, or politics.

The moral decay behind fame: a look at Hollywood. This reality becomes evident in some famous people, especially in

Hollywood, where many spend most of their time and resources on vices and abuses related to fame and wealth. These vices and abuses can range from substance abuse to reckless behavior. Many of these celebrities ends up in scandals in public places and on television and even proudly boast about them.

The facade of wealth and the true inner rot. Behind the facade of wealth lies a haunting inner decay. Beneath their polished exteriors, some of these individuals are hollow, lacking morals and empathy, spreading destruction wherever they go. They may appear impeccably groomed, but their lives are plagued by disorder and excessive like demons, as we've come to see more clearly of late.

Many end up in court or even jail, where their reckless behavior and extravagant lifestyles turn into public scandals. It's a stark reminder of the toll that fame and fortune can exact, often driven by reasons for darker and more misunderstood than the public can imagine.

The distortion of reality and the false image of celebrities. Most of the followers of these famous people have difficulty distinguishing between fact and hyperreality. This is often perpetuated by many of these celebrities delegating the management of their social media profiles to external people or companies. Consequently, what they believe are their favorite characters' most intimate thoughts and feelings are often scripted by people hired for that purpose. This awareness can prompt a more critical view of celebrity culture.

The culture of "I am like this." It reminds us that there are no fixed patterns of behavior to achieve fame. You must look at the internet platforms to see that anyone can gain recognition and generate significant income. The doors are open for those with the intelligence and cunning necessary to get there.

Fame and emotional wounds. It is important to remember that most celebrities and famous people were once ordinary people. Like any human being, they have emotional and psychological wounds caused by various factors such as abuse, abandonment, aggression, deception, and disappointment. Understanding their journey can foster empathy and a more nuanced view of their actions.

The fact of achieving fame does not eliminate these harmful and toxic emotions, which, over time, can become a regular part of their lives. Sometimes, a celebrity can become a reflection of a disastrous emotional state, living a life that could be a cause for sadness. This can include problems such as alcoholism, sexual challenges, substance abuse, criminal acts, domestic violence, insults, promiscuous behavior, excessive pride, and resentment.

The dark side of fame. Following a famous person is often like entering a black market and choosing what kind of emotional discomfort you want to acquire. Violence, vices, betrayal, promiscuity, resentment, conspiracies, heartbreak, theft, fraud? Any of these choices makes you a potential candidate to face health problems, loneliness, or even jail. It's truly a shame!

Fame does not imply emotional health. Being famous and popular is not a sign of an emotionally healthy person. In fact, people may sometimes use their talent to vent their negative and toxic emotions and, unknowingly, transmit their toxicity to those who have given them success and fame.

The potential for transformation is within all of us. Everyone, including celebrities, can reflect, repent, and make positive changes. We all have our 'desert' to traverse, facing various obstacles. For celebrities, this could mean overcoming vices and traumas such as alcoholism, drug abuse, theft, domestic violence, insults, sexual promiscuity, hatred, pride, resentment, and more.

231

The key is to acknowledge these issues and work towards healing and growth.

True wealth extends beyond recognition and fortune. What good is fame and wealth if it leaves you isolated without a meaningful legacy? Instead, consider the impact of celebrities who have used their influence and resources to improve the world. These individuals have chosen to invest their money and experience in building a more just and equitable world, sharing with those who need it most. Their actions are a powerful reminder of the potential for positive change, even in the celebrity world.

If you find yourself in a position of fame and wealth, able to acquire anything and fulfill any desire, yet still feel a lack of peace and a sense of unfulfillment, it may be time to consider a different path. Seeking emotional and spiritual healing can be a decisive step towards a more fulfilling life. It's about changing your mindset and attitude and embarking on self-discovery and growth.

SOCIAL RESPONSIBILITY

Be aware of all celebrities in show business, sports, politics, etc. Their words and actions strongly impact the lives of one or thousands of people. From fashion trends to political opinions, the appeal of a celebrity's lifestyle can influence people's beliefs, interests, and behaviors. The influence is so significant that it can easily change the minds of thousands or even millions of followers worldwide.

Because of this, you must know what you are conveying to the public, to thousands or millions of fans. You have a social responsibility to your followers because they become something like *"your adopted children, your adoptive family,"* so to speak.

Consequently, it would be best to have certain obligations and responsibilities with all of them.

Celebrities profoundly influence youth, particularly among adolescents and young people. Their fame often serves as an emotional refuge and can profoundly shape the identity of many. However, followers may sometimes struggle to differentiate between admiration, idolatry, and awe. Therefore, celebrities must recognize their potential to influence and be prepared to assume this significant role positively.

Being a celebrity is not just about fame and wealth. It's about the responsibility that comes with your public image. You are not criminals, drug traffickers, or bearers of evil. Every decision you make and every word you speak can shape how the world sees you. Your actions must be carefully considered, as they can send a powerful message. Do not compromise your integrity for fleeting emotions or selfish advice.

The power of influence. If you feel it's time to do something different, consider dedicating yourself to helping those who desperately need what you have in excess. A little of your time, money, and ideas can make a difference beyond a conventional relationship. Organizations like UNICEF have a long list of celebrities committed to children's programs, health, environmental conservation, and the eradication of poverty and ignorance, such as Antonio Banderas, Ronaldinho, Maná, Nicole Kidman, Angelina Jolie, Gisele Bundchen, Katy Perry, Nicolas Cage, Harry Belafonte, the Vienna Philharmonic Orchestra, Shakira, Juanes, and many others.

You are exploring new ways to do good. In addition to supporting organizations like UNICEF or the UN, you can explore other ways to do good that you may have yet to dare to try, either due to lack of knowledge or skepticism. You can start by approaching

God with sincerity and a genuine desire to change. Be sure He will hear and help you in ways you can't imagine. God manifests himself to those who call upon him, respecting their free will, and faith, love, and hope are found in patient waiting.

Now it's your turn to express your opinion about your favorite idol or character. I am a fan of it.

_____

_____

_____

_____

_____

I think it does well why.

_____

_____

_____

_____

_____

Also, I know he has done things he shouldn't have done.

_____

_____

_____

_____

_____

My idol or favorite character should have.

_____

_____

_____

_____

A Call to Social Responsibility for Celebrities

I call on the famous figures of show business, entertainment, sports, politics, social media, and other media to be aware that we are all human and carry with us our flaws, weaknesses, and emotional traumas. We understand that the pressures of fame can be immense, but we urge you to use your platform for positive influence. Do not wait to have a tragic fall to lose everything and regret it later.

Lessons from history.

We can take examples of famous people who have already left this world. Some left a valuable legacy worth following, while others left a bad example and a trail of misfortune. It is important to remember that the cemetery is full of people who were once millionaires and famous. Some considered themselves irreplaceable, believed they had unparalleled intelligence and prestige, and came to think that the world could not go on without them.

However, despite their fame and fortune, many have been forgotten, and no one remembers them. Among many examples, the following figures stand out:

Jean Simmons Bob Marley Ernest Hemingway Michael Jackson Gianni Versace Cristian Silva Skater Ronnie James Dio, and Steve Jobs.

What matters. The list of famous people is endless, but undoubtedly, what we will be remembered most for are the marks we leave on the lives of those we love and those who love us. How are we acting with the loved ones we have by our side?

The true greatness of human beings.

I ask you a question: How many of the famous figures in show business, entertainment, sports, and politics will be the most famous and most prosperous in the cemetery? And if any of them were to be, what good would it do them? Whenever we are at the peak of success, fame, and money, we must remember that the greatness of a human being lies in our ability to recognize our smallness before God and the universe. The pinnacle of success and the most incredible wealth a human can achieve is conquering that which cannot be bought with money.

Message to the Famous:

Remember, your fame is not just a personal achievement but an opportunity to influence positively. Your actions and words can inspire, educate, and uplift millions. Embrace this power and use it for the greater good. Do not wait for a tragic fall to realize the impact of your actions. The regret that follows such a fall is not just personal but a stain on the legacy you leave behind. Act responsibly now so you don't have to regret it later. Use your position of influence to leave a legacy worth following. Let your actions inspire others to do good and live with integrity. Remember, true greatness is not measured by fame or wealth but by the values we uphold and our positive impact on others.

"Fame is an illusory act of man that increases his ego and pride, clouding his conscience and damning the soul."

THE CIRCLE OF WISDOM

Wisdom dwells within the human being. Thanks to the broad and deep knowledge acquired through study, intelligence, and experiences, it is infinite and eternal. Wisdom is also prudence and understanding, and it increases with time. Likewise, it is the quality developed in applying intelligence, experiences, and study. In this way, we gain knowledge that gives us greater understanding and discernment of truth and falsehood, good and evil.

Wisdom, prudence, depth, and humility. Wisdom, once acquired, is distinguished by prudence and good sense. It gives the individual a greater understanding and depth of knowledge about the circumstances determining all existence. Likewise, we discover that everything is relatively futile and that there is nothing new under the sun because the past, present, and future are related in all creation. In fact, the supreme wisdom is not found in the mind of the living (Job 28:[13]) but in the essence of God.

The beginning of wisdom is awakening and nurturing; embracing it will give you prestige. Wisdom is a precious gift from the creator; it is a spirit friend of man and the force that moves and shines by itself. It molds man and makes him perfect in prudence and work. Its seat is the mind, the center of the intellectual and moral decisions of the human being. In the circle of wisdom, graduation does not exist, and anyone who feels too wise has abandoned his ability to learn.

Striving for excellence. He is not wise, but he is the one who says, "*I know everything,*" but he is the one who says I need to learn more to educate my ignorance! He does so by looking inside himself and recognizing his limitations because knowing a lot and intellect differentiates him from others but does not make him better than anyone else. All rivers go to the sea, and the sea is never full, so is wisdom; no matter how much you learn, you will never know enough. This invites us to seek higher levels of consciousness to reach excellence. Nothing can compare with wisdom, so much so that all the wealth and luxury of the world is just a handful of sand and mud next to it.

An investment greater than any material wealth. Invest in wisdom more than anything else; it is worth more than gold, money, jewels, and more than any property. Once acquired, it can be compared to nothing. Wisdom excels foolishness, as light excels darkness. Riches, gold, and luxuries will always abound, but the most valuable thing is wisdom on expert lips. Better is a poor and wise man than a rich, old, and foolish man. Wisdom is worth more than strength, more than weapons. Analyze the conflicts and notice that the great wars have been won more with wisdom than weapons.

He who seeks wisdom never tires, and he who finds it, his face is radiant, his eyes shine, and his attitude has grace and firmness.

He is not interested in hurtful feelings. Wisdom is possessed by those who are worthy of it. Books must be respected because they cure the most dangerous diseases: ignorance. However, wisdom is not about knowing but rather about the treatment given to others and the ability to keep silent when the ignorant make noise.

Wisdom cannot advance in closed-mindedness; a person may have high intellectual knowledge. But it does not mean that he is emotionally intelligent. Study with dedication, according to your strength, but not too much because it will damage your health if you overdo studying. It is the same as writing many books; it will be never-ending. For this reason, wisdom is carved in the failures, pain, and tears, *with the tests and the passing of the years,* and above all, when acquired with humility. Learning to have peace and self-control under challenging circumstances and value those who dedicate time to you can never be recovered. The wise man does not grieve for the things he does not have but rejoices and is happy with what he has.

WISDOM IN SEARCH OF A HOME

Long ago, wisdom went out to look for someone worthy of possessing it. She searched in the squares, temples, companies, schools, and universities. With authority, she raised her voice.

--- Listen to me, all of you, humans, how long will you love inexperience, arrogance, and pride? How long will you hate wisdom?

--- How long will they remain blind, deaf, and ignorant?

- Do they think that with pride, they can manage reason, and, with violence, they can always dominate? - You fool! -

---- I am calling you; I am addressing my voice to the sons of men, inexperienced and reckless humans; listen, I am going to tell you important things!

--- I am going to speak sincerely; listen to me!

--- I am wisdom, my palate tastes the truth, my lips abhor evil -- all my speeches are fair, there is no hypocrisy in me, my ways are not twisted.

--- All my acts are explicit and suitable for those who act uprightly and justly.

--- I seek someone worthy with whom I can live, someone who will accept my instructions before gold and fame.

--- For I am of more value than fame, more than gold and jewels, nothing earthly valuable can compare to me.

--- Listen to me, imprudent humans; I wisdom only coexists with truth, prudence, and discretion.

--- Rejected, he hated pride and arrogance, the evil way, the false tongue, the reckless have no ways with me,

---- I love those who love me. Those who seek me with eagerness, find me; whoever can possess me will indeed have wealth and glory, solid fortune and righteousness,

--- My fruits are of great value and the best health; my harvest is worth more than gold and choice wealth.

--- My paths are righteousness and justice, to distribute wealth and treasures to those who can live with me,

---Blessed is he who allows himself to be instructed in my ways, listen to me and become wise, you will live healthy and happy, accept me.

--- Whoever can possess me finds life, peace, prudence, health, progress, and respect. I will watch over his entrance door, and nothing can harm him.

--- Listen to me, humans; blessed is he who listens to me; I will let myself be possessed by whomever I find worthy of me.

--- Think, think again. Look, I will tell you something you will not forget.

--- You manipulate machinery and flints, and you can go into the interior of the mountains and deep into the sea.

--- They can open the rock, take out precious objects, and discover medicines and some mysteries in the laboratories.

--- It is intelligence that comes unity to the mind, the body, and its needs, with intelligence doing a lot, even.

--- They can conquer cities, go into space, and visit planets.

--- Could someone tell me what wisdom is, where it comes from, where it lives, and who has it?

---Come on, ask anyone who can answer. And they began to answer.

--- In my half-hearted wandering, I have been able to touch it. Says the wind.

----- It has not fallen here. Says the abyss.

--- He is not with me; he has not sailed this way. Says the sea.

--- With me, you can't buy it; I haven't seen it. Says the gold

---*We know his fame and power* by *hearsay*. They say doom, hatred, and pride.

---I do not *know her*," I am not allowed to approach her. Says death.

--- So, *will there be any human worthy of possessing me and feeding his soul*? Will humans pass the test and roar, "I have it, wisdom is mine," and we can walk in joy together?

Therefore, there was a great silence; in fact, all human beings wanted to possess it. They tried to catch it and not let it escape. The most daring began investigating and planning how they could have so much wonder together. But no matter how hard they tried, they could not. The disappointed and sad wisdom said the following.

---What a misfortune, in these times, no human is worthy of possessing me totally.

--- Some do temporarily, but envy, selfish thoughts, pride, and arrogance make me turn away from them.

--- Humans, listen to me at least once in your short life; intelligence dwells in your minds; it pleases the soul and its needs, but nothing more.

--- Wisdom absorbs intelligence, surpasses understanding, and nourishes and strengthens the soul. You can find it **inside you** if you know how to look for it*!*

- They did not heed my voice when I called and disregarded my warnings.

--- So, humans, eat the fruit of your actions!

- Beware of enjoying your rebelliousness; you only enjoy what fills your senses, deluded ones; the world is a disguise; it is a vain illusion!

- Pure vanity, this world is whole of nothing but **vanity and pride!**

- Never forget, where your riches are, there is your heart!

--- There is not a single human being who is entirely just, upright, and worthy of me. How sad; everyone is concerned with the shell, and no one thinks about the seed!

--- I will leave with great sorrow for the place I came from.

--- From everlasting I was formed, from before the earth's and water's origin.

--- I will play again with the eternal father, architect of the heavens and the orb.

--- You want to know what wisdom is, you humans, sons of men, so much you read and do not learn, so much you look and do not recognize, so much you hear and do not grasp, so much you study and do not understand, in fact, the more you are lost!

---I have said it thousands of times, for centuries and centuries. Complete wisdom *is the knowledge of God the Father to understand, enjoy, and care for His creation!*

--- And if anyone thinks himself worthy and wants to possess me, I will not speak to him, but he will have to ask God to have me.

Now, I invite you to write what wisdom means to you in your own words. And, to whom and why do you consider that you are a wise person?

Wisdom for my is.

_____

_____

_____

_____

_____

The people he considered wise are.

_____

_____

_____

_____

_____

_____

A person knew is strong in.

_____

_____

_____

_____

Wisdom: A Treasure to Cultivate. Once we have attained wisdom, we must understand the importance of nurturing and preserving it. Over time, we realize the ephemeral nature of many important things. The clouds follow their cycle without changing their essence, the rain benefits everyone equally, and the sun shines without distinction. All rivers flow into the sea, and it never fills up. Our responsibility is to cultivate and preserve this treasure of wisdom, motivating us to do so.

The relativity of existence. Humans assume various roles in this profound life journey: prophet or pagan, wise or ignorant, rich or poor. However, in the end, we all share the same destiny. The only truly immortal thing we possess is our spiritual soul and the wisdom we have acquired. This journey of life is a philosophical exploration we are all engaged in.

The level of human knowledge can be categorized in a circle or set of levels:

- Simple knowledge
- The necessary knowledge

- Transcendental knowledge
- The supreme knowledge

What circle or level of knowledge are you in?

We are all situated at various points along the spectrum of knowledge. Contemplating our position on this continuum can illuminate areas where we may enhance our wisdom.

"Intelligence must never be confused with wisdom. Intelligence serves us to subsist; wisdom reveals to us the mysteries of life".

THE CIRCLE OF CHANGES

Human beings experience four primary stages of change in their evolution: birth, growth, reproduction, and death. However, it's important to note that we constantly and inevitably change within these main stages. These changes largely determine the course of our existence, our way of life, and our relationships with others. Motivated by pursuing happiness, love, faith, fame, personal development, and motivation, we change various aspects of our lives.

- Changes in possessions, clothing, vehicles, furniture, and tastes.
- Changes in emotions and feelings.
- Changes in diet and preferences.
- Changes in life plans.
- Changes in profession and work.
- Changes in ideas and opinions.
- Administrative changes.
- A divorce, a breakup.
- Changes in partners.
- Changes in friends.
- Changes in residence.
- Changes in beliefs, including religious beliefs.

If we analyze carefully, we must make many adaptations and changes throughout our existence, often without being fully aware. It is difficult for us to accept that everything can and must change! Some changes, even the small ones, involve time, effort, risk, stress, etc. In addition, most of them entail a renunciation, a loss, or a transformation.

For those who are in their comfort zone, facing life changes can be like facing death. The reasons we must do so are varied, but regardless of the cause, we must prepare ourselves to face these changes, however difficult they may seem.

One of the most frequent reasons is that we lose focus on our life plans, losing our way. It is like when we are behind the wheel of a vehicle: if we lose focus and get distracted without seeing the road, we are likely to have an accident. The same thing happens in life: if we get distracted from our purpose, we lose focus, and sometimes, we do not assimilate life changes.

«*Where there is no vision, the people go astray*. »[1.] Without vision, we are nothing. A clear and defined vision of life must guide every change we undertake, thus avoiding falling into entropy.

The Path of Change. It isn't easy to embark on a journey without a clear destination, and even more challenging to do so without knowing where we are starting from. The map shows us the route but not the territory itself. Finding a way out of a maze is no easy task. To make effective life changes, we need a clear goal, a talent to develop, a well-structured plan, the decision to act, and the action itself.

Purpose, the engine of change. No action can be effective if it is not linked to a specific goal. Defining our purpose and why we want to make these changes is essential. Rome was not built in a day, but bricks were laid every minute. With discipline, time, and perseverance, we can build an empire or, in this case, rebuild our lives. Little by little (step by step, brick by brick), we will achieve essential and intangible changes in our existence. Dreams can come true if we maintain a constant commitment to them.

Don't let yourself be carried away by the idea that the world is ending or at its worst. History teaches us that there have been many more challenging times. Our planet, the universe, is in constant evolution, with permanent changes. Empires have risen and fallen. Throughout history, we have faced viruses and plagues that have claimed millions of lives.

Many moments in history have been perceived as the end of the world, including the First World War, the Second World War, and, more recently, the COVID-19 pandemic. However, we have overcome these adversities. The key is to know history, read, educate oneself, prepare, and understand that we exist in cycles of life that repeat themselves.

It is true that, at first glance, it may seem that "there is nothing new under the sun." However, this perception does not consider the depth and transcendence of the changes we experience. While events and situations may repeat themselves throughout history, each has a context, an interpretation, and a unique impact on our lives.

To effectively face life changes, it is essential to have a series of determining factors that drive and guide our process. These factors are self-love, faith, knowledge, intention, evaluation, decision, passion, and action. These factors help develop our potential to achieve coherent and profound changes. I will cite some frequent changes and the necessary knowledge to leap at change.

The Importance of Assimilating Change

The most beautiful drawing of flowers does not smell like flowers. Everything you can say about love is nothing if you have never felt it. Action, planning, and intervention are essential. In the beginning, you must get used to the new aspects of these experiences and show an open attitude to the changes that occur.

A positive attitude, faith, tolerance, patience, and a sense of humor are key to adjusting to any change in life. Getting ahead of the changes allows you to get a complete picture of what is needed for a new way of working, a new partner, or a new lifestyle. Another advantage of not leaving everything to the last minute is having time to assimilate the changes, for example.

The following should be considered when accepting changes in a couple or solving a conflict. In most cases men, we do not read women's minds; sometimes, we do not know what they want because men are direct, and women are indirect. For example, when a couple is in a vehicle, and they pass by a restaurant, the woman suddenly says, look at a restaurant; you are thirsty, and the man says, let's not go on. What the woman wants to tell him is that she is thirsty. Men are more direct, tenths; I'm thirsty. Let's get some water.

In love, if we are not reciprocated, we must know how to walk away because clinging despite being in love is martyrdom. Especially if you get tired of holding on to someone who has never wanted to stay and never wants to be close, it is better to leave in silence because everything you wanted to say was already said when you were together. Don't give your heart or love to someone you like because you could use illusions and lies. But who truly loves you, values you, and accepts you with all you are?

What to say about work and family: We often get so involved in our work and professional role that we forget the world, and our family does not see our faces. To realize this, to assimilate it, and to make changes is to move forward. Because we are neither our profession nor our work, we are a unit that makes up a whole, so we have a family. Only in this way can we work appropriately as a source of motivation and growth. We must open our intelligence and conscience to be more open to life's changes.

Worry also affects us; it is one of human beings' most damaging emotions and destructive states. The physical and mental effects of worry are diverse and problematic. While it is true that some people experience nothing more than constant headaches, many people end up developing psychosomatic disorders. It affects mental health, which is the food of stress. It produces fear and anguish affecting different areas, such as:

The psychological effects of worries

- Fatigue
- Feeling tired.
- Difficulty concentrating
- irritability, restlessness and impatience
- Stress

Physical effects, among others, are.

- Back and neck pain
- Headache, migraines
- Stomach pain and digestive disorders
- Insomnia

About changes and success in my personal experience, I have never seen anyone who has a fulfilled life. Even if they succeed in all areas of life, they have had to make severe changes. They have succeeded because they have failed, humbled themselves, suffered, cried, sweated, struggled, and sacrificed, keeping their focus on their goals with faith. If you have a dream, don't be afraid of drastic changes; you must fight and keep at it until you achieve it. The only way is to do it yourself because no one will do it. Every human being has an enormous untapped potential, which lies in your spiritual dimension. First and foremost, you are a loved and beloved being for God, linked to everything else by the power of love.

For some people, it is difficult to reinvent themselves with change. If this is your case, the wisest thing you can do is to use your *"**creative imagination.**"* Which is to go out, look for, and find what other people have done work and do what they have done until they have done it and made it better. In other words, it's attracting and doing things and ideas we never thought possible. That is the facility to devise or project new things.

To discover what you want from a change, you must first know precisely what you want. Please do not allow a change to change your nature, no matter how difficult. For this, in moments of solitude, close your eyes and communicate with yourself, with your conscience and heart. Knowing that there is also a part of God in the inner self, focus on what you can manifest and what you want.

For changes to be effective, you must practice forgiveness. But do not self-pity or self-justify, for it does not allow you to see your potential. So first, you must forgive yourself. Then, your parents, siblings, relatives, and whoever has offended and hurt you. But before you do this, know yourself and ask yourself what peace of mind is. If you are a person of faith, pray and thank God. Prayer gives strength and hope. First, we must have an inner dialogue with ourselves; you can do it as you are used to or do it in the following way.

--- Dear me, I know that among so many things in life, we have failed in many things, but we have also won our battles.

---This is destiny, and there are still roads to travel, some battles to fight, and thousands of obstacles to overcome. ---many mouths to shut, many things to learn and lessons to teach, and great potential to demonstrate.

---And, with God's love and discipline, we can win this war.

If you have true faith, you can talk to God. He appreciates what you have in your memory but loves what you have in your heart much more.

--- My God and Lord, no matter what the circumstances, please help me move forward and learn to overcome difficulties. I am learning to be strong and patient, to wait for your time.

--- Remind me that you would never give me a burden that I cannot bear, for where my strength and willpower end, yours begin. Amen, Amen, Amen.

Now, I invite you to express your opinion and how you face changes. I believe that to make changes.

_____

_____

_____

_____

_____

_____

"He who refuses to face life's changes is refusing to live, allowing obstacles to affect his nature."

THE CIRCLE OF FAITH

What is the definition and meaning of faith? What can we say about faith?

Faith hurts when it is a relentless battle, like the walls that break the earth. For this reason, every human being has been endowed with a body, soul, conscience, feelings, and knowledge. We also enjoy free will to choose our path and work on our preferences. Likewise, we should believe in our choice's ideologies, beliefs, and religion. In the same way, we can accept, deny or reject everything.

The Power of Self-Reflection in Spiritual Discovery. It is crucial to understand that we are not bound by the preconceived notions ingrained in us, our level of education, or our life experiences. These are all shaped by the sociocultural context in which we were raised and currently reside. The Creator of the universe has left an indelible mark on our hearts, spirits, minds, and our entire being. At any given moment, we can access our inner knowledge and establish a connection with the Creator. We are His children, heirs, and bear His spiritual DNA. The Creator has given us all that He created, an 'all' that most of humanity in the 21st century does not fully comprehend or value. It is our responsibility to discover and make use of this legacy.

God is not a stranger or distant, but many treat Him that way. It is not a question of whether God exists but whether He matters in your life. So, relate to the Creator by developing intelligence, faith, awareness, and authentic trust. Gain personal experiences that are key to the process of spiritual awakening. Wherever and however, you seek God, you will not be alone. Secretly, the Holy Spirit will be with you, guiding you.

We all thirst for God, and for this reason, man has invented theological ideas at his whim that only benefit the one who invents them, not God. Theologies, in turn, have their divisions and differences in an endless search for eternal truth without realizing that this truth is within them.

Therefore, faith is believing in God without evidence and without seeing, but it is lived and something more than that. Faith is neither emotion nor proof. It is not a feeling, much less a leap into the void. *Faith is the strength of inner growth; it is knowing,* having the sense and certainty that I believe thanks to my free will, and I think because I live it, I feel it, and I choose to believe. Faith always trusts God and believes everything comes from him; it eliminates pain and makes me grow in love.

In everything that happens, the Creator of the universe directs us to understand it. Faith sees the invisible and believes in the unbelievable, and *he who has faith receives the impossible,* making it possible. Therefore, faith is the certainty of things hoped for, the demonstration of things not seen. Faith is also a tiny word, capable of moving great mountains. It is to have the certainty that it will happen even if you do not know how it can happen, which is called trusting in God. And this trust grows when we get closer and know Him more; in fact, the more we know about ourselves, the more we know God.

He who believes walks by the greatness of faith and not by sight. If you look for logic in faith, you will only find absurdity and meaninglessness; faith has the strength that logic does not know. It also has a deep meaning with a criterion of life amid spiritual valorization because God has ways of acting that we cannot yet understand. In fact, most human beings are ignorant of an airplane's principles and operational aerodynamics, but we do benefit from it. So, with God the Father, we ignore his principles and great mysteries and benefit from him and all his creation.

There are times when the Creator would instead feed the hungry than recite a psalm, although there are times when prayer should occupy our time, investing in faith. This world is made in duality and spirituality; we seem like tourists. It is as if we were crossing the desert, where theological ideas appear with their differences **(today, there are more religions than political parties)**.

Some seem to be merchants, where each belief has deep theologies, assuring that a certain religion is the only way to true faith. They offer salvation and a better world, forgetting the instructions of God the Father and the true teachings of Jesus. However, some of their messages have been altered or misinterpreted in the translations of the Bible (Note: *some biblical translations are not faithful to the original written in Hebrew*).

Divisions only bring confusion to believers, creating false interpretations of God, distorting the messages of the Bible, and changing light into darkness with wrong translations. Many take individual, egocentric, and aggressive attitudes, interpreting according to their thoughts and conveniences, instead of building, dividing, and destroying without considering that *"pride itself humbles men."* Undoubtedly, there are great theological divisions in all religions (with some truths)

This is a demonstration that some have knowledge that others ignore. Each has its reasoning and expertise with its theological foundations according to its faith. Each religion, in its way, claims to have the absolute truth about God, life, its origin, and death. Many seek to save what they cannot because they do not conform to the concepts and precepts of God in the Bible. They lead the people with doctrines invented by man that cannot save anyone. We all fear mistakes and honor the creator in the wrong way.

If truth precedes any belief or religion, *what would you do if you knew the whole truth?* If you knew *"all in all,"* You would make it known, but unfortunately, no one would believe you, and they would call you "crazy." Apart from that, a man's brain would not fit all the truth; no one is prepared, nor do we still have the mental capacity for that.

There was only one and more than 2,022 years ago when he revealed great secrets and mysteries to us, but they killed him in the same way that they murder the truth today. Many follow the search for absolute truth in psychology, philosophy, theology, and belief. Each one believes according to his ideology, which evolves according to his knowledge and interpretation of God. This indicates that knowledge and absolute truth in humans do not exist because they are subjective truths. After all, it is inaccurate, circumstantial, ideological, and partial. Only the eternal God has the absolute truth.

The different theological foundations confuse and separate men because each theologian believes according to his doctrinal ideas. These become dogmas or religious traditions, but despite everything, the *JEWS* with their ethnic differences (Azhkenazis, Sephardim, Falashas, Lembas, Beta Israel, Tiu-Kiu-Koui, Netzarites, Mandaean-Sabeans) and messianic, continue believing, praising and serving God according to their theological knowledge and their faith.

CHRISTIANS are approximately 2.400 billion believers as of this book's publication date, with significant theological differences and divisions. They include the Catholic Church, the Coptic Church of Egypt and Ethiopia, those of Serbia, Bulgaria, and Romania, the Orthodox Christians with the Greek Church, the Slavonic Church of Moscow, the Calvinist and Presbyterian Church, the Methodists, the Baptists, the Presbyterians, the Evangelical Church, and the Assyrian Church of the East.

Within Christianity, we also have the so-called Protestants, currently more than 800 million, who emerged after the schism of Martin Luther, Calvin, and Zwingli, who continue to practice different interpretive lines of the bible, with marked divisions between them (Jehovah's Witnesses, Pentecostals, etc., etc.) and the Anglican Church founded by Henry VIII,

All of them continue to believe and exist. Still, we have a scripture that gets us out of this mess. Jesus Christ said, "And I also tell you that you are Peter, and on this rock, I will build my church, and the gates of hell shall not prevail against it."[1]. Important note: He said "church" in the singular; he did not say "churches," which is plural.

ISLAMICS have the same roots as Israelites and Christians. However, since the foundation of Islam in 611 B.C. as a religion, the Muslim community has been divided into two main branches: the Sunnis and the Shiites. The two main branches of Islam, Sunnism, and Shi'ism, clashed to decide who had the legitimate right to lead Muslims. There are approximately 1.2 billion believers, and despite their divisions, they continue to believe and exist.

With about 230 million followers worldwide, *the BUDDHISTS* also have the divisions They also have their divisions (Theravada and Mahayana Buddhism). Buddhism was born in northern India about 2,500 years ago, thanks to the teachings of Siddhartha Gautama, the Buddha par excellence. It developed parallel with Hinduism, producing some of its most profound and abstract philosophical texts. It is governed by ideas, not by gods or doctrines. They do not know the notion of holy war; in their way, they continue to believe and exist. Incidentally, however, we imagine God, we will never have an exact idea of his entire essence and greatness.

We do not need to be experts in analogy to conclude that God inspires us with faith, love, and trust. Mary of Nazareth was the only Jewish woman the Creator chose to give life to the Word and be the flesh of His flesh and blood of His blood. Through her, Jesus Christ was born to teach, redeem, and unite us to the plan of salvation.

Deny Mary of Nazareth is like denying Eve in creation or Sarah in the origin of the Hebrews. In fact, it would be like denying Jesus Christ and contradicting God the Father. Mary of Nazareth has an Israelite meaning and background that should not be ignored. She is the mother of Jesus Christ by the creator's choice, and no one can deny that.

God the Father does not want people subdued by fear, living in fear of everything and for everything. We must follow God, not from exaggerated fear, nor imposition or inertia, not with a resigned spirit or because there is no other way. The Creator does not impose love or respect; God proposes, and you decide.

It may be that nobody knows you or is famous or recognizes your efforts. But don't forget that the Creator has His reward and will give it to us the day we least expect it. When you least expect it, God will surprise you with new opportunities; trust in Him, and everything else will follow. We can believe and have faith without allowing religion to become a yoke with evasion of reality. It bogs down our understanding, our way of being and living. Nor can we ignore that God also evolves from age to age, so to have faith and grow.

- Don't try to change your whole life; improve it.
- Do not seek to be humble; it is enough to perform acts of humility.
- Please do not pretend to be virtuous; it is enough to do acts of virtue.
- Please do not pretend to be wise; it is enough that you understand
- Please don't pretend to give everything; it is enough to help your neighbor
- If you can, analyze the scriptures and respect God and his precepts.
- Cultivate your gifts and your faith, which pleases God.

To have faith is to pray, love God, and walk with a heart full of names. It is to obey the inner voice that speaks to us of what is right, what is beautiful, what is accurate, and to see our surroundings knowing what is right and wrong. To understand that God's decisions are mysterious but, in our favor, and to say aloud:

--- My God, my Lord, be my promised land and the reason for my hope! Be the light that gives meaning to my feelings and answers my needs.

--- Be my refuge in the storm, comfort in sorrow --- be my light, your Lord, my strength in weakness; amen, Amen, Amen, Amen.

May the fruit of your life be love and service. May your goals make you a better human being each day, making you addicted to love, understanding, and gratitude, and with the light of the Creator of the universe within and around you, guiding you to be of service wherever you are needed and uniting us all in that light. Remember, God does not always give us what we want, but He always gives us what we truly need.

In any society and country, the need for laws of conduct is undeniable, just as it exists in the scriptures. Even for those who lack beliefs or faith, it is essential to recognize this. On social media, unfortunately, there is a tendency to mock God, the Bible, and the teachings of the Creator, along with ridiculing everything related to faith. The eternal God does not persecute anyone, which reflects a limited knowledge of God and the scriptures. Remember, most of a person's good or bad actions carry rewards or punishments due to the law of cause and effect. This is a powerful reminder of our responsibility and the impact of our choices.

God does not need money either (*since he owns all that exists*). The money people give is for their ministers; this applies to any religion. The collection is for the maintenance of the church and personal expenses (salary, paying for electricity, water, telephone, food, etc.). Some give themselves luxuries. If money is still left over, it is supposed to help others with various community needs. Some religions help worldwide with disasters and needs.

In every wheat harvest, there will always be tares. In this world, there will always be excellent and bad believers and atheists. The same happens in religions and churches, but this does not define God but man. Because we men are divided in mind and heart, some are very twisted. Just as there are scoffers, there are also defenders of faith in God. Anyway, to each one according to his words and actions, and of the fruit of his harvest, each one shall eat.

"A believing man is filled with blessings." (Proverbs 28:[20]).

THE CIRCLE OF ATHEISM

What is atheism, and what does it consist of? Atheism is a position or an ideological current that denies the existence of God. There is no absolute atheist in virtue of the fact that *'every atheist is a god to himself'*. Radical atheists, by completely denying the existence of God, overlook the complexity of the universe and existence itself. Their position is based on negation and lack of faith, falling into an intellectual and experiential reductionism, such as reducing the beauty of a sunset to a mere chemical reaction or the love between two people to a series of neural firings that limit their understanding of reality.

Faith in everyday life: A clear example of this limitation is the trust that atheists place in the quality of products such as food or medicines they consume (milk, cereal, aspirin, etc.). This trust, necessary to live, is a faith in humanity's ability to create and provide. It is a practical demonstration of their confidence in the belief that everything is in order and that they can trust manufacturers.

This trust in the practicality of atheism is as essential to their lives as the sun is to our galaxy, making the elimination of God from the universe as illogical and absurd as trying to remove the sun from our galaxy, something impossible besides being irrational and unreasonable.

- Can science discredit religious beliefs?
- Does neuroscience knowledge contradict religious belief and experience?

These are questions that arise in the debate between science and religion. In my opinion, science cannot discredit religious beliefs, as there is no scientific argument or evidence to prove that God does not exist. On the other hand, there is a lot of scientific data and evidence that supports the existence of God and, therefore, strengthens the faith of believers. This lack of scientific evidence against the existence of God is a testament to the strength of religious beliefs. Science and religion are different fields with different methodologies and scopes, so they cannot be used to delegitimize each other.

It is essential to remember that cognitive science, which includes neuroscience, is a multidisciplinary discipline based on evolutionary biology, psychology, and anthropology. While neuroscience can identify neural correlates of religious experiences, this does not constitute scientific evidence against the existence of God. Ultimately, religious beliefs and faith are deeply personal and spiritual matters that go beyond the scope of science to evaluate definitively. This depth of the topic makes the debate between science and religion so intriguing and complex.

How to explain the existence of the Universe Man, and everything else

It is fundamental to consider the notion of existence itself to comprehend the existence of the Universe, human beings, and everything else. According to the dictionary, existence is the mere act of existing. That which exists, therefore, is that which is present, and existence is the capacity of something to be.

Consider *the existence of everyday objects,* such as a house, a watch, or a cell phone. All of them, without exception, must have a creator. This is a fundamental truth, even if we don't know or have any idea who it is. Without a creator, there would be no explanation for their existence.

To explain the existence of these objects, we logically affirm that there must be a creator, someone who conceived, designed, and manufactured them. This is because things do not arise from anything on their own. They could not simply exist just because.

If the need for a creator is evident in inanimate objects, it becomes even more compelling when considering living beings. Logically, human beings must also have a creator. Consider the wonder of our existence, with its complex internal systems: the *ability to speak*, *think*, *devise*, and perfect. Such marvels could not have come into being on their own.

The same applies to animals, the Earth, the wind, and water, which are sources and sustenance of life. Someone had to plan the water cycle so that rain would give fertility to the Earth. Someone had to prepare the existence of the Sun and its usefulness, providing the necessary heat for life.

The complexity of the Universe is genuinely awe-inspiring. How can the vast and immense Universe exist with its thousands of galaxies and planets, all governed and coordinated with impressive mathematical and geometric precision? All this could not exist without a great geometer and mathematician of infinite and valuable intelligence.

This entire Universe must have a more significant and magnificent ideologist, Creator, and inventor than anything it has already created, a determined, creative source with the capacity for evolution, such as the Creator of the Universe.

Logic and Faith. When applied, logic, theology, and philosophy allow us to make comparisons based on analogy for understanding, emotions, and sensitivity and, importantly, on the knowledge of God through logic.

In summary, logic, and reasoning lead us to conclude that everything that exists, both within and outside our understanding, must have an origin, a creator, and that creator is God, the eternal and supreme being whose awe-inspiring nature is responsible for the existence of the universe and all things.

Great minds, great questions. For example, we cite some great geniuses from various fields:

Michel Foucault Friedrich Nietzsche Denis Diderot

Richard Dawkins Bertrand Russell David Hume

Sigmund Freud Stephen Hawking Karl Marx

These scientists, psychoanalysts, geniuses, and astrophysicists shared that they did not believe in God, the Father's creator, but there was a curious thing. None of them could, in their own words, explain the existence of the universe with its galaxies, of the man, and everything existing on the planet.

Astrophysicist Stephen Hawking, who postulated that the universe arose from a state of *'nothing,'* has ventured further in his explanation. His assertion that the universe exists *'because it has to exist'* is an unsatisfying conclusion for someone of his intellect. Note that this *'nothing'* is not a mere absence of things but a state devoid of any physical laws or properties; *consequently, nothing exists or could exist in this state*.

Albert Einstein's famous phrase 'God does not play dice' is often interpreted as rejecting the idea that the universe operates on random chance. Stephen Hawking's counterargument, 'not only does God play dice, but He throws them where we can't see them,' suggests that there may be elements of randomness or unpredictability in the universe that are beyond our current understanding. This opens a debate about the role of chance and the nature of the universe.

As proponents of Stephen Hawking's ideas, we advocate for randomness as inherent in the cosmos. This contrasts with common sense, often suggesting a particular order or predictability to the universe. If God were throwing invisible dice, wouldn't we, with our human audacity, seek to seize victory from Him? The devil's absence in our path does not imply his non-existence; perhaps we are advancing in harmony with him.

The limitation of human knowledge. Regardless of social status, power, education level, political, scientific, intellectual, or emotional standing, we must admit that no human being has access to the essence of God. If we did, we would be like God himself.

Humans, in our limited capacity for comprehension, try to fit the nature of God into our brains. *It is illogical*! If we cannot understand ourselves, much less the heart and thoughts of another human being, how can we pretend to understand the thoughts and actions of God the Father, architect, and creator of the universe?

WHERE DOES GOD THE FATHER COME FROM?

Whoever invented the watch first had the idea, then conceived it, then created it, and finally, designed it; all this he made possible outside the watch. He could not have created it inside the watch, so he invented it and created it outside the watch, likewise, with an airplane, a car, a household appliance, etc.

God the Father: The Awe-Inspiring Transcendent Creator The living Father and God of Jesus Christ, the God of Adam, Enoch, Abraham, Isaac, Jacob, Israel, and Moses, of whom the Bible speaks, who planned and executed the creation of the universe, is unaffected by time, space, or matter. He is self-existent, meaning He does not rely on anything else for His existence.

The timeless nature of God. If God were affected by these elements, He would not be God because time, space, and matter were established simultaneously. This is like imagining a triangle without three sides or a circle without a circumference. For example, where would you put it if there were matter but no space? And if matter and space existed but no time, when did they exist? Matter cannot exist without space, and these could not exist without time, independently of each other.

God the Father: beyond our comprehension. In other words, God the Father exists above our imagination and understanding limits because He is self-existent, omnipresent, omnipotent, and omniscient. These divine attributes, which we can only begin to fathom, underscore His transcendence, making it difficult for us to conceive of Him before any creation, to understand time, space, and matter before creation, or to comprehend the concept of nothingness.

God the Father made the Invisible Visible while being Himself Invisible.

Analyze the following (*the spirit of God moving over the face of the earth, dark and formless*): [2.] Therefore, before there was time, matter, and space, God existed. Before creating the universe, God the Father was delighted with himself because he is pure immanence, the energy that fills the universe; he is everything and more significant than everything [3.] His essence is intangible, "not knowable," and the source of all things. God joyfully dwelt in eternity as the unmanifest beginning.

Limiting questions. Asking how and when God existed is like trying to catch the wind in a net. It's a limited question that seeks to define the infinite in finite terms, like a baby asking why the sky exists. In doing so, we restrict ourselves to our understanding, confining God to the dimensions of time and space, concepts that He created. It's like trying to measure darkness with a ruler.

Instead of seeking an origin, we could ask why anything exists. Perhaps the real question is not how God came to be but how the capacity to ask questions arose. This apparent paradox of seeking to understand the infinite with finite terms invites us to consider that God may be beyond our rational comprehension and that His existence may be a mystery that transcends time and space.

The higher logic. Not understanding and not having logic is madness. If you analyze well, you will realize that you are a person who limits himself and others. I analyzed: When have you ever loved someone with all your heart?

Higher logic existed before deductive logic in human intelligence, forming the harmonious union of logic and reason. Love, solidarity, nobility, and cooperation are the product of an evolving universe, just like God.

Reflecting on life, mind, and the search for God

Revisiting the age-old question: How long have you been pondering the existence of God, only to find it slipping through your fingers? You might feel trapped in a maze of uncertainty and unexplored territories. How long has this puzzle been weighing on your mind? What insights have you managed to uncover so far?

Evaluating our capabilities. Let's take a moment to assess our abilities. Consider your mental and analytical skills. What is your IQ? How do you fare in terms of emotional intelligence? Can you grow a plant? Could you create a worm? Could you bring a dead bird or rabbit back to life? And most importantly, do you believe you can advise God?

Our limitations. The truth is, we can't even naturally change the color of our hair. In the grandeur of the sea, we are but a drop of water. And in the vastness of time, we are not even a second. This stark realization should humble us and foster respect for the universe, reminding us of our small place in the grand design.

It is possible that you do not understand your own life, and much less that you cannot know the thoughts and heart of another person. So, with what mentality and heart do you intend to understand and analyze the unfathomable architect of the universe, a being whose thoughts and ways are far beyond our comprehension?

God the Father is infinite, inexhaustible, and unimaginable love; " he *who does not love does not know God, for God is love.*" [4.] Our imperfection and the bondage of the senses do not let us see beyond what we can perceive and understand. We are conditioned by our senses and how we see things due to how we have been educated and developed. It is unnecessary to make a great effort to understand that we will never fully understand the Creator because to understand Him would be to limit Him.

Using the brain: a myth and a reality

For example, it has already been proven that 100% of the human brain is used in all activities.

According to the Spanish Society of Neuroscience (SEN), in its research, every neuron in the brain is continuously active. However, we believe that we only use 10% of our brain capacity. This statement originated in the early 20th century when the first electroencephalograms were used, which could only detect a small percentage of the brain's activity.

In fact, there is evidence that this is not true. Humans use only 10% of their brain capacity; we do not use all our intelligence. The most intelligent people use 10% or less.

Mind, brain, intelligence, and the search for God. The mind is a complex entity, distinct from the brain, and intelligence is a separate capacity altogether. The mind is the seat of reason, the faculty of thinking, feeling, and perceiving, while the brain is the physical organ that supports it. On the other hand, intelligence is the ability to learn, understand, and solve problems, a unique aspect of human cognition.

The intelligence quotient (IQ) is a tool that measures some aspects of intelligence but does not define it in its entirety. IQ does not evaluate other types of intelligence, such as emotional, social, or creative.

The human limitation in the face of God's vastness is a humbling realization. It is true that, from an analogical and theological perspective, it is impossible for a human being to comprehend God fully. No matter how developed, human intelligence will always be limited by its nature. God, in His infinite wisdom and power, transcends our capacity for comprehension. Yet, we can only approach Him through the profoundly personal avenues of faith, revelation, and personal experience, which make our connection to Him even more profound and meaningful.

Divine creation and the animation of the human being

Whoever created the vehicle, the computer, the clock, and the airplane created them while being outside. First, the idea is perceived, then the creation, and finally, the animation. In the same way, God created us and gave us animation through the soul and feelings through the spirit. Our mind is only chemistry and glucose, so how can it trust its reasoning and conclusions? More interestingly, where do they come from, and *why do they originate?*

God the Father exists before creation, before everything, and is responsible for his creation. Before creation, only God existed, and if creation did not exist, the only one who would exist would be God. In fact, if the world were to cease to exist, God could only continue to exist. If an atheist, as a human being, has not been able to understand himself, how can he expect to understand

God and his complex and perfect creation? Many resists belief, falling into the attitude of criticism and the obsession with denial. They must search and open their mind and conscience without falling into the obsession of the intelligent psychologist.

God does not force but reveals Himself to those who seek Him

God does not force us to believe in Him. He respects our free will. However, He reveals Himself to those who seek Him with sincerity and an open heart. One must know how to seek, wait, and discover God. Indeed, there are no atheists, only rebels against the creator.

Some do so because they reject what the scriptures say, which does not suit them. Others do so because of unfortunate acts or events that happened to them in the past, and the only one they find to blame is God. Others adopt a defiant attitude.

Imagine a world where we doubted everything until it was proven. It would be a world at a standstill. Yet, all doubt is reasonable, even when it comes to God.

Doubt, in fact, can be a catalyst for seeking truth. We may not doubt the true God of faith but rather a god of our limited understanding. I encourage you to write down your thoughts, question and seek, and discover the truth lies beyond your doubts.

Therefore, it is crucial to delve deep within yourself, striving to transcend the limitations of the senses without allowing your ego to dominate. This introspective journey is a significant part of the search for God.

I don't believe in God, and I'm an atheist because.

I invite you to a profound encounter with yourself, lock yourself in your room (*mind*), and ask yourself the meaning of your life, where you come from, where you are and where you are going in the physical world, and if we have spirit and what is the soul? If you conclude that there is no spirit or soul, you will also conclude that there are no feelings. The human being who ignores his spiritual value also ignores the values that come from that dimension; that is to say, he ignores his being.

Analyze the following fable. On one occasion, two old friends met; one was a neurosurgeon and believed in God; the other was an astronaut and an atheist; he did not believe in anything. The Astronaut, wanting to ridicule the surgeon's belief and faith, says to him.

---- I have made more than five trips to outer space; I have had the opportunity to see planets and the cosmos.

---And you know something, I have never been able to see heaven as your bible says, let alone your God, so I don't think it is real.

---- For me, the only real thing a human being has is his mind and his ideas, his capacity to think and analyze to achieve a goal.

So, the surgeon replied.

---- My friend, I have performed more than 1,225 open brain operations; I have inspected the skull, the head, and the human brain in all its parts and dimensions.

--- I have searched but have never seen an idea inside the brain.

---- If so, said the astronaut, --- Tell me, where is God?

To which the surgeon replied, ---- Tell me, where is it not?

--- However, let me clarify something: God is seen by those who seek him from their hearts, by those who acclaim him, call him, and need him. --- In the Bible, it says.

--- "Call unto me, and I will answer thee and teach thee great, mighty, and secret things" [5]

--- "For everyone who asks receives, and he who seeks finds, and to him who knocks it will be opened."[6]

--- For everyone who asks receives, and he who seeks finds, and to him who knocks, it will be opened.

Search your inner reality with freedom impeccably. When you decide to believe in God and place your trust in Him, you are also committing yourself to the Creator. Consequently, His obligation would be to protect and guide you because, for God, you are not a genetic chance but a prophecy being fulfilled. You were born for inner growth and life purpose: to help perfect creation by transcending and to help others transcend.

Always remember that the Creator is love that wants to be loved, conveying a feeling that goes beyond the exuberant enjoyment of the senses. Many people had the excuse of time and fundamentals for not believing in God. Well, now God is giving you the time and everything you need, so you have no excuses.

"Faith, love, and hope are all contained in waiting." (TS Eliot, English poet and playwright, 1888-1965).

THE CIRCLE OF OPPORTUNITIES

In the whirlwind of life, opportunities, like fleeting birds, appear and disappear in the blink of an eye. Capturing them requires luck and a precise dance between preparation, cunning, and a dash of audacity. In this scenario, the "Circle of Opportunities" concept arises, a space where proactivity and intelligence become the keys that open the doors to success. When opportunities present themselves, they must be seized, like the exhilarating rush of taking advantage of good weather.

Knowing how to take advantage of the Sun, not the Darkness: Life, like an erratic climate, offers us sunny days full of possibilities and gray days full of obstacles. However, in those moments of prosperity, we must make the most of the opportunities that arise without allowing cloudy days to paralyze us. Indecision and fear of failure are often the worst enemies in this game, as they rob us of the opportunity to flourish under the radiant Sun of possibilities. Sometimes, for fear of taking risks, we let go of good opportunities. Among them, love, a job, a trip, and almost always, there is no valid reason to let them pass.

Opportunities are like wildflowers: they can wither and disappear if we do not pick them up in time. However, we should not be discouraged if one escapes us. The value lies in the ability to try again, to pursue our dreams with tenacity, and to learn from past experiences. This learning is our guide to identifying future opportunities better, instilling a sense of reassurance and confidence.

Time as a Catalyst: Time, like a master of ceremonies, orchestrates the encounter between people and opportunities. It is in that magical moment when our decisions become actions, which, in turn, transform our lives. Life surprises us with new faces and scenarios that open doors to a promising future. What would existence be without the intrigue of exploring the unknown and contemplating the possibility of reinventing oneself?

Complacency, like an invisible cage, limits us and prevents us from moving forward. It traps us in a circle of proportionality, where we only receive what we give. To break this cycle, we must go beyond expectations and provide more. The opportunities that lead us to success germinate in this act of generosity and proactivity.

Expanding Horizons: Traveling the world, experiencing diverse cultures, and immersing ourselves in new experiences not only enriches us as individuals but also opens our minds to a world of possibilities. Traveling allows us to break down prejudices, broaden our perspective, and develop the intuition necessary to identify the opportunities hidden around every corner.

The Nose for Opportunities, which are like hidden treasures, not always evident, requires intelligence and imagination. It is necessary to have a 'nose,' take risks, and act with faith. Recognizing them involves seeing beyond the obvious and detecting the subtle signs that indicate the presence of a great occasion. Like a skilled hunter, we must develop a 'nose' for success, a skill that allows us to discern between mere coincidences and genuine opportunities that can change our lives. Your intelligence and imagination are not just tools but your most potent weapons in this journey, empowering you to see what others might miss.

When an opportunity arises, attitude and action are decisive. We cannot allow fear or doubt to paralyze us. We must be proactive, take the reins of our destiny, and act decisively. Opportunities do not wait for us to be ready; we must be prepared to make the most of them. The value of essential things allows us to seek them out again and bring them back. We should not wait for things to come to us, but we should go out and seek them with determination and courage.

Work and Intelligence, the Foundation of Success

Opportunities are not the result of chance but of hard work, perseverance, and persistence. Seeking motivation and setting clear goals are the engines that drive our path to success. In its wisdom, destiny often places us in the right place at the right time as long as we have done the previous work and are prepared to seize the opportunity. Your determination, resilience, and ability to bounce back from setbacks will pave the way for your success, making you stronger and more determined with each challenge you overcome.

Recognizing and seizing opportunities. Life offers us endless possibilities, but they are not always eternal. We must learn to identify them in time, to pay attention to the details, and to act quickly. Our intuition, that powerful inner voice that guides us, plays a fundamental role in this process. Remember that second chances do not always exist, so we must make the most of the present.

Motivation: the engine of success. Seeking motivation is the main engine that drives us to achieve our plans and goals. Having a defined purpose allows us to maintain interest and perseverance in the search for the long-awaited opportunity that, by design of destiny, might be right where we are now. We can take advantage if we know when to say things, pay attention, take risks, and pay close attention to intuition. It's the determination to keep going that will lead us to success.

Attitude towards opportunities: key to success. To take advantage of opportunities, we must know how to express ourselves clearly, pay attention, take risks, and pay close attention to our intuition. For example:

- In an African tribe where everyone goes barefoot, some go out crying, and others see an opportunity to make big shoe sales.
- If they throw lemons at you, you can cry or make lemonade. As you can also see, it is a matter of attitude because when opportunity knocks at your door, you must let it in immediately and not wait too long to open it.

The "Circle of Opportunities" is not a physical place but a metaphor for life itself. It is a space where proactivity, intelligence, and a positive attitude become the tools that allow us to achieve our dreams. Let us embrace opportunities enthusiastically, learn from experiences, and never stop relentlessly pursuing our goals. Success is not a destination but a journey that is built with work, perseverance, and a positive attitude.

Next, I invite you to write down the opportunities you want.

_____

_____

_____

_____

_____

Some opportunities only appear once, and I am ready to take advantage of them and change my life. I know I can miss a chance, but if I don't take risks, I will be ready to.

_____

_____

_____

_____

_____

I must get through the personal desert and overcome the sandstorms to make my plans a reality. So, I plan to do the following.

_____

_____

_____

_____

_____

*--- **I have my plan but need action, will, faith, and attitude.** **These** are the most valuable and profound qualities I need.*

It is about maturing, growing, and changing harmful attitudes for positive ones. Opportunities open every moment in our lives. I now understand that missing opportunities that can change my life is unpleasant.

God gives us opportunities, but that does not mean that everything we desire will always be available. That's life: time goes by, and opportunities run out, so don't let them slip away. Always remember that the best of life is before you, but the most beautiful is inside you. Although everyone sees what you do, very few know what you are worth. That is why knowledge and reason show opportunities, while ignorance and mistakes hide them.

Remember your mind and thoughts; they know all your strengths, weaknesses, and limitations. And, just as it is your best friend, it can also be your worst enemy. Use your imagination and remember that logical things can lead us to the correct meaning, but imagination opens possibilities and takes us everywhere. A good opportunity is recognized when.

- Feel that you are the one who finds it, not the opportunity for you.
- Learn that being happy is not something that happens by chance but is a decision.
- Knowing that it is not about looking important but being important.
- Know that others speak of your achievements and not your mouth.
- Be aware that there is always more coming to you who expects nothing.

Analyzing and recording what he said is good (William Ward, 1812-1882, English theologian). Opportunities are like sunrises, if we wait too long, we miss them.

"The real sign is to seize opportunities more than judgment and knowledge; we need our imagination and intuition at its highest level."

THE CIRCLE OF SUFFERING

Suffering is universal because even the Creator of the universe has suffered when he has seen the ingratitude and behavior of his incredible creation. Because we have eyes, but we are still blind; we have ears, and we do not listen; we have brains, and we do not grasp; we have soul and spirit, which is what we care for the least. We read and do not understand; we walk and do not know where we are going. When we can understand something, we ignore it because it does not suit us or accommodate it to our image, belief, and convenience. That is, we are comfortable walking in ignorance.

Suffering as part of inner growth. If the Creator has suffered, if his prophets have suffered, if Jesus Christ suffered in body, soul, and spirit, *who do you think you are not suffering*? Pain and suffering are inevitable for developing intelligence, wisdom, and soul growth on this planet. In fact, from grief and sorrows have emerged the strongest souls, the most significant characters that have changed destinies and the history of the world.

To want to live without suffering is to refuse to face inner darkness and hidden ignorance. It is not wanting to learn the lessons of life that make us grow.

Affliction: temporary and transformative. Affliction rarely stays forever since it alternates with the joy of learning a lesson. The leading cause of suffering is living with it without seeking definitive solutions. Suffering is often confused with pain, which is sensitive in human organs and directly affects the body. Suffering is something else; it is to suffer moral and mental damage, and it is a torturer that takes hold of you.

Suffering: a universal experience. Regardless of our character, economic level, or intellect, we all share the experience of suffering. It is an integral part of the human condition. We all grapple with various forms of suffering: moral, economic, physical, or from ignorance.

Blaming others: a delusional trap. It is common to seek culprits for our ills and misfortunes. However, no one is exempt from suffering. Instead of falling into this trap, we should focus on finding solutions and overcoming difficulties. This shift in focus can bring hope and optimism, as we all grapple with the inevitability of suffering.

- Why did he reject me?
- Who abandoned me?
- Who stole from me?
- Who broke my heart?
- Who tricked me?
- Who made me suffer and why?
- Who made me lose money?
- Who took away my happiness?
- Who stole my illusion?
- Who took away my peace of mind?
- Who controls my emotions?
- Who controls my life?
- Who decides for me?

Are your parents, your job, your partner, your spouse, your past, your family, your lover, a vice, your neighbor, your boss, a ghost who controls your life and makes you suffer so much? In the face of all this, I let you know the following.

- Whoever prolongs suffering too long will end up being possessed by that suffering.

- Whoever prolongs a grief too long ends up being possessed by it.
- Whoever prolongs hatred too many ends up being possessed by that hatred.

The planet and our world are an emotional laboratory, full of problems, difficulties, and sufferings but also full of overcoming. Possibly, you can make a long list of suspects and culprits for your suffering. You will indeed find that many people have failed you; you will also find others who have given you what you deserve. However, how to point the finger at others is more convenient; indeed, you already have the culprits of your suffering. And, possibly, you say.

---- uufff What a relief to find the culprit after so much searching finally. How easy I would have done it sooner. Well, you should know that looking for culprits *doesn't solve anything!*

Suffering: An echo of past wounds. Suffering: An echo of past wounds. Some suffering is the price we must pay for not having fought before. Mistakes, abandonment, abuse, parental divorce, bad choices, failures, and violent reactions are consequences of inner wounds caused in childhood, and we are not aware of that.

The stored pain of the mistreatment in childhood and adolescence remains inside our minds in the unconscious. We carry it in our brain, and at any moment and in the least expected place, a minor situation or external pain brings up that pain, which explodes, causing more pain.

Internal pain and anger are unconscious responses. Those who have deep emotional wounds are offended by any small detail. They explode in anger and pride, overwhelmed by inner pain. The wounds of the soul are still with open scars, allowing pride and violence to control their joy and sadness.

Lack of understanding and the need for healing. We do not understand why we do not take on suffering or know its causes or effects. Suffering comes from our memories, making us suffer. This increases our pain, ignoring that there are two types of tiredness. The first is an extreme need for peace; the second is the need to sleep peacefully.

Knowledge through suffering: A paradox. As the theologian François Fénelon said, "*He who has not suffered knows nothing; he knows neither good nor evil; he neither knows men nor knows himself.*" We cannot even control our thoughts. Many do not know the need nor know themselves, nor will they be able to know the thoughts of others.

It's often overlooked that silence and a smile are two powerful tools for achieving true emotional peace. A smile, in its warmth, can ease conflicts and foster understanding. Meanwhile, silence acts as its wise ally, not just reacting to problems but preventing them from arising in the first place. It gives us the space to reflect before reacting. Silence and a smile help us resolve challenging situations, strengthen our inner calm, and bring us closer to a more balanced and mindful life, putting us in control of our emotional well-being.

The crucible of suffering: forging resilience and love. Like a trial by fire, suffering can transform the soul. Just as fire refines metal, so does suffering, which refines humanity, testing our faith and courage. In this life, suffering is inevitable, but how we carry it is a choice. The past cannot be changed, nor what was done or said, but the future can be changed. This depends on what we do today: avoid living in the past because nothing can be changed.

The present is a canvas on which to build the future. It is being optimistic, visionary, and pioneering, which means breaking limiting patterns and embracing new possibilities. It is believing in one's potential and that of others, yearning for everyone to achieve happiness and fulfillment. The present is not just a moment in time but a powerful tool in our hands to shape the future. It would be wonderful if our ten could become the one for others, for them to start.

To alleviate suffering, we must first heal our inner selves. It is not about seeking strength or power but achieving freedom and enjoying life's blessings. In the face of suffering, it's important to remember that God tests us not to lead us into sin but to help us develop our light and share it with the world. This philosophical concept encourages us to find meaning in our suffering and use it as a catalyst for personal growth and the betterment of humanity.

Humility is the prelude to true love. It is essential to heal to help others heal, and this is achieved with humility of spirit because one cannot be humble without being humbled. For this reason, I ask myself: Is suffering anything else? We can genuinely connect with others through our shared experiences of suffering and healing.

Love: the antidote to suffering. Love, in all its forms, is the only tangible reality we can experience. It is the most powerful force to combat suffering, connecting us with humanity's essence and God. This is the only tangible reality we can have, thanks to the fact that we can precisely feel and perceive love.

Healing Through Profound Experience. By profoundly immersing ourselves in suffering, we can ascend to higher states of consciousness. This 'profound experience' refers to a deep, transformative journey where we confront and learn from our pain. We heal past wounds such as anger, resentment, guilt, anxiety, failure, depression, fear, rage, envy, hatred, and trauma, freeing ourselves from the chains that bind us to happiness.

I invite you to embark on an introspective journey, closing the doors to distractions and opening your spiritual dimension. Allow suffering to speak its truth. Dare to acknowledge your flaws and weaknesses without self-pity or excuses.

KEYS TO OVERCOMING SUFFERING

Self-Awareness and Evaluation: Begin by understanding yourself deeply. Ask yourself: Who am I? What is my purpose on this planet? Am I ready to let go of the causes of my suffering?

Embrace and Understand Pain: By accepting your pain and seeking its root cause, you empower yourself to overcome it and emerge stronger.

Seek Support: Remember, it's okay to lean on loved ones and consider professional help if needed. This support system is there to provide comfort and reassurance in your journey.

Connect with Your Faith: If you have faith, turn to prayer and spiritual practices. Remember, your faith can be a source of spiritual nourishment and guidance in your quest for well-being.

Practice These Guidelines:

- Avoid Judgment: Refrain from judging others or making assumptions.
- Speak with Integrity: Be true to your word and treat others respectfully.
- Let Go of the Past: Release old, painful memories.
- Go the Extra Mile: Always strive to do more than is expected.
- Appreciate Others: Value those who support you.
- Practice Forgiveness: Both giving and receiving forgiveness.
- Find a Hobby: Engage in activities you enjoy.

- Respect Nature: Honor the Earth and all living beings.
- Embrace Your Purpose: Recognize that life is a purposeful journey.
- Follow Your Faith: Adhere to your spiritual beliefs.
- Remember, Love Endures: Love is eternal.

I suffer for the following reasons (if necessary, use separate sheets of paper or a notebook).

_____

_____

_____

_____

_____

_____

_____

Love, tolerance, and hope help to heal pain if we understand and recognize our inner suffering and are willing to overcome it and leave it behind. Man grows and matures in suffering because pain tempers and enriches him inwardly. To do this properly, we need to follow a plan, a goal with serious purpose, and faith in what we do and believe because he who lacks God lacks everything, and he who has God lacks nothing.

We also suffer because we are blind to understanding; we need to know that we are right and that everyone else is wrong. We suffer for fear of being wrong for not being perfect; that is to say, we suffer because, in many opportunities, we self-reject and self-blame. Humanity's search for happiness, truth and beauty is an eternal quest that invites us to find ourselves. Now, my plan to overcome suffering is,

_____

_____

_____

_____

_____

_____

_____

I promise to strengthen myself by making concrete plans, and I will start with.

_____

_____

_____

_____

_____

_____

---I know I need to focus better on my life purposes. I have learned that suffering is a choice and not a lifestyle.

---I need to learn to live in peace, applying basic behaviors to overcome the emotional suffering I am in.

God knows you suffer in this life, but you don't have to endure it alone. He wants you to seek comfort and healing. "Blessed are those who mourn," Jesus taught, "for they shall be comforted. [1.] "Trusting in God and others can heal your pain. Remember, if you will give up, let it be at the feet of God. We must have the humility not to feel superior to anyone, the courage to face our mistakes, and the wisdom to ignore the foolishness that others say. These virtues are ideals and tools that empower us in our healing journey. As Saint Augustine said, "God had a son on Earth without sin, but never one without suffering."

"Suffering helps us to know ourselves and teaches us the right path to correct life's mistakes".

THE CIRCLE OF VIOLENCE

In the whirlwind of human history, violence has stood as a persistent ghost, plaguing our societies and leaving a trail of pain and suffering. Violence is at an unprecedented scale and intensity in human history. We see psychological, mental, and physical violence. Likewise, we have gender-based violence, domestic violence, violence in schools, cults, politics, state violence, and violence for power. And as if that were not enough, we also have digital violence. We need to come together and take collective action to address this pervasive issue. I wonder...

- Why cruelty and hostility among human beings?
- Why violence in the family?
- Why violence in schools and universities?
- Why so much violence at work and in society?
- Why is there such a thirst for political and military power?
- Why are we who inhabit this planet so aggressive?
- Why do we create so many unnecessary conflicts and wars?

The Roots of Violence: Violence does not arise by chance but results from a complex interplay of factors rooted in culture, education, economics, and power structures. Inequality, discrimination, poverty, and lack of opportunities create a breeding ground for resentment, frustration, and, ultimately, violence.

In its rawest form, violence manifests as inflicting physical or psychological harm on another person. However, its tentacles extend further, permeating family, work, and social relationships with a climate of fear, hostility, and distrust. This invisible violence erodes social cohesion, hindering development and perpetuating misery.

We are unable to measure the long-term consequences of using violence. Some try to justify themselves by saying that we are human and therefore imperfect, trying to justify attitudes and actions by feeling more potent than others. Many others seek justice and rights through violence, forgetting that *"violence begets violence."*

Some media make us believe that violence and war are ordinary and necessary activities on this planet, valid means of resolving social problems, achieving peace, and achieving a better balance of power abuse. This is conveyed to us in movies, newspapers, books, and television series.

In our world, we learn that success and power can only be attained through abuse and violence on many occasions. We don't need to be geniuses to know that what is obtained through violence is only preserved with more violence. - Woe to him who builds a city with blood and finds a people with violence! Dark clouds announce a stormy existence!

The Right to Violence: A Questionable Concept. From a particular perspective, states and organized labor are two legal entities that historically granted the right to sanction violence legally. This right, often justified to maintain order and security, is contentious. However, allowing violence to erupt over problems known to the rulers that have not been adequately addressed is inexcusable. Similarly, for the working class, destruction and looting do not build.

It is crucial to understand that development and peace cannot be achieved through incendiary bombs. The act of hurting police officers or looting supermarkets and stores has never led to an improvement in a country's conditions. Burning buses and trucks, destroying a hospital, and leaving hundreds of people without work only exacerbates the existing problems. Violence, whether by workers, the state, or individuals, has always led to destructive consequences.

If we need examples, let's look carefully at the history of Adolf Hitler, Saddam Hussein, Osama bin Laden, Idi Amin, who was president of Uganda, or the president of Syria, Bashar al-Assad. Look at the countries where violence is the daily bread; violence always begets more violence and solves nothing. Now analyze, for example, where and how that person from whom you inherited your violent attitude is, surely nothing enviable.

The Power of Nonviolence: History has shown us the incredible transformative power of nonviolence. Figures like Gandhi, Mandela, and Martin Luther King Jr. have demonstrated that peaceful resistance can potentiate social change without violence. The eradication of violence is not a distant dream but a realizable aspiration that requires everyone's commitment and action, starting with oneself.

Violence begins to germinate in the mind and your heart, and according to how you think, so will your actions. As it is fed, it becomes more hurtful, giving way to the branches of resentment and the stems of hatred. Without realizing that on the day of the harvest, they will only reap the fruit of contempt, abandonment, and loneliness. Because from the fruit of their actions, man shall eat, and the actions of the violent shall be their destruction.

The Long Days of Pain Inflicted by Violence: The days are long and filled with pain inflicted by violence, not only because of the thoughts it leaves behind but also because of a sad and aching heart. With the painful marks left by bad memories filled with bad experiences, with torturous memories that don't let you live.

Who likes to drink the wine of violence, which, when ingested, only brings more violence? The violent person believes they have everything under control and feel like the master's themselves, not realizing that they are merely an expression of their fears. With this attitude, they find what they least seek: the rejection of others! Because the violent man, rejection, loneliness, and evil will continuously pursue him relentlessly.

Do not allow the waves of violence to separate you from your shore, nor let what you have learned in so many years become a distant memory—leaving bitterness in your heart, sleepless nights surrounded by loneliness, and tears streaming down your face. Remember, in violent seas, there will always be a storm.

Look at your surroundings, at your sons and daughters; what memory do you want to leave them? A vulgar and violent inheritance? Don't look at how much you will leave your children; look more at what kind of sons and daughters you will leave the world. You must be aware that violence is only an expression of your inner fears of the abuse you were a victim of, leaving you with emotional wounds.

Look at your loneliness, your spiritual misery, thanks to your way of acting. Look at yourself; you act like a rabid animal that will end up attacking itself. That is the fate of the violent because if they do not correct their attitude or rectify it, they do not deserve another end.

Ask yourself, what do you gain by being violent to your brother and friends? What do you gain by being violent to your parents, to your sons and daughters? What do you gain from being violent to your family and neighbors? What do you gain by being violent to your body, soul, heart, and life? By chance, have you ever asked yourself these questions?

- What are the deep wounds you have?
- Why is loneliness greater every day?

What do you expect to reap if that is what you have sown? Don't expect to sow pineapples and reap guavas! Each one reaps what he sows: the pay and reward. Amid violence, sometimes it is necessary to stop and look at the horizon to visualize how far one can go with this course of action. He who is violent will be violent, just as he who plunders will be plundered; he who deceives will be deceived, and he who plunders will be plundered. This is because we live on earth amid men and not in heaven.

Do not forget that life gives back what you have provided; the same will happen when you die. You will die of the same thing you have lived because, just as violence rises, so does justice. And, those who have sown violence and confusion, nothing will remain of them, nor of the joy they had among them, nor of their deeds, nor their wealth. Remember that one of man's missions is to help bring order to this imperfect world, thanks to his actions.

But not in a violent way, because violence in the end only makes victims, and the world already has enough of them. Violence comes from the mind and heart of man, so it is the heart of man that has to heal it. What harms man is what comes from within, not outside. If the primary goal on this planet is peace and forgiveness, then you have found a reason to live and remember what; not all who wander are lost.

Now, I invite you to voluntarily remove yourself from worries and make an internal retreat of "silence" of consciousness. Do it with your stomach half full or empty but without hunger; strengthen it with water or fruits. Look for a quiet place, if possible, in contact with nature, away from the noise, worries, your watch, or your cell phone. Forget your routine, give peace to your mind, relax more, and leave the usual mental activities. Please do not allow the other to harass, blame, distract you, and tell you that abandoning everything is not worth it.

Quietly, he concentrates until he feels he is traveling in a vacuum and arrives at a place where nothing exists. There is no noise, no voices, no figures, where he is still, static. Yes and no mean the same thing, opening to his accurate spiritual level. In that place, you overcome your fears and limitations.

A place where you can achieve a genuine openness to change because you are in the antechamber of God's presence in your life. Because God dwells in us, he is at the root of our being in secret (Matthew 6:[6-13]). We must be willing to open ourselves to new values when we reach a new level of understanding in our spiritual life and accept God in our existence.

This is what is known as "*awakening to spiritual attention*". You must be aware that life evolves in the same way as the universe. Likewise, our consciousness and spiritual life must develop and evolve, and we must seek higher levels of consciousness and spirituality. This will be new if you do not know that we must take care of our spirit. So, look inside yourself, examine yourself thoroughly, and ask yourself the following:

- What have you gained from their violent acts?
- What do you gain by living by threatening and randomizing others?
- What has he gained by mispronouncing his language?

Has he not noticed that his mouth excites violence, which he has turned into his necklace and lifestyle full of lies and manipulation? This is holding back the miracle of reconciliation and forgiveness. Now, make an inner examination without lies and in full use of your conscience.

I recognize that I am violent because of .

_____

_____

_____

_____

_____

--- I am aware that I need to change; violence only attracts people just like me.

--- I am going *to change*! My attitude does not help me; it only brings me problems. --- I need to heal my emotions and traumas of abuse and aggression.

--- I will practice understanding and empathy to find the path of peace, love, learning, and self-discovery.

--- I know I am like this because I do not recognize that I have inner wounds; I have rejected God because of falsehood, injustice, and contempt for others, their dignity, their goods, and their achievements.

--- I recognize that creation is an act of love and surrender. It is not an act of violence; God is not violent; he is just, and he loves and protects us. Help me, my God, and forgive me for my arrogance, pride, and ignorance.

--- Forgive me for thinking only of my pain, not knowing the pain I was causing others. I want to change, and I will start by.

_____

_____

_____

_____

_____

_____

_____

--- I wish to heal the mistreatment I was subjected to, the abuses and violent acts I experienced. I recognize that I have emotional and inner wounds to heal. I ask for help from God. Hear me, Lord, help me; do not leave me alone; I bow before you confidently. Make me whole again. I have faith and trust and place my life in your hands.

"God tries the righteous and the wicked, and his soul abhors him who loves violence." (Psalms 11: 5).

THE CIRCLE OF VICES

The word "vice" encompasses a wide range of meanings, from the moral and spiritual to the psychological and social. Essentially, vices represent those destructive behaviors or patterns that enslave us, make us sick, and can lead us to personal ruin. They range from immoral acts to negative habits that, regardless of their specific definition, have the potential to weaken and destroy a person.

Vice: An Internal Enemy. Vice, an enemy spirit, is like a parasite with one sole purpose: to destroy you, to gradually wear you down, and guide you towards the lowest forms of human behavior and misery until nothing remains of you!

While we are born free of vices, bad memories, and hatred, we are universally exposed to various behaviors and customs that can influence our personal development during childhood, adolescence, and learning. We observe the vices and customs of parents, siblings, relatives, friends, neighbors, teachers, and acquaintances. Some of these vices, so fatal, can become infernal behaviors that mark our existence, making us feel less alone in our struggles.

WHAT VICE IS NOT INFERNAL AND DESTRUCTIVE?

Everything that enslaves and destroys deserves that term, such as drug addiction, smoking, alcoholism, overeating, gambling, addiction to depraved sex, lying, drug dependence, ludopathy (gambling addiction), corruption, lying, envy, and many more not mentioned.

Vices affect our physical health and profoundly impact our psychological and social state. They impoverish our perception of life, the world, and ourselves, becoming addictive disorders that lead to severe consequences such as:

- Destroys dreams and life
- Ends with a happy home
- A mother's suffering begins
- A wife's weeping and suffering begins
- The sadness of a family and the disappointment of children
- Ends faith in the future and hope
- Leaping from success to human misery

The insatiable thirst for vice. We human beings create multiple needs for ourselves, but those of vice have no satisfaction because they always grow more. Thanks to many men, they only see the sad glow of their vices. Some perditions have no masters, but most come as something necessary and passing. Then, they stay for a while as guests, and finally, they remain as masters and lords of our lives.

Universal Enemy. Vices, with their insidious nature, do not discriminate. They infiltrate all walks of life, affecting people of all social conditions, races, colors, jobs, religions, sexes, and places of birth. If we don't monitor what enters our lives, vices, like emotional relaxants, take hold of us. Once settled in, vices act like roaring, hungry lions, always seeking someone to devour.

Excuses and Justifications. The answers are usually unsatisfactory when faced with questions about unpleasant and uncomfortable vices. The addict takes refuge in comfort and necessity, inventing excuses to justify the unjustifiable. Even a viceless vice becomes something necessary and fair in their distorted mind, a dangerous perception. For many, a vice is only bad when it is addictive and leads to extreme ruin. They ignore the silent damage it causes daily in relationships and overall well-being.

When does a person with an addiction know excess? Never! Vice, besides being cursed, is treacherous. It infiltrates as a passing occasion and takes root as an unbreakable habit.

Self-Imposed Slavery. Each person chooses the vice that enslaves them. The one with vices is not their master, no matter how much they shout it to the four winds. The person with an addiction is not accessible; they are a prisoner of their customs and ties. People with an addiction seek illusory satisfaction in their mental illnesses, falling into loneliness and bordering on madness. They come to know the depths of bitterness, a bottomless abyss.

The False Excuse of "Everyone Does It." It is common for people to deceive themselves with the philosophy of "everyone does it, so why shouldn't I?" I advise these people to stop being "monkeys" who imitate everything, even if they don't like it. The fact that millions of people share the same vices does not turn them into virtues. Imitating others without questioning only leads us down a path of self-destruction, a path we must be cautious not to tread.

We already live in the days when what is beautiful and correct has ceased to be so, and they call it "abnormal." Everything that is vice and destructive is something "normal." because the most devastating of all is practiced, which is to do evil out of vice and wickedness! *How necessary it is to awaken the conscience!*

Ask yourself the following question: what benefit has vice brought you, --- oh, what a pity, nothing to say, right?

The harmful consequences of vice. The vices only bring problems, diseases, and equally vicious people to you, affecting you directly. You may also notice that it never affects those not involved. The practice and persistence of a vice becomes deceptive euphoria.

Just as lousy conversation corrupts good manners, so does vice to your life, soul, and spirit. Finally, it isolates him and plunges him into its domain of perdition to strike the final blow with no one to help.

A Path to Misery: Drug addiction, alcoholism, gluttony, smoking, bulimia, gambling, theft, dishonor, betrayal, and death. These become a daily need that leads you to perdition, ultimately leading to misery and finally to death. But before you die, it will take its toll. You will surely end up in a hospital on an oxygen tank, locked up in a mental institution, on an operating table, or bedridden, begging for compassion.

In any case, you will have to pay for your audacity and mockery of God, life, and your family, with diseases, pain, and suffering, having a humiliating, miserable, and painful death.

In this life, everything is a process. It was a process to acquire a vice, and it is a process to leave it because nobody leaves a vice or a habit by throwing it out the window. Vices are left with mental reasoning and spiritual will, step by step. They must be removed by the ladder, rung by rung. Remember that each person reaps what he has sown, what he deserves.

- Don't pretend to have healthy lungs if you have smoked all your life.
- You don't have a healthy liver, stomach, and heart if you are an alcoholic.
- Do not pretend to have a good memory and a healthy brain if you are a drug addict.

Every vice has a price to pay. Whoever gives in to evil becomes a slave to that evil, damages his health and plans, and is out of tune with his own life. Many people stop practicing the least common of the senses, precisely common sense! What irony and lack of understanding. Next, I invite you to think about the vices you have.

I recognize that I have the following vices.

_____

_____

_____

_____

_____

Every vice has a cause and a reason. So meditate deeply and write down the cause and origin of your vices.

_____

_____

_____

I know that one is a slave to the one who defeats him. For this reason, vices have brought me the following.

_____

_____

_____

_____

I know I need help and healing for my emotional wounds and shortcomings. I need personal reconciliation and the help of God, from whom I have been so far away. I need professional help and to ask forgiveness from my family and my loved ones for so much pain and problems caused. Help me, my God, renew my heart, and allow me to correct and live again. The plans and actions I must take to give up my vices are as follows:

_____

_____

_____

_____

--- My God, feed my soul; you are the lamp that lights my path, the bread that feeds my life, the road that leads my way. Remember that God's specialty is taking pieces of something broken and making a masterpiece out of it.

"The vices that manifest themselves are lighter; the dangerous ones are those that hide under virtue." (Seneca).

THE CIRCLE OF OLD AGE

Embracing the Life Cycle. Old age, an inevitable stage in every human being's life cycle, is not a destination to be avoided. It is the acceptance of a natural process from the moment we leave the womb until the day we return to the mother of all. A gradual decline in physical and cognitive abilities characterizes old age. The body no longer possesses the same elasticity and resistance, and the mind may experience some slowness in processing information.

Vulnerability to Diseases. Our immune system weakens as we age, making us more susceptible to diseases, viruses, and infections. COVID-19, for example, has proven to be a particular risk for older people—difficulties with Technological Advancements.

The rapid evolution of technology and science can challenge older people. Constant innovation and information overload make adapting and understanding new developments is difficult.

The path to old age makes us sensitive, slow, and with tired eyes. It makes us prone to diseases, announcing to us that it is the final stage of life and that we are nearing the final departure. On the road to old age, we notice that time and life pass quickly and that it is a fleeting journey for those who succeeded and those who did not.

A Laboratory of Emotions. Throughout our journey, life has presented us with a rich tapestry of emotions: joys, satisfactions, sorrows, anger, envy, worries, resentments, discord, and fears, especially the fear of death.

The Importance of Reflection and Repentance. Old age, a time for introspection, allows us to reflect on our actions and decisions. We must be consistent with our experiences, repenting for what has harmed us and seeking to improve our attitude.

Others prefer to remain oblivious to life's lessons. Despite their experiences, they stay unobservant, unresponsive, and uncomprehending. As a result, while they rest, their nighttime dreams trouble their thoughts, leaving them confused and ashamed.

HE WHO PLANS FOR OLD AGE

Aging with wisdom and inner peace. The elder who reflects on their journey, on caring for their family, their health, and their finances, on managing their assets and the legacy they leave, experiences a sense of fulfillment and satisfaction. Climbing the mountain of old age brings fatigue and weariness but also a broader and freer perspective. The spirit feels calm and serene, for it has learned to live in harmony with the body, time, memory, oneself, God, and others. This harmony with oneself is a key to inner peace, thanks to the fact that prudence and experience are the crowns of older people.

Every prudent elder finds happiness and inner peace in God, leading a well-lived life, rectifying mistakes, and achieving goals. Having raised their children well, with pride and seeing their grandchildren as their crown, they play a crucial role in transmitting knowledge, harmony, and love. A beautiful old age is the best reward for leading a well-managed life, leaving footprints worth following and passing on to all their descendants.

The wisdom that comes with age. The elder who possesses experience, knowledge, and prudence, what human being can blame them? With time, we must seek values within ourselves and outside. Likewise, we learn that it is not the young who know the rules who should be happy, but the old who know the exceptions and know how to manage their existence to reach a greater age—living an acceptable life that, despite the passing years, remains young, only with a little more effort.

WHAT YOU WILL REGRET WHEN YOU REACH OLD AGE

If you could live and take advantage of the precious moments that life gave you, you deserve to have a peaceful and pleasant old age. That is ordinarily the reward for having led a good life. But if you let the beautiful moments and the best opportunities pass you by, you may regret the following.

- Not having taken that trip he dreamed of when he had the chance
- Not having learned a little more because of his stubbornness, because he thought he knew everything.
- Having been in a stormy relationship for such a long time
- To have stopped doing so many things out of fear

306

- Not having taken more physical care of oneself, exercising more
- Not having resigned from the job I hated so much
- Not having been happier, a choice I let go of
- Not having said "I love you", when he had the chance
- Not listening to his parents' advice, he realized everything they told him was authentic and for his good.
- Not having forgiven that person for whom you feel resentment
- Not having lost forgiveness due to ego and pride
- Failing to help people in need, living indifferently, and not serving others
- Not having devoted more time to your family, your partner
- Failure to complete the project he started
- Not having played and dedicated more time to the "little ones," most of the time was wasted working with jumping jacks.
- Not having taken risks, especially in love
- Not having been faithful to his dreams
- Having lost contact with friends and valued people
- Not having more faith and trust in God

HE WHO DOES NOT PLAN FOR OLD AGE

The consequences of neglect in youth. Suppose you chose to live for pleasure and disregarded your family and health during success, well-being, and good work. If you couldn't manage or save during your good streak. If, when you could, you didn't gather anything and found yourself trapped in the prison of vices, pleasures, ignorance, and pride. How do you expect to have anything for old age if you didn't gather anything? If you don't consider that old age affects everyone and requires preparation, as all stages of life do.

How can you expect to have something if you didn't sow anything in your youth? When you reach old age, what do you anticipate finding?

- Were you happy?
- Did you give happiness?
- Did you make someone happy?
- What good will you have?
- What right do you have to complain if you can't take care of anything?
- If you can't manage your life, what will you teach?
- If you only lived for yourself and couldn't give anything to anyone, what can you claim in old age?
- Who can you claim anything from?

You can only hope to live on charity. That is the reward for the foolish and careless.

What wisdom can you have if you don't know how to care for yourself? What kind of good can your gray hairs bring? What experience and reflection can you share if you have no judgment and don't know how to live? What will they inherit from you if you can't set an example? What did you do with your life? How did you utilize your talents and gifts? What did you do with your abilities? What legacy did you leave? What did you teach? Did you leave joy and peace, or did you only leave sadness, fear, and desolation? Did you have faith? How much love were you able to give and receive? How much service have you rendered?

Sowing and reaping: An inescapable law. I will remind you of something the Bible and logic say in this life: you reap what you sow! Amid your pain, you may say, "If only I could live again,"

"If only I could go back." You would try to make fewer mistakes and not have waited so long to grow. But it's too late, and you only have to wait for the day of death to justify yourself. Even then, it will be of no use; you will be a corpse without memory or honor, and your memory will be lost.

The Final Lesson. Let us not forget that each of us receives according to what we do, and life charges and pays us according to our deeds. The consequences of our actions are inevitable, and ultimately, we all face them. Some have erred all their lives, living closely with vices. In the end, they discover that they are not truly afraid of death but of their conscience, of the final judgment. Too late, they realize that they were never scared of darkness, for they had lived in it all their lives, but they were afraid of their light, the light of truth that now confronts them.

A call to conscience and forgiveness. My words do not intend to judge, condemn, or point fingers. I am not a judge, nor do I aspire to be. I plan to awaken spiritual consciousness and invite recognition of mistakes. To know how to forgive, to ask for forgiveness, and to rectify if necessary. How many days remain for older adults with tired eyes, labored breathing, and illness? We do not know. But whatever little remains, I advise you to dedicate it to God. Let this call to conscience and forgiveness inspire and motivate you.

Indeed, what is done is done; nothing from the past can be changed. The reality is that we live in a society that marginalizes, forgets, and neglects older people. Regardless of their actions, older people become vulnerable in almost all areas of life. Society should always keep this in mind.

To older people, I can only say: Look deep within yourself and try to discover if, after leaving this world, you will be a troubled soul. The answer may be no, or it may be yes. The good news is

309

that all suffering has a purpose, and all heartfelt repentance has redemption. The purpose of life is to evolve and grow spiritually, and the final lesson is to learn to love, returning to eternal love even in the last hour. This emphasis on self-reflection should make you feel reflective and contemplative.

"I thought that the days would speak and, the many years would teach wisdom." (Job 32: 7).

I invite you to express your conclusions about old age.

_____

_____

_____

_____

_____

_____

_____

The elderly must have a deal.

_____

_____

_____

_____

_____

_____

_____

I help or would help the elderly as follows.

_____

_____

_____

_____

_____

"A great book is old age. It is a pity that man must die when he begins to read it with profit!". (José María de Pereda - 1833-1906). Spanish writer.

THE CIRCLE OF PEACE

Regardless of our title, wealth, education, position, or power, we all share an everyday struggle—the battle to achieve inner peace. This struggle arises from our emotional wounds, painful experiences such as hatred, resentment toward those who hurt us, or the inability to forgive ourselves.

Achieving inner peace is impossible without the ability to forgive and reconcile, not only with others but also with that wounded "inner child" we carry within. We must acknowledge our mistakes and accept our imperfections and fragility. However, through the transformative power of introspection, self-knowledge, and emotional cleansing, we can find the balance and peace we crave.

Challenges to Inner Peace. Our current society presents numerous obstacles to inner peace. We live in a frantic world that bombards us with stimuli through social media, the media, and technology. This avalanche of information confuses our senses and distorts our perception of reality.

The technology industry strives to capture our attention, often manipulating us through various platforms that harbor a dark side. Video games, for example, can fuel warlike fantasies in young people, contributing to an increase in indifference, fear, anxiety, and sadness. These external pressures add to our internal struggles, creating a cocktail that robs us of peace.

The Roots of Violence and War. Why do wars exist between individuals, families, groups, cities, and nations? The root lies in the ambition for power and the presence of leaders and rulers who do not have peace with themselves. A person who does not have inner peace is at war with themselves and with the entire world. A leader or ruler with unhealed emotional wounds is like a time bomb that can explode anytime.

The Masks of Hidden Pain. We live in a world where almost everyone wears personal masks to hide our wounded inner child. These masks can take many forms, from a facade of confidence to a tendency to avoid emotional intimacy. Additionally, we use different personas to cover up emotional wounds of abandonment, abuse, aggression, and disappointment. We trade our inner peace for populism, power, and ignorance, falling into spiritual exile.

But there comes a time when we must stop. We must set aside worldly concerns and search for inner peace. This search is crucial, regardless of our social position or personal achievements. Inner peace is not just a destination but a journey that empowers us to build a complete, meaningful, and fulfilling life.

Inner Peace: A Universal Right. Inner peace is not a privilege reserved for a few but a universal right of every human being. It is a state of well-being and balance that arises from the harmony between our body, mind, and spirit.

Embracing inner peace empowers us to live life fully, confront challenges with resilience, and foster healthy, enduring relationships.

Inner Silence: The Key to Peace. Nurturing inner silence is crucial to attaining inner peace. This entails quieting the mind, soothing the emotions, and creating a space of openness. In this state of tranquility, we can listen to the voice of our soul, think clearly, and make decisions that resonate with our life's purpose.

Stress and daily worries are obstacles that distance us from inner peace. It is essential to learn to manage these emotions effectively, developing relaxation techniques, meditation, and faith. Inner peace is the foundation for building a more peaceful world.

Inner Peace: A Personal and Collective Journey. Inner peace is not an individual achievement, but a path built from the inside out. Finding peace within ourselves can radiate it to our surroundings, creating a ripple effect that benefits our families, communities, and the world.

KEYS TO FINDING INNER PEACE

Stop Blaming Others: Taking responsibility for our actions and decisions frees us from blaming others. Pointing the finger at others for our own mistakes is a sign of ignorance, deep inner wounds, and a wounded heart. Not doing so can lead to strained relationships, increased stress, and a lack of personal growth.

Accept That You Cannot Control Everything: Embracing the fact that there are and will be situations and experiences we cannot control is a liberating realization. It allows us to focus on what we can change, relieving us from the burden of trying to control the uncontrollable.

__Let Go of Unnecessary Burdens:__ We have specific responsibilities and obligations to fulfill. That includes dealing with the tasks in our daily lives, and there will undoubtedly be unnecessary burdens that we will have to let go of. Learning to balance life and activities brings a sense of calm, allowing the mind to stop creating and fighting unnecessarily and find the elusive peace.

__Abandon Malicious Criticism and Gossip:__ It harms everyone. We get into more trouble for what we say than we do. It causes depression, low self-esteem, emotional and psychological imbalances, and stress, and in some severe cases, can lead to suicide. An uncontrolled and rude tongue is the result of unhealed emotional wounds. Those who gossip only find loneliness and rejection and are considered toxic people, living in constant conflict.

__Abandon manipulation,__ stop insulting and speaking ill of others, and stop comparing yourself to anyone.

__Practice gratitude__: Focusing on the good things in our lives generates positive emotions and well-being. It can improve our mental health, enhance our relationships, and increase our happiness.

__Cancel debts,__ and do not go into debt again. Do not allow yourself to be used intentionally. Do not believe that you are more or less than others. Overcome complexes and traumas.

__Connect with nature__: Spending time in nature calms us, renews us, and connects us with our inner selves.

__Meditate:__ This technique helps us quiet the mind and connect with the present.

Serve others: Helping others connects us to a greater purpose and generates personal satisfaction.

SEEK GOD. Authentic faith is, in fact, the most indicated way since it is the only one that can give us total peace. In the bible, peace means to be free from conflict, contention, or war. It is the inner calm and comfort of the spirit. When the peace that God offers us appears, worry and fear disappear, and we face each day, each duty, and each challenge with security and confidence in the results. It will be easier for you to return from your spiritual exile; it is like taking a shortcut and leaving aside the bonds of the mind. Pray with authentic and true faith and remember:

- Prayer is the strength of man and the weakness of God.

Forgiving and Asking for Forgiveness. Humanity's failure to seek forgiveness and forgive is a significant issue. When we judge solely based on our emotions and feelings, we create a barrier to inner peace. The absence of forgiveness and the accumulation of resentment act as chains, trapping us and preventing us from achieving the inner peace we desire.

Judging others based on our emotions and feelings only plunges us into a cycle of pain and bitterness. We must recognize that we all make mistakes, a shared human experience that connects us all. Forgiveness is not a momentary act but a conscious and courageous decision to free ourselves from the emotional bonds that prevent us from moving forward. We are hard to forgive and even harder to ask for forgiveness, but we are all in this together.

The Path to Healing and Inner Peace. To achieve healing and inner peace, we must let go of self-justification, self-pity, and victimization. It's essential to recognize and accept our imperfections and understand that we all make mistakes. Forgiveness, both toward us and others, is the key to emotional healing. It allows us to release the toxic burdens that weigh on our hearts and move forward.

In a deep examination of conscience, I invite you to ask yourself the following questions and write down the answers. Also, write down the behaviors and habits that keep you away from inner peace.

- What gives you fulfillment?
- What interests you in life?
- What are your values?
- What do you think inner peace is?
- What has helped you become more of a person?
- How far would you go to achieve inner peace?
- What would your life be like if you could balance intelligence and wisdom between the emotional and the spiritual?

Now, you can answer those questions. I believe that.

_____

_____

_____

_____

_____

In the search for inner peace, I need.

_____

_____

_____

_____

_____

I am willing to start with.

_____

_____

_____

_____

I also suggest you attend seminars, workshops, and retreats and read self-help and self-improvement books. My book, "Emotional and Inner Healing Workshop," *will significantly help you*. If you can get a life coach or a spiritual coach, it will help you a lot.

BENEFITS OF HAVING INNER PEACE

We must abandon bad habits and elevate our consciousness, establishing a spiritual connection in harmony with ourselves and the world. This can be achieved through meditation, mindfulness, and self-reflection. These allow us to distinguish between good and evil and help us change our perception and way of life. Often, we are the ones who complicate our lives, and enjoying each moment is up to us.

Inner peace is a sanctuary of calm and serenity, empowering us to confront challenges with emotional control and optimism. It brings deep satisfaction as we learn to channel our thoughts and actions toward our goals and balance our soul, mind, and purpose. In whatever form it takes, faith is a guiding light that brings us closer to God, nature, and our fellow human beings. It teaches us to listen to our inner selves and find balance amidst our daily concerns.

Remember, the path to inner peace is a profoundly personal journey. It demands effort, dedication, and patience, but the rewards are boundless: a more prosperous, happier, and more meaningful life. Don't be afraid to take that first step and embark on this journey towards inner peace. You're not alone.

"In peace I lie down and sleep, for you alone, Lord, make me live confidently." (Psalm 4:^{8}).

THE CIRCLE OF DEATH

From the moment we draw our first breath to the instant we exhale our last, life guides us on an unalterable path toward the inevitable destination of death. This is a fate that all living beings, regardless of their form or function, share. While the fear of this ultimate end is a natural part of our human condition, we must also acknowledge our biological reality and the life cycle that defines us.

Death: A Transition, Not an End. Death, rather than being a frightening conclusion, is a natural transition—a return to the essential state we existed in before birth. It transcends the roles we play in life, such as mother, father, sibling, or spouse, and touches the core of our being, our very essence. Death is not about losing identity or social roles but a passage into another realm of existence, where we leave behind earthly limitations and the roles we embody.

We are making the Most of Time. It's crucial to be mindful of life's fleeting nature, but it's equally important to remember that, in the grand scheme of eternity and total existence, it's a relatively brief period. This certainty should not lead us to despair but be a powerful motivator to seize our time and make the most of it.

We are living a Full Life. In this process of fullness, taking care of all aspects of our existence is essential: the physical, the emotional, and the spiritual. Healthily nourishing our bodies, cultivating meaningful relationships, and nourishing our spirits with attitudes that bring us peace and meaning are essential pillars for living a whole life.

We were reflecting on Our Footprint. As we progress on this path, we must reflect on the mark we leave on the world. This involves asking ourselves questions such as: how have we lived? What legacy do we want to leave behind? What impact have we had on those around us?

Have we made good use of our time? Reflecting on these questions can help us evaluate our lives and make necessary adjustments to live more meaningfully.

We should be present in each moment, appreciate its unique value, and act with intention and purpose. As the saying goes, "Everything in this life has its time," such as:

- Time to love and time to hate
- Time to cry and time to laugh
- Time to be silent and time to speak
- Time to fix and time to break
- Time to be happy and time to suffer
- Time for peace and time for war
- Time to build and time to destroy
- Time to be born and time to die

Facing Death with Serenity. Indeed, death is not only the end of our earthly existence but also the moment when we account for our actions and the impact we have had on the world. It is a final exam of the conscience, where not only what we have achieved but also how we have lived, and our decisions are evaluated.

For many, death does not represent a punishment but a liberation from the burdens and limitations of earthly life. It is a moment of peace and rest where we finally free ourselves from the material world's pain, suffering, and attachments.

For those who are old, worn out, and burdened with worries, for the needy and the weak on their deathbed, death is not a punishment but a sweet sentence that every living being must fulfill. Do not cling too much to your riches, luxuries, needs, hatreds, or fears. Just as you came naked from your mother's womb, nude, you will return to the grave. Nothing you have treasured, the things you have suffered or fought so hard for, can you take with you. We were born bringing nothing, and we die taking nothing with us.

In this sense, we must detach ourselves from the riches, possessions, and luxuries we accumulate. These material things will not accompany us to the afterlife; clinging to them only generates suffering and unnecessary attachment. What attachments bind us if we resist leaving? Why is there so much resistance to something inevitable?

Both the wise and the ignorant, both the strong and the weak, die. What truly endures after death is the legacy we leave in the world. This legacy is not just a collection of our actions but a reflection of our character, our values, and our impact on the lives of others. It is the actions we have taken, the relationships we have built, and the positive impact we have had on the lives of others.

But those who have not known how to live or have only lived according to their vices and passions. They must consider the conditions in which they have lived, who they have harmed, and what mark they have left. Life has drastic and traumatic changes, and the 'last move' refers to the final transition from life to death. Will we be ready for this ultimate change, and what will it reveal about how we have lived? In the end, our contemplation of death should not be a source of fear but a catalyst for living a life of purpose and meaning.

WHICH CIRCLE HAS HE CHOSEN TO DIE IN?

Depending on the circle we have lived in, we could die in the same one. Our actions, values, and beliefs determine the legacy we leave and the path we trace toward our final destination. Some choose peace, kindness, and an honest life, building a circle of harmony and satisfaction.

Others, on the other hand, immerse themselves in vice, theft, betrayal, and violence, creating a circle of darkness and pain. Some others choose to die in the circle of sex and fornication, and, very possibly, death will surprise them in one of those moments.

The greedy, the proud and arrogant, the liar and the gossip, the manipulator, the murderer, etc. Our circles and levels of life are as numerous and diverse as people's faces or the fingerprints of our fingers.

Wealth, pride, luxury, fame, and the power you hold in life will be meaningless in the end. When a person dies, all that remains is dust, destined to return to the earth, inheriting only worms, insects, and decay. Death is the great equalizer, erasing wealth, pride, fame, arrogance, and ego. Reflect deeply before your final hour arrives.

So, what do you expect in return if you lived in pride?

- What do you expect in return if you lived amid pride and arrogance?

- If you lived amid adultery and prostitution, what do you expect in return?
- What do you expect in return if you lived in falsehood and betrayal?

If you lived in hatred and emotional misery, what do you expect in return? What do you expect in return if you lived on greed, cheating, stealing, and deceit? If drunk or drugged, you liked to live, what do you expect in return? What do you think you can find when you cross the threshold of death? We are very lost; we have lost the meaning of life. We almost always die in the circle or how we have lived because *he will repay each one according to his deeds* [1.]

But if we change and rectify, we will surely leave heavy burdens. You better be prepared to give an account of your freedom, free will, and how you have lived. Have you taken care of your gifts? Have you realized your mission and fulfilled it?

Did he take advantage of the gifts he was given? Did he use them? What did he do with them? On the threshold of death, days, hours, and minutes before leaving this world, the body feels pain, but the soul feels more pain. Fear is felt by those souls who, analyzing their lives, look back and find no inventory, action, or decision to have done something beautiful and imperishable in their lives.

They are empty souls because their desire to have and receive surpassed their desire to give. Their desire to judge overcame their willingness to forgive, and their material desires overcame their spiritual desires.

What is total existence? Total existence is living beyond the confines of death; it is reaching a life that knows no end. In spiritual understanding, immortality is more than the absence of physical death—it is a perpetual connection with the essence of God, who is eternal. According to Scripture, God created

324

humanity in His image [2], with a purpose of immortality and transcendence, reflecting His eternal nature.

However, humanity often strays from this purpose. In our shortsightedness, we place more trust in our own reasoning and the limited interpretations of others, overlooking or undervaluing the promises God has made. The hardness of the heart and resistance to faith prevents us from embracing the fullness of the eternal life God offers. Clinging to earthly explanations, we lose sight of the wonders that God reveals to us, forgetting that our true destiny is to transcend in unity with Him.

The Bible says, "Cursed is the man who trusts in man and makes flesh his arm, and whose heart departs from the Lord.[3] " We complicate things by seeking explanations and answers for everything; we want to reason and understand God when we cannot understand ourselves.

--- *My God,* what ignorance is not knowing how to live. I lived according to my needs and emotions, lost without knowing how to live. I did not think I had a purpose and mission to fulfill. I forgot that you, my God, protected me in my mother's womb. I have lived ignoring that in your inscribed books are the days you have set for me without the first one existing. I ignore the purpose of my existence and my mission on this planet.

Humans have the problem that most of the things we are taught are learned and used as **"basic information,"** storing it and nothing more, and that does not help much because we do not assimilate much.

The phrase that says, "We *are just passing through on this planet,"* but they can't even imagine what they mean by that. Others say: "We all have a mission to do," but they don't even bother to find out what it is. What's more, they don't even know the purpose of their existence, living in nothingness. *How sad to live without meaning in life*!

We live an impressive spiritual atrophy and exile; we only care for what is ***physical and material***. For example, I am hungry, thirsty, need to study, want a dress, need a car, cold, hot, want a car, go on a cruise, get married, pay the house, and pay the mortgage.

My business is growing, and I need to go to the gym, have plastic surgery, and diet. Just imagine the needs of modern life with all its complications: business, resources, buildings, and transportation. It has no end; we are too focused on physical and material development.

Embarking on a Journey Towards Truth. It's time to awaken from the spiritual slumber in which we often live and embark on a profound journey toward consciousness and the purpose of our existence. This journey requires courage, as it calls us to explore our inner world without fear, to question the beliefs we have accepted without reflection, and to open ourselves sincerely to the possibility of truth beyond what we currently know.

Seeking truth means dedicating time and attention to our essence, to that part of us that longs for something greater and enduring. Truth is not a set of rules, dogmas, or doctrines imposed from the outside; it is a deep wisdom that reveals itself through personal experience, inner discovery, and a connection with something transcendent—something that surpasses our limited understanding. When we seek with an open mind and a sincere heart, we align ourselves with a truth that cannot be fully defined by words but is profoundly felt, transforming us in the depths of our being.

This journey is an invitation to live consciously, to find purpose in the everyday, and to experience the peace that arises from knowing we are connected to a greater reality and a purpose that gives meaning to our existence.

Many ignore spiritual care because they don't tend to or nourish it. They only notice it when they are on a deathbed, dying and confused with fear of death, as we consider it a punishment. This is due to the preconceived ideas instilled in us, and we are ignorant of the truth because we have no idea what it is. Is it fission? Is it an invention? We are blind; we have no time because we are busy with daily living, satisfying the physical and material needs we invented.

We only pay a little attention to our spiritual being when we know that we are about to die. As I mentioned, we are afraid of our brilliance, of the spiritual light, because we do not know it.

Fear is often a product of ignorance. If we fear something, it's because we don't understand it. This is particularly true when it comes to our spiritual potential. We are often uninformed and ignorant about our spiritual level. Overcoming this fear through knowledge and understanding is crucial in our spiritual journey.

It's as if it were still the age of the caves. Both life and death have their mysteries. However, we must analyze that we are going through stages. In my opinion, being born is one stage, and dying is the beginning of another. Your understanding of this depends on your study and knowledge of the levels of consciousness and spirituality.

Spiritually, to be born and to die is the same process

Only at different times. That is, when a baby comes out of the womb, his days begin to count from that moment, and he can live 25, 40, 65, 85 years, and even reach the limit of years allowed by the Creator, which is 120 years.[1]"

For example, some "Tzadik's" in Judaism (*secrets of longevity*). We also have the French **"Jeanne Louise Calment, who lived 122 years," according to the information of the book "record Guinness. "** Understood this, let's explain them in more straightforward and more understandable terms, but to do so, you need a minimum level of *knowledge and spiritual awareness*. Otherwise, you will be unable to understand absolutely nothing and end up confused.

The Soul in Gestation. From the moment of conception, a remarkable transformation takes place within the womb. Cells divide, organs form (heart, arteries, hands, feet, brain), and the physical body takes shape. But along with this physical development, a non-physical aspect also emerges the essence of who we are, encompassing consciousness, intuition, and the spark of our being. This spiritual nature of the soul, a fascinating mystery, has driven exploration and contemplation in all cultures throughout history.

The Mystery of the Soul: A Fascinating Enigma. The soul, this spiritual entity, remains an enigma that has inspired exploration and contemplation across all cultures throughout history. Its origin, nature, and destiny have been the subject of deep discussions, theories, and beliefs at every level of human understanding.

However, it is essential to remember that when we speak of the soul, we enter the realm of the spiritual domain that can only be described through symbols that point toward its essence without fully defining it. Words and concepts are merely reflections that bring us closer to reality, yet they can never capture its mystery and greatness in their entirety.

While the nature of the soul remains a mystery, the evidence of its existence is found in our own experience. With its ability to feel, think, and be conscious, the soul is a significant part of our existence, indicating the presence of something more than a mere physical body.

The only credible origin we have for its formation says thus, "And the LORD God formed man of the dust of the ground and breathed into his nostrils the **breath of life,** and man became a living soul"[1.] The word "breath of life" comes from the Hebrew word *(Neshama)*, which means breath of life or spiritual soul, better known on this side of the planet as "spirit."

FORMATION OF THE BODY AND UNION OF THE SOUL

In the awe-inspiring biblical account of creation, God forms Adam from the dust of the earth, but he does not come to life until God breathes into him "the breath of life," infusing him with a spiritual soul. He was animated after God the Father gave of Himself and breathed into him the breath of life; that is, He gave Adam a spiritual soul (life, movement, consciousness, feeling, thought, power). This union between the physical body and the spiritual essence is a mystery that has captivated humanity for centuries.

The Enigma of Gestation: Science and Faith Unite. Similarly to how science describes the process of gestation, where the union of the sperm and egg initiates an extraordinary physical development, for many believers, this process transcends the physical. It's not just about the body form, but in a spiritual sense, it's also about the creation and incorporation of the soul, marking the incarnation of a complete being, both in its physical and spiritual dimensions. This union of science and faith, emphasizing the spiritual significance of gestation, offers a profound perspective on the mystery of life and its origin, connecting us to the divine aspect of life.

This approach connects both biological and spiritual dimensions in a way that highlights the importance of understanding gestation as a physical phenomenon and a profound expression of the eternal God's intervention in the creation of life.

From this perspective, man and woman, in their physical union, contribute to the creation of life, while God infuses the spiritual soul. As the Bible says, "If you do not know how the spirit comes to the bones in the womb of her who is with child, neither can you know the works of God who does all things" [2.]

It also says, "For you formed my inward parts; you knitted me together in my mother's womb" [3.] And further, "Your eyes saw my unformed substance; in your book were written, all the days that were formed for me, before one of them came to pass" [4.]

A Mystery Shared by Science and Faith. While science cannot definitively affirm the existence of the soul or its union with the body during gestation, it provides valuable insights into life's physical processes. In this, science and faith find common ground, facing mysteries they cannot fully explain but are eager to explore together. Science, with its understanding of the physical body, and faith, with its belief in the spiritual soul, can work in harmony to deepen our understanding of the union of the two.

Spiritually and in terms of faith, a body without a spiritual soul would be merely flesh. 'The spirit gives life; the flesh profits nothing' [5.] Therefore, when the baby is formed in the mother's womb, its spiritual soul also unites with it so that it may have life, for God made us in His image and likeness 6. This union, which we usually call *'being born,'* is a profound moment when the spiritual soul, infused by God, animates the physical body, bringing it to life.

From a scientific perspective, 'being born 'can be seen as when the physical body, having completed its gestation, is ready to be animated by the spiritual soul. This process is still a mystery to science but is deeply ingrained in the faith tradition. At the same time, another birth comes physically but at a spiritual level because the soul returns to its origin.

A Dual Existence. At birth in the physical world, a human being begins life on the material plane, receiving a name, an identity, and an earthly purpose. Yet, from a spiritual perspective, a deep and eternal being is also born or incarnates within, though initially overshadowed by the experiences and distractions of the physical world. *(..and the spirit shall return unto God who gave it)*. This dual existence defines our nature: we are both material and spiritual beings. Our highest purpose is to integrate these two dimensions so that the spirit can express itself through our earthly life and guide us toward a full and transcendent existence.

Return to the Source: As we said before, in this context, physical death is not the end but a transition to a profound spiritual journey. The soul, liberated from the physical body, embarks on a wondrous and awe-inspiring voyage toward its spiritual home, a journey of discovery and enlightenment. The question is: When are we formed in the mother's womb and are born materially? Is the spirit born or incarnated? The answer is in the book of Ezekiel, in the story of the valley of dry bones.

A Transcendent Purpose. We are born with a profound purpose: to learn lessons that transcend both the spiritual and material realms. Regrettably, we often overlook the spiritual aspect, concentrating solely on the tangible and earthly. This is a consequence of the social and cultural environment in which we are nurtured.

We learn all the other socioeconomic and cultural needs of modern life without considering and completely forgetting about the spiritual being. We are entirely ignorant of the phases and development of the spiritual soul. We are completely unaware that we were born with a greater purpose and a mission to fulfill.

The Ignorance of Our Spiritual Being

The fear of death is deeply rooted in our psyche, stemming mainly from a disconnection with our spiritual nature. When we lack understanding of who we are, our purpose in this life, and the destiny that awaits us beyond physical death, uncertainty arises that transforms into fear. This fear is not simply of life's end but of emptiness, of the loss of meaning and transcendence.

However, as we reconnect with our spiritual dimension, fear dissipates, replaced by a deeper understanding of life and our true essence. Spiritual awareness allows us to view death not as an absolute end but as a transition in a much larger journey. Embracing this understanding grants us peace and inspires us to live with greater purpose and fulfillment, knowing that our existence doesn't end with the physical body.

Actual spiritual knowledge invites us to live more consciously, where the fear of death transforms into an opportunity for transcendence and purpose, strengthening us and leading to a more complete relationship with life and the eternal.

Death: A Distorted View. We perceive death as an enemy, as an abrupt and painful end. But it represents liberation, a transition to a higher state of existence where earthly suffering and hardships vanish, and we find peace and tranquility.

Dr. Elizabeth Kübler-Ross is an expert in thanatology (*the study of death*). Dr. Kübler explains the processes and faces of death, where her research and experiences led her to affirm that: "*Dying is not something to be afraid of; it can be the most wonderful experience in the world; it all depends on how we have lived."* Likewise, Dr. Elizabeth Kübler-Ross affirms. *"Death is only a transition from this life to another existence in which there is no more anguish or pain."* Jesus of Nazareth told us about the same thing in Matthew 22:[29-30].

Living on this planet is a spiritual exile. What is of the earth returns to the world, and the spiritual soul returns to God, who gave it. Spiritually, we are born twice. A person dying on the physical level (death of his body of flesh) is born again on the spiritual level to a higher level of life without pain.

We Pave the Way for the Soul to Return to Its Place of Origin. The death and resurrection of Jesus Christ represent the most compelling evidence of life after death. His sacrifice offers us the hope of redemption and the possibility of attaining eternal life.

Divergent Paths: Honor, Justice, and Rectification: Not all of us will reach the same level after death. The path of the honorable noble leads to a higher existence, while the path of the wicked and unjust will require a process of rectification and learning.

The True Fear: Insignificance and Emptiness: The fear of death does not lie in death itself but in the possibility of having lived an empty, meaningless, and purposeless life. Panic arises when we recognize that we have only focused on the material, fleeting pleasures without cultivating our souls.

At the end of our days, the final exam is not faced by the physical body but by the spiritual soul. The soul will answer our actions and determine our destiny in the afterlife.

In the following lines, I invite you to take an inventory of what you would like to do and have not done.

_____

_____

_____

_____

_____

_____

Now, write what you would do if you were near death.

_____

_____

_____

_____

_____

_____

If you analyze the result of your life, you will notice that of all the things you have done, you missed some that were important, not knowing how to use and take advantage of life. You let wonderful things pass you by because you did not know how to choose, and if you did not know how to choose, you did not know how to live either.

St. Francis of Assisi, in his bed, said, "Welcome, my sister's death." The Bible compares death with dreams more than 50 times. When we die, I can tell that we imitate butterflies. When they are born, they come out of the cocoon. For us, it is like escaping from an endless captivity, returning spiritually to the place of origin, because the spiritual soul never dies.

It is not a question of living in fear, but if we were more aware that our lives can end anywhere and anytime. We would stop wasting time on trivial things without being fooled by what the supermarket of artificial happiness offers.

"Death is nothing more than a detachment from the physical body, like the butterfly from its cocoon. It is a transition to a higher state of consciousness where you will continue to perceive, to understand, to laugh, and where you can grow." (Dr. Elizabeth Kübler-Ross).

THE CIRCLE OF GOD THE FATHER AND MAN

God: The Eternal and Ineffable Being. With its innate capacity to bestow meaning, the human mind faces a titanic challenge when comprehending and describing God, the eternal being and architect of the Universe. His transcendent essence lies beyond our limited human understanding. Throughout history, countless prophets, Israelites, pontiffs, theologians, philosophers, thinkers, and writers have dedicated their lives to paying homage to God through books, poetry, and other works inspired by their faith.

The Audacity of Human Comprehension. In our relentless quest for God and our unyielding desire to fortify our faith, we, as humans, have dared to conceive the Creator of the Universe in our minds despite our imperfect understanding. It is a testament to the audacious spirit of humanity that we strive to contain the magnificence of God in our minds, even in the absence of complete wisdom and comprehension. If some possessed such wisdom, would they share it? In my case, I am compelled to share the limited understanding I have gathered.

The Spirit of the Creator: Origin of Being and Life. The spirit of God, the architect of the Universe and all galaxies, is rooted in the origin of being and life. He created us in His image and likeness, not in a physical sense, but spiritually. In other words, we were spiritually conceived to reflect the essence of God. We all come from the same source, which makes us His descendants and bestows upon us a part of His greatness. We must recognize our spiritual DNA and live in harmony with it.

Within us resides *God's spiritual DNA*, an inheritance revealed as we delve deeper into His knowledge and, therefore, into self-knowledge. Created in His image, we possess talents, the capacity for transformation, ingenuity, and a natural impulse toward organization. These qualities have allowed us to advance in science and technology, from quantum physics to space exploration.

While we are blessed with exemplary leaders, their errors can influence their followers. In His infinite love, the Creator cares for and guides us like children, surpassing maternal care. However, it is disheartening that many humans ignore the words and warnings of their Creator, who has communicated with us through prophets, messengers, and His son Jesus (Yeshua). It is truly astonishing that despite the scriptures and the displays of power and love, many fail to recognize their divine origin and the guidance that comes with it.

ORIGIN OF LIFE AND THE PROCESS OF EVOLUTION

Researchers from the Jet Propulsion Laboratory (JPL) and the NASA Astrobiology Institute suggest that the naturally generated electrical energy on the ocean floor, around 4 billion years ago, could have been the catalyst that triggered the emergence of life.

Although the hypothesis of *"life's emergence from underwater alkaline hydrothermal vents"* had been proposed earlier, this study does not contradict biblical accounts. Instead, it offers a detailed explanation of the processes that the Bible describes metaphorically. This approach is based on decades of fieldwork, laboratory experiments, and theoretical research, providing a solid scientific foundation for an ancient mystery.

Incredibly, this is also in the bible: "For they are willfully ignorant of how long ago there was a heaven and an earth out of the water, and **established among the waters,** by the word of God. [1]" This verse pairs, where it says that on the fourth day, God said, **"*the waters roar with living creatures...* *and God created the great sea monsters and every living creature that makes the waters roar* [2] "**. Science says that the origin of life is in the water and shows us that mammals *(whales are mammals)* were the last species to develop on Earth. Genesis says that man was created on the sixth day, completing God's creation, and science confirms the same (but with different words), affirming that man is the last superior form of animal life. Science exists to explain in detail what God says in Genesis.

The Bible also indicates that man was created on the sixth day, completing God's creation. Science confirms that humans are one of the higher forms of animal life that appeared most recently on the evolutionary scale. Science does not seek to contradict the Bible but rather to offer a tool to understand its symbolic and spiritual descriptions better, especially when considering the original languages in which it was written.

History of Biblical Translations

The literal interpretation of the six-day creation, as described in Genesis, has been a topic of discussion and reflection over the centuries. For a long time, these six days were considered 24-hour periods.

The concept of "days" in the creation account. In the context of ancient writing, the word "day" does not always refer to a 24-hour period, as we understand it today. In Hebrew, the word **"yom"** (day) can have several meanings, including a broader period of time or even a specific stage within a process. This suggests that the "days" of creation should not necessarily be taken as a rigid chronological account but rather as a metaphor for describing the divine order in which creation unfolds.

The metaphorical interpretation of the "days" of creation not only opens up space for deeper reflection on the origin of the universe but also invites us to view creation as a continuous and dynamic divine act rather than a one-time event. This approach recognizes that the Genesis account should not necessarily be understood as a literal manual but as a profound revelation of a divine process that encompasses both the spiritual and material realms, inviting us to explore creation as a masterpiece that evolves and is revealed over time.

Translations with Crossroads. Biblical translations have faced challenges since the Jews' deportation to Babylon (586 BC—537 BC). The loss of the Hebrew language and the rise of Aramaic as the dominant language made the accurate transmission of the scriptures easier. In 538 BC, the Persian king Cyrus liberated them, and the only ones who spoke Hebrew were Daniel and Ezra. When they taught the scriptures, they did so through Targums or interpretations.

The Septuagint: A Milestone with Reservations. Around 300 BC, King Ptolemy II ordered the Hebrew Bible translated into Greek, resulting in *the Septuagint, or the Seventy*, as a group of uninitiated Essene scholars translated it.

Another group, *the initiated Essenes,* played a crucial role in preserving the scriptures. Among them were esteemed elders and wise rabbis of the tribe of Judah, who were the custodians of the written and spoken scriptures, instilling a sense of reverence and respect for their dedication.

From this perspective, the translation of the Septuagint remains shrouded in some mystery. The Essenes, out of reverence for God and the people of Israel, chose to conceal certain biblical secrets from a foreign and pagan audience unfamiliar with the Hebrew faith, sparking curiosity and intrigue.

Translation as a Tool, Not an Absolute Revelation. The earliest biblical translations, such as the Masoretic Text in Hebrew, the Targums in Aramaic, and the Greek Septuagint (3rd-2nd centuries BC), were initiated when the books were written. Understanding the historical context of these translations is crucial, as it encourages readers to consider their interpretive nature critically. It's also important to remember that Ptolemy II, a foreign king, ordered the translation of the Bible, and it was not a divine command.

It is important to emphasize that the order to carry out the biblical translation came from a foreign, polytheistic, and invading man of Israel, not from God. Traditionally, wise rabbis received divine instructions from prophets in ancient times.

When analyzing the story of Adam and Eve in the Greek version of Genesis, discrepancies can be observed with the original Hebrew text. A notable example is Adam's response to God's question about the forbidden fruit. In Hebrew, **"and I will eat"** (((

וְאָכַל – it is pronounced as *ve'okhal*). His response implies that he had already eaten and would continue to do so, defying the Eternal God.

Who Was the Serpent that Spoke to Eve?

The figure of the serpent that spoke to Eve in the biblical narrative has been a subject of diverse and intricate interpretations. Traditionally, it has been perceived as a literal reptile. However, the serpent, as a representation of humanity's lowest aspect, stands at the highest level among animals because humans can reason, manipulate, and question their own existence. This multi-layered symbolism invites us to delve into the complexities of human nature and the struggle for spiritual harmony.

In Genesis, it is mentioned that "*the serpent was the most cunning of all the animals,*" and the Hebrew word used for cunning (עָרוּם) is arum, which not only means "cunning" but also "shrewd" or "prudent." This term does not simply describe a physical characteristic of the serpent; it points to a mental and psychological quality, something more related to instinct and the ability to manipulate than to an animal's behavior in its natural state.

The Serpent as an Internal Metaphor

Therefore, the serpent represents not only a reptile but also a metaphor for human beings' most primitive and animalistic impulses. It symbolizes the internal struggle between our divine essence and our earthly limitations. Eve was not speaking with an external entity but with herself, with her own material and animal side.

This *'animal side'* can be understood as the internal part of our mind: <u>doubt</u>, <u>confusion</u>, <u>curiosity</u>, <u>internal contradiction</u>, <u>restlessness</u>, and <u>mental fragmentation</u>. These are not just Eve's conflicts but the universal human conflicts that arise when a person disconnects from their divine essence and faces the limitations of their earthly nature. In this way, the serpent's symbolism resonates with each of us, reflecting our shared struggles and the quest for spiritual balance.

Therefore, the serpent that spoke to Eve is not just an animal that tempted the woman but a profound symbol of human nature's internal and material aspects. It represents the conflict between the spiritual and animal parts of our nature, a duality each individual faces when making decisions and interacting with the world around them.

This biblical metaphor speaks not only of a historical fall but of an internal fall, a timeless struggle where humanity faces its own nature and limitations, temporarily distancing itself from the divine to sink into the confusion and unrest of its lower self. This narrative, with its profound insights into the human condition, remains as relevant today as it was in ancient times, engaging us in a dialogue about our own instincts and spiritual journeys.

The apple: Translation error or theological accommodation

It's important to note that the word "apple" only began to be used about the forbidden fruit in the 16th century, long after the events described in Genesis. However, this term was introduced into some Bible translations as if it had existed in the original text from 5,785 years ago. This is a clear example of how cultural interpretations and theological adaptations can influence Bible translations, introducing elements that were not part of the original message.

The original Hebrew term used to describe the "fruit" that Eve takes in the Garden of Eden is "פְּרִי" (pri), which means "fruit," without specifying what type of fruit it is. However, the biggest twist in this interpretation lies in the word mistakenly associated

342

with the apple. The Hebrew word "זֶרַע" (zeráh), which in its root means "seed," "offspring," "lineage," or even "semen," reveals a much deeper truth or meaning than the simple idea of a literal fruit or an object that Eve ate.

A Legacy of Translations: Since 300 BC, the Septuagint version has been considered the accurate Greek translation of the Old Testament. Almost seven hundred years later, in 390, Saint Jerome produced the translation known as the Vulgate. Translations into English were also carried out, attributed to John Wycliffe and William Tyndale. In 1515, Cardinal Ximenes published a translation in three languages in each column: one language, the Hebrew version, the Latin Vulgate, and the Greek version.

As these translations unfolded, someone's negligence resulted in the loss of the original Hebrew passages, along with some of their keys, enigmas, and secrets. This loss raises questions about the authenticity of most current biblical translations, which merely reflect the original Hebrew text before the deportation to Babylon.

Interestingly, no one considered that the Septuagint might not contain all the original biblical doctrines in Hebrew, which the wise rabbis of the tribe of Judah and the initiated Essenes had concealed.

Foolish Leaders and Erroneous Doctrines: Some religious leaders, in their presumption of wisdom, have become irrational, diverting God the Father's glory and straying from the truth. They teach erroneous doctrines and theologies motivated by ignorance, greed, power, pride, and dishonesty. They distort the messages of the Bible, turning light into darkness, which generates confusion and spiritual loss for both them and their followers. God, the

Father, thus becomes one of the world's most misunderstood and betrayed beings.

Exploitation and Manipulation: These leaders, who claim to guide God's people, often promote human doctrines that lack the power to save. They exploit people, shamelessly appropriating their faith, wages, and even possessions, taking advantage of their ignorance. They manipulate and alter the scriptures to suit their purposes, generating confusion and a lack of understanding.

Despite reading the Bible, these leaders fail to comprehend its true meaning. They have lost the ability to discern the sacred from the profane, being ignorant of and distorting the true nature of God and His messages.

Distortion of Biblical Truth: Some self-proclaimed guardians of the faith do not promote discernment between the pure and the impure. They ignore the truth of the Bible and God's holy days God's holy days, interpreting the scriptures to suit their own purposes. They believe themselves prophets with vain visions and speak arrogantly, disregarding God's perpetual commandments.

- There is a way that seems right to a man, but its end is the way to death. *(Proverbs 16:25).*

It is astonishing that, as human beings with limited intelligence, we try to confine God, who possesses unlimited intelligence, to theological doctrines. Even more problematic is our desire to claim exclusivity over the gifts and blessings of life and healing from Him.

There are many false leaders because they exploit people's vulnerability in search of power, wealth, or influence. They often distort the truth and manipulate the faith of their followers for their own interests rather than guiding them with integrity and wisdom. These leaders, who sometimes present themselves as spiritual authorities, lack a true understanding of divine teachings and principles and seek to control the masses with empty promises. True faith requires discernment, and it is essential to be cautious when following those who deviate from the genuine message for their own benefit.

The omnipotence of God: According to the Bible, "He made and made all things" [3], and it also says, "Behold, the heavens and the heavens of heavens belong to the Lord your God, the earth also, with all that is therein" [4]. It also says, "But Jesus said to them, 'Do not hinder him, for he who is not against us is for us.'" [5].

Likewise, it says, "Not even a sparrow falls to the ground apart from your father" [6,] much less the works of man. The prayers and celebrations that are done in one way or another ascend, invoking God and His spirit. Because God the Father is the perfect ruler of the spiritual world, His omnipotence is a source of awe and reverence. Father is the ideal ruler of the spiritual world.

Universal hope is a unifying truth that "all religions unequivocally unite in one hope, which is eternal life" [7]. This shared belief in a higher being who transcends us and offers us life after death is a powerful bond that unites humanity.

When it rains, it is for a few and all. Likewise, in the air, all living beings can breathe freely. Different theologies clash over their way of interpreting the messages of God and His prophets, the way of worship, prayers, and the days dedicated to Him. So, we are generally doing well, but undoubtedly, we could do much better. And whoever contradicts without proof, in this way, contradicts himself.

Moreover, many political leaders have caused violence, abuse, and fraud. They have damaged the environment by polluting the air, water, and land with various destructive activities. We have neglected the planet and filled it with problems such as ambition, atheism, betrayal, weapons of mass destruction, murder, uncontrolled idolatry, and the endless pursuit of wealth and materialism. Our solemn responsibility is to address these problems and care for the garden God entrusted us. We have the power to make a positive change through ethical action, and we must do so.

- Many kill in the name of the God of life.
- Others wage war in the name of the God of peace.
- Others hate in the name of the God of love.
- Others practice cruelty in the name of the God of compassion.

Indeed, the most significant challenges for creation and its Creator arise from our actions as human beings. Despite the advances that science has given to humanity, certain scientific statements sometimes remain as mere assertions without solid evidence. This is where critical reflection becomes crucial. We must question and analyze these statements, such as the 'Big Bang' theory, the mystery of different blood types, and the enigma of dark energy in the universe.

- The "Big Bang" theory is just a theory or an unproven hypothesis.
- The different blood types in human beings and the reason for this phenomenon are still unknown with certainty.
- Dark energy in the universe cannot be detected, and science cannot prove that it really exists. The expansion of the universe is the only explanation they have found. They also believe that this energy represents 70% of the universe.

The Missing Link in Evolution: The quest for the missing link has long captivated the field of paleontology. However, as our understanding deepens, it becomes increasingly clear that evolution is a richly complex process, far from a linear path with a single, definitive ancestor. Fossil evidence reveals a web of intricate relationships between species, punctuated by numerous gradual evolutionary transitions, a narrative that continues to unfold.

Creation and Science: It's crucial to recognize that the concept of creation also encompasses its own evolutionary stages, as articulated in 2 Peter 3:[5:] ***"For this they deliberately forget that long ago by God's word the heavens existed, and the earth was formed out of water and through water."***

This suggests that the creation of the universe, as depicted in the book of Genesis, could resonate with scientific data, particularly when delving into the original Hebrew texts. The notion of an evolutionary creation beckons us to deeply contemplate the potential harmony between science and faith, offering a hopeful perspective that they can coexist and enrich each other.

Language and Translation: The issue of biblical translations and the numerical significance of Hebrew is pertinent. By their very nature, translations can strip away the subtle nuances of the original language, making it challenging to grasp the texts in their entirety. This cautionary note encourages a critical approach to understanding the scriptures.

Psychoanalysis and Spirituality: Psychoanalysis, despite its value in exploring the mind, does not directly address spiritual aspects such as immortality, the soul, or God. However, Carl Jung's perspective on numbers as primitive elements of the mind and their use by the unconscious for organization opens an exciting door to the connection between the mind, numbers, and the spiritual.

Jung's Theory and the Blue Brain Project: Carl Jung's theory on numbers and the unconscious finds an intriguing echo in the "Blue Brain Project," a Swiss scientific project that seeks to create the most detailed digital model of the human brain. The coincidence that neuroscientists have discovered that the brain functions in a network of eleven mathematical, though not physical, dimensions resonate with Jung's idea of archetypes and the collective unconscious.

Exploring the Dimensions of the Brain: These digitally modeled mathematical dimensions can help us uncover fundamental mysteries of neuroscience and better understand the brain's multidimensional world. This innovative approach leads us to consider that the brain not only processes information in a three-dimensional manner but also operates on much more complex levels.

The dimensions we are exploring, including the soul, spirit, dreams, intuition, memory, and the perception of time, hold the potential to unlock the secrets of the human brain. This research could reveal the profound mysteries of our brain and the divine greatness within us, sparking a new era of understanding and appreciation for the complexity of our minds.

By understanding the dimensions of the brain, we can develop more effective methods for preventing and treating mental and physical illnesses by integrating natural, organic, and technological approaches. My book, the Emotional and Inner Healing Workshop, explores this holistic view of health in depth and equips readers with practical tools for achieving overall well-being. It's a guide that empowers you to take control of your health.

What does God expect of us? Nobody wants to live their life and think they have wasted it without fulfilling their mission. The prophet Micah, a significant figure in the Old Testament, shares what God expects of us in one verse, with such influence that it is written on the United States Library of Congress building. The verse, often called the 'Micah Mandate, 'calls for justice, mercy, and humility in our actions.

Micah 6:[8] . "It has already been declared to you what is good! You have already been told what the Lord expects of you: practice justice, love mercy, and humble yourself before your God."

"He who validates the precepts of man, ignoring those of God, satisfies man, but is a spiritual exile for God."

AN OFFENSE AGAINST THE CREATOR

In a world saturated with distractions and trivialities, it is easy to lose sight of the greatness of God the Father, our Creator and Lord. Limiting eternal God to human characteristics would be a mistake, as 'God the Father is all, pure immanence,' omniscient, omnipotent, omnipresent, and immutable, a concept that signifies His omnipresence and immeasurable nature, infinite in the universe and beyond our comprehension.

God the Father and his relationship with humanity: Despite infinity, we can conclude that God has feelings, as He created us in His image and likeness. Moreover, as the architect and Creator of the universe and supreme being, He desires to be recognized and honored by humanity throughout history. We are His most incredible creation and, at the same time, His weakness. Thanks to this, He gave us power **over all one that exists** [1,] on earth and instructions to live, manage, and correct. We are not just His creation but an integral part of His divine plan.

Despite this invaluable gift, it's humbling to acknowledge that humans often forget the Creator's greatness. Those who delve into the biblical scriptures can glimpse God's will. Guided by devotion to Jesus Christ as the Son and sent by the Father, an entire week commemorates His passion. Mary of Nazareth, chosen by the Creator and mother of Jesus according to His design, is honored in many ways, even more than anyone else.

Angels, saints, and the righteous are also honored with special dates and days in their names. This wide range of celebrations forms a complex tapestry of devotion, uniting us in our shared faith. In addition to religious celebrations, we also remember and celebrate significant events in human history. These events include, among others:

- **Day of the Race in honor of the discovery of America:** Columbus Day (in honor of the discovery of America)

- **Independence Day:** Independence Day

- **Flag Day:** Flag Day

- **Mother's Day:** Mother's Day

- **Father's Day:** Father's Day

- **Christmas and New Year's Day:** Christmas and New Year's Day

- **Secretary's Day:** Administrative Professionals' Day

- **President's Day:** President's Day

- **Women's Day:** International Women's Day

- **Day of the Dead:** Day of the Dead

- **Innocents' Day:** Holy Innocents' Day

- **Labor Day:** Labor Day

- **Constitution Day:** Constitution Day

- **We celebrate the Birthdays of:** We celebrate the Birthdays of

- **We celebrate and remember the death of:** We commemorate and remember the death of

- **We remember the dates of the World Wars:** We remember the dates of the World Wars

- **Reformation Day:** Reformation Day

Likewise, as a sign of gratitude, we celebrate the outstanding characters in each country's history, such as Independence Day (Martin Luther King Day) in the USA and Benito Juarez Day (Benito Juarez in Mexico). In Argentina, they celebrate several days for the immortality of their local heroes.

In a world saturated with noise and superficiality, it's easy to forget the greatness of God the Father, our Creator and Lord. While religious celebrations can be expressions of faith and gratitude, focusing solely on them can distract us from cultivating a deeper relationship with Him. God the Father is also known as: Yahweh, Jehovah, Hashem, El, El Shaddai, Elohim, Adonai, and the Eternal Father whom Jesus of Nazareth taught us about.

It is essential to examine the teachings of Jesus Christ, who revealed the Kingdom of Heaven and introduced us to God the Father in a unique and unprecedented way. Let's look at some of His teachings.

The centrality of Jesus Christ in the will of God the Father: Jesus emphasized His mission to fulfill the Father's will when He said, "***For I have come down from heaven, not to do my will but***

the will of him who sent me." [1]. This powerful statement highlights the central role of Jesus Christ in His mission to fulfill the will of God the Father.

Jesus Christ, in His acknowledgment of the Father's superiority, also reveals the importance of understanding this distinction: "You have heard me say, 'I am going away and will come back to you.' Now, if you loved me, you would be glad I am going to the father, because *the father is greater than I."* [2].

This concept is complemented by His statement, "Which of the gods has ever shown such love? As for us, we praise our God and Father, who, with great power, raised Jesus from the dead.[3]" Respecting the distinction between God the Father and Jesus Christ is not just essential but crucial, as they stated and as it is affirmed in the Bible.

The distinction between God the Father and Jesus Christ: God the Father makes a clear distinction in the scriptures: "This is my beloved Son, with whom I am well pleased."[4] And He also says, "Behold, my servant whom I have chosen, my beloved, with whom my soul is well pleased. I will put my Spirit upon him, and he will proclaim justice to the nations." [5].

The distinction between the Eternal Father and His Son, Jesus, is crucial to understanding the Scriptures correctly. The Father is the supreme authority, while Jesus, though divine, is subject to His will. Any interpretation that ignores this fundamental distinction risks distorting the message and misinterpreting the scriptures.

Faithfulness to the Scriptures and False Interpretations

Misinterpreting the Scriptures is akin to disregarding the truth conveyed by prophets like Isaiah, Jeremiah, and Paul. The Scriptures, particularly the Old Testament, contain 44 specific prophecies about the coming of the Messiah, woven into foundational texts such as Genesis, Deuteronomy, Isaiah, Jeremiah, Psalms, Daniel, Hosea, and Malachi. These references point to the fulfillment of a divine plan and affirm the interconnectedness and harmony of the Scriptures as a whole.

The New Testament further deepens this unity, citing the Old Testament 516 times, emphasizing the connection between the two and the importance of interpreting them faithfully. It's important to remember that the Holy Spirit plays a crucial role in interpreting the Scriptures, guiding us to understand the deeper meanings. Each passage serves a purpose that, when appropriately understood, allows us to grasp the full scope of God's messages without distortion, revealing a coherent and divine guidance that spans all of Scripture.

When Jesus officially presented Himself to His people as the Messiah, He did so by quoting a verse from the Old Testament: "The Spirit of the Lord is upon me, because he has anointed me to bring good news to the poor. He has sent me to proclaim release to the captives and recovery of sight to the blind, to set those who are oppressed at liberty, to proclaim the year of the Lord's favor..." [6].

In all His works, Jesus imitated the Father. He told them: "Truly, truly, I say to you, the Son can do nothing by himself; he can do only what he sees his Father doing. For whatever the father does, the son also does likewise." [7]. Jesus' messages and desires are that we may know and praise the Father in heaven.

Indeed, Jesus was persistent in prayer; He prayed during the day, at dusk, early in the morning, and, on occasion, spent the entire night praying. Did He pray to Himself? To whom did He pray? Clearly, He prayed to "Abba," His Father, and our Father.

This prayer underscores the profound relationship between Jesus and His Father, inviting us to contemplate the depth of this divine connection.

All this underscores the profound connection between Jesus and God the Father, a relationship that is not to be taken lightly. It inspires wonder and admiration but does not imply a literal identification between Jesus and God. Jesus himself said, "The Spirit of the Lord is upon me, because...)

RESURRECTION OF JESUS CHRIST

The resurrection of Jesus Christ is the most meaningful event in Christianity, the foundation of redemption and salvation for believers, and the promise of eternal life. However, a fundamental question arises: *Who resurrected Jesus?* Throughout the New Testament, several passages offer clear and direct answers, highlighting *God the Father as the primary source of the resurrection* and Jesus as the redeemer.

The resurrection of Jesus is not only a historical event but also a Trinitarian act that reflects the unified work of the Trinity: the Father, the Son, and the Holy Spirit. In this divine act, *God the Father, the author and finisher of life, resurrects Jesus from the dead*, demonstrating He is the author and finisher of life. This divine act marks victory over death and sin and fulfills Jesus' promise of the hope of eternal life.

Below are some key passages from the New Testament that assure that *God the Father is the one who resurrects Jesus Christ* and invite us to reflect on the profound meaning of this event:

This Jesus God raised from the dead, and we all witness it. [8.]

(...But God raised him from the dead...) [9.]

God has fulfilled this promise to us, his children, by raising Jesus from the dead, as it is written in the Psalms:

'You are my son, today I have begotten you.' [10.]

(…He who was raised from the dead, Jesus our Lord…) [11.]

(…just as Jesus was raised from the dead by the glory of the Father…) [12.]

If the Spirit of him who raised Jesus from the dead dwells in you… [13.]

(…and you believe in your heart that God raised him from the dead, you will be saved…) [14.]

We would be false witnesses of God, for we have testified against God that he raised Christ… [15.]

Paul, an apostle—sent not from men nor by man, but by Jesus Christ and God the Father, who raised him from the dead— [16.]

"Having been foreknown before the foundation of the world but made manifest in these last times for your sake, and through the gospel, you have heard and believed in which you have also put your hope in God who raised Jesus from the dead." [17.]

Therefore, the resurrection of Jesus Christ is much more than a historical event: it is a Trinitarian work that reveals the sovereignty and power of God the Father. Through His glory and power, *God the Father resurrects Jesus, thus granting victory over death* and the promise of eternal life to all who believe in Him.

Why Didn't the Resurrection Occur on a Sabbath?

Have you ever wondered why Jesus did not rise from the dead on a Saturday, a Friday, or a Monday but rather on a Sunday? The answer is not merely theological but deeply biblical. The resurrection of Jesus Christ by God the Father, as recounted in the

Scriptures, holds profound significance. Sunday, rather than any other day, was chosen with purpose.

According to the Bible, after completing creation, God established the Sabbath as a day of rest—a day when the eternal God does not work. The choice of Sunday for the resurrection aligns with this pattern, connecting it to God's rest after creation and highlighting the Sabbath's significance in the biblical narrative.

Those who have studied the Bible thoroughly conclude that Jesus' resurrection on a Sunday fulfills the word and promise of the universe's architect, a theological term referring to God as the creator and sustainer of the universe, not to work on the Sabbath. God the Father demonstrated His power over heaven and earth, nature, life, and death on a day other than the Sabbath.

This day of rest, established at the world's creation, is not a privilege limited to a specific group but has a universal significance that reaches beyond nationality and religion to embrace all of humanity. It stands as an act of divine love and care, part of a larger, universal plan for every individual.

Jesus Christ, following the example of his heavenly Father, presented himself as Lord of the Sabbath. He demonstrated his divine authority to interpret and apply the law, showing that its original purpose was human welfare, not an empty legalistic burden lacking love for one's neighbor. His teachings inspire us to apply and live the Sabbath in a way that truly honors God and benefits humanity.

Jesus taught that the law is flexible in situations of need and in mercy toward others, for the Sabbath was made for man, not man for the Sabbath. Jesus said, "Love God above all things and your neighbor as yourself," and he applied this to the Sabbath without invalidating it.

Jesus of Nazareth observed the Sabbath but did not break the law; he offered teachings on its application. Quoting the prophet Hosea, he highlighted the importance of mercy over ritual sacrifice. Not a single word of Jesus states that the Sabbath was invalidated for a reason; *in the book of Exodus, it is a perpetual mandate.*

The Resurrection of Jesus Christ, which is celebrated on Sunday, has a profound and transcendent meaning beyond a mere historical event. It symbolizes God's power over creation and victory over death. It represents the fullness of divine plan and law, a theological concept encompassing God's ultimate purpose and moral and ethical guidelines, where mercy and love manifest.

The Unity and Distinction between God the Father and Jesus Christ

When Jesus of Nazareth said, "I and the Father are one," 19 He was not asserting that He and God the Father were precisely the same person, but rather expressing a profound unity in their divine nature. Jesus also declared, "But of that day and hour, no one knows, not even the angels in heaven, nor the Son, but only the Father." This verse underlines the sovereignty and exclusive knowledge of God the Father regarding specific events. Jesus also says, "Truly, truly, I say to you, the Son can do nothing by himself; he can do only what he sees his Father doing." 20.

To better understand this relationship, imagine a president sending a minister to represent the government. The minister, invested in the power of government, acts on behalf of the president but is not the president. They are two distinct persons, although they share the essence of power and authority.

This analogy illustrates the unity and distinction between Jesus and God the Father without belittling Jesus Christ's divinity. Unlike a minister, Jesus acts on behalf of God and shares his divine essence. However, in his role as Son, he respected the will and sovereignty of the Father. This relationship teaches us the importance of humility and obedience, virtues that significantly impact our lives since Jesus himself submitted to the will of the Father, being a perfect model for us.

In the Bible, God is referred to as Father approximately 172 times, with greater prominence in the New Testament, highlighting the tenderness with which Jesus calls Him Abba ('Daddy'). This love and affection are not one-sided but reciprocal, inviting us to share in this intimate relationship, as can be read in the book of Psalms: "As a father has compassion on his children, so the Lord has compassion on those who fear him." 21.

Jesus, as the Son of God, has authority, but the Father gives that authority. Given this father-son relationship, two significant questions arise:

- *Where and on what date is God the Father's Day celebrated?*
- *Where and on what date is Creation Day celebrated?*

In this part of the world, no date universally and exclusively highlights God the Father and Creation. This absence is striking, considering that the Bible presents God as the architect of the universe, the One whom Jesus, our brother and Savior, uniquely revealed to us.

God the Father is known by many names, each reflecting a different aspect of His divine nature: "I am who I am," "Yahweh, Jehovah, Hashem, Adonai, He, Elohim, El Shaddai, Abba." These names have been present in the Scriptures from the time of Adam, Abraham, Moses, the prophets, and finally, in the teaching of Jesus. In fact, the prophet Isaiah tells us that <u>Jesus of Nazareth is the servant of Yahweh</u>. [22].

This absence of a universally recognized date for celebrating God the Father and Creation raises profound questions about our understanding and relationship with Him. It prompts us to reflect on our lack of recognition according to the biblical teachings of Jesus and the prophets.

- What about the Holy Trinity?
- Which day would be the day of God the father?
- What day and date would be the day of creation?

God the Father, the sole source of life for the Holy Trinity, is a figure of immense reverence and respect. He is the Father, the Son, and the Holy Spirit, the one who knows, is knowledge, and is the knowledge of himself. As we contemplate the unity of the Holy Trinity, we are drawn to the awe-inspiring question: who is God, and where does He come from? Who formed Him? Who commanded Him to come among men?

God the Father, the Eternal One, is the first person of the Holy Trinity and the source of life within them. His eternal nature is reflected in the continuity of His role on earth. Whom do they represent on earth? God the Father. What do they do on earth? They do, know, and love God the Father. We will observe that prayers are directed to God the Father in different religious traditions, whether in Catholic Mass, Jewish synagogues, or some Protestant churches.

Therefore, the following questions arise: ***What would be the day of God the Father and the day of creation?*** From Genesis to the Acts of the Apostles, the Bible guides us in understanding these profound questions. It indicates one of those days, leading us to a deeper understanding of God the Father's role.

- Moreover, as the Scriptures themselves say, "...and if anyone sins, we have an advocate with the Father, Jesus Christ the righteous," [23] it also says:

- And behold, a voice from heaven said, "This is my beloved Son, with whom I am well pleased." [24].

- This is my beloved Son; listen to him." [25].

- "For I have come down from heaven, not to do my will but the will of him who sent me." [26].

- "Whatever you ask in my name, I will give it to you." [27].

- "Pray then like this: *'Our Father who art in heaven...*"" [28].

- Jesus said to her, "Do not touch me, for I have not yet ascended to my Father; but go to my brothers and say to them, **'I am ascending to my Father and your Father, to my God and your God**.'" [29].

Jesus Christ came to reveal God the Father and establish a personal relationship with humanity:

- "Anyone who has seen me has seen the father." [30].

- "Believe me when I say that I am in the father and the father is in me." [31].

- "That you may be children of your heavenly Father." [32].

- "If anyone confesses that Jesus is the Son of God, God abides in him, and he in God." [33].

- "You will drink my cup, but to sit at my right hand or my left is not mine to grant, but it is for those for whom my father has prepared it." [34].

- "This Jesus God raised from the dead, and we are all witnesses of it." [35].

- "Let it be known to you all and to all the people of Israel that by the name of Jesus Christ of Nazareth, whom you crucified, whom God raised from the dead—by him this man stands here before you healed. [36].

- "Grace, mercy, and peace from God the Father and Jesus Christ, the Son of the Father, be with us, now and always, in truth and love." [37].

- "You have heard me say, 'I am going away, and I will return to you.' If you loved me, you would be glad I am going to the father, for the father is greater than I." [38].

- At the ninth hour, Jesus cried aloud, "Eloi, Eloi, lema sabachthani?" which means, "My God, my God, why have you forsaken me?" [39].

Unity in Celebrating God the Father

It's crucial to remember that the divisions we sometimes see in our celebrations are at odds with the message of unity and love that God the Father conveys to us through Jesus Christ. Understanding the essence of Jesus' mission, we realize his greatest desire was to reveal and glorify God the Father, who sent Him into this world.

Jesus' mission was to highlight God the Father, who is active and present in our lives. Jesus came to reveal the truth and free us from our limitations and preconceptions about the divine. His teaching guides us toward emotional freedom and offers us profound existential lessons.

Jesus declared: "*I am going to my Father and your Father, to my God and your God*. [40] " This is not just a declaration but a profound truth that Jesus has one God and Father, which clearly indicates that he is our elder brother, and our savior. God the Father has not just wanted but always wanted us to know and experience His immense love. However, we often forget and do not give Him the importance He not only deserves but demands, as we do not celebrate a day in His name or honor His work.

Recognizing the presence and love of God the Father in our lives is not just a suggestion but a necessity. This recognition is not just a key but a powerful tool that can unlock a deeper relationship with Him and the gateway to the spiritual freedom that Jesus taught us. It's a source of enlightenment and empowerment.

- We say you are our light but do not see it.
- We say you are our way, but we are lost.
- We call your life, but we die without You.
- We call you "The Eternal One," "Elohim," but we do not seek You.
- We say, "You are good," but we do not trust him
- We say, "Almighty God," and do not respect You.
- We call You "Lord," "Adonai," and do not obey You.

Honoring God the Father

In the book of Leviticus, we deeply honor celebrations and feasts in reverence of God the Father and His creation. These perpetual and unalterable feasts profoundly reflect God the Father's desire to be present among men and draw attention to Himself and His work.

However, what happened to the Trinity? The Trinity is honored as such. The Word and the Holy Spirit are celebrated in their manifestations and missions.

The sacrifice of Jesus on the cross, a profound act that transformed the material into the divine, brought God the Father closer to humanity. The Eucharist, as the divine presence through Jesus and the Holy Spirit, offers us a pathway to connect with the Father when we are in grace. It is a spiritual union between humanity and God, a beacon of hope through Jesus and the Holy Spirit.

Claiming *that every day is the day of God the Father* or that honoring the Son is honoring the Father, while true, is not a complete response but rather a convenient interpretation. It is true that God is always present and that honoring the Son is honoring the Father, as Jesus taught. However, the absence of a specific day dedicated exclusively to God the Father, as seen in the

Scriptures, leaves a gap that may dilute the importance of acknowledging and honoring God the Father uniquely.

Jesus, in His teachings, highlighted the centrality of the Father in God's divine plan. While the Christian faith focuses on redemption through the Son, we must not lose sight of the importance of honoring and recognizing God the Father through Jesus and directly, as established in Scripture.

Jesus did not come to change the law. Instead, He is the way to the law, the living "Torah" for Christians. Neither God the Father nor Jesus changed the law. This is reinforced when He tells us that loving God consists of keeping His commandments, which are not burdensome. [44]. So, who will change these commandments according to his judgment? The scripture says, "Thus have you made the word of God of no effect, through your tradition." [45].

In our contemporary world, we commemorate many holidays to express gratitude for diverse reasons. We erect statues in honor of scientists and create works of art that, though aesthetically pleasing, often fail to resonate deeply with our spirits. It is a cause for concern that no universally recognized day is dedicated to revering the eternal God.

He is neither honored nor remembered through a special celebration in His name. No holiday reflects His greatness and merit in this part of the world. No theology or ideology has addressed this issue despite this desire having existed since creation. This forgetfulness and neglect constitute an unforgivable offense. The created is worshiped more than the Creator, which makes no sense.

By setting aside our biases, broadening our understanding, and delving into the scriptures, theologies, and beliefs of all Christians who believe in the Holy Trinity, we notice a stark disparity. The second person, Jesus Christ, is honored with holidays, and the third person, the Holy Spirit, is celebrated. But what about the first person, God the Father? This imbalance calls for our attention and action.

Pentecost celebrates the coming of the Holy Spirit and the beginning of the Church's activities. Therefore, it is also known as the celebration of the Holy Spirit. In the Catholic liturgy, it is the most critical feast after Easter and Christmas. Different days are celebrated for the Virgin Mary. A persistent question remains: what happened to the first person of the Holy Trinity, God the Father? Where and on what date are celebrated:

- THE DAY OF THE CREATOR
- THE DAY OF CREATION

If any doubts remain, let us carefully consider these words: "Yet a time is coming and has now come when the true worshipers will worship the Father in spirit and truth." [46]. This aligns perfectly with other scriptures that address this topic. [47].

Jesus said, "You shall worship the Lord your God, and him only shall you serve." [48]. This reaffirms another scripture: "You shall have no other gods before me, for the Lord is a jealous God." [49]. If this does not align with our current understanding of the Bible, it may indicate that the translation is incorrect or altered or that our interpretation is flawed. In such a case, revising and correcting our understanding of these texts is imperative.

The absence of a specific celebration dedicated to God the Father in our religious traditions reflects a significant disconnect between our practices and the essence of the bible. Honoring God the Father with a special day would be an act of divine justice and a testament to the righteousness and fairness of our faith, strengthening our spiritual relationship with God and helping us abandon many erroneous ideas and practices.

Another Offense Against God the Father

Incorrect worship, whether due to ignorance or practices that do not align with biblical teachings, is an offense to God the Father. In His infinite wisdom, He has made it clear in the Bible how we are to worship Him. This worship is not about superficial rituals or ceremonies but rather a complete and sincere surrender of the heart, mind, and spirit to the Eternal God, as taught by Jesus of Nazareth. Therefore, true worship involves not just living in obedience but understanding the necessity of obedience, humility of spirit, and love, following the example and teachings of Jesus, and honoring God the Father in spirit and truth.

The complexity of this issue lies in the fact that worship is not limited to idolizing physical images and idols. In a broader sense, it can be defined as anything that takes the place of God in our hearts. This includes an excessive attachment to material possessions, social media, power, money, status, interpersonal relationships, or even ideologies. The subtlety of idolatry lies in its ability to disguise itself, camouflaged within our beliefs and values, elevating the created above the Creator.

This transgression occurs when we elevate human interpretations above the divine word, substituting revealed truth with human opinions. One of the most significant errors that Israel committed, and for which they were exiled, was undoubtedly idolatry. The consequences of this transgression, as seen in the biblical narrative, were severe. They led to a loss of divine favor, moral decay, and exile. These consequences serve as a cautionary tale for us today, highlighting the dangers of idolatry.

There are approximately 987 biblical verses that address idolatry. To put this into perspective, this is equivalent to the length of three New Testament books or a book as extensive as Deuteronomy, which contains 982 verses.

It is crucial to remember the sacred and immutable words: "You shall not make for yourself an image in the form of anything in heaven above or on the earth beneath or in the waters below. You shall not bow down to or worship them, for I, the LORD your God, am a jealous God." 50 To this day, no biblical evidence has been found to suggest that this commandment has been invalidated or replaced by another. It was given as a perpetual law.

Human beings are prone to cognitive biases that can cloud our judgment and affect our interpretation of information. These biases, such as confirmation bias or anchoring bias, can lead theologians and ideologues to interpret verses on idolatry in a way that confirms their preexisting beliefs rather than analyzing them objectively. Awareness of these biases and striving for objective interpretation is crucial.

My understanding of the Bible is based not merely on casual reading but on seven in-depth analyses, each covering the entire text from Genesis to Revelation. These analyses were conducted with great effort and from various perspectives, including faith, history, linguistics, theology (Christian and Hebrew), philosophy, archaeology, science, psychology, textual criticism, and other related fields.

Despite these in-depth studies, I encounter recurring paradoxes. What I affirm is supported by the Bible; these are not my ideas, nor are they intended to offend but rather to correct. Here, I present two of them: on one hand, those who do not accept the Messiah, and on the other, those who practice idolatry. One of these paradoxes lies in the difficulty some theologians seem to have in interpreting and addressing the 987 biblical verses on idolatry despite their extensive wisdom and biblical expertise.

It is striking that these verses, which contain enough information to fill a 285-page book, pose a challenge for some theologians, even when they interpret other much more complex scripture passages very well.

The historical context: It is essential to consider that in the time of the Old Testament, there were no photographs, canvas paintings, or cinema. Neither did they have the Internet, social media, AI, or sufficient information. One might then ask: how would they have interpreted the biblical texts on idolatry if these visual representations had existed?

Psychologically and emotionally, humans react differently to images, photographs (whether of family members or others), statues, characters, or situations. These responses are not random; they are deeply influenced by our cognitive biases, which arise from our expectations, pre-existing beliefs, and the inherent need to find meaning and purpose in life.

These biases, which lead us to interpret and react in particular ways to visual stimuli, reflect our perception and our constant search for connection, identity, and understanding in a complex world.

A work of art, an image, a statue, or a photograph can evoke memories, feelings, or ideas about what happened, what was, or what something or someone is, and this is not bad. However, it is essential to remember that these representations should not be worshiped or have all our energy and faith placed in them, as they are objects created by human beings. This not only goes against biblical teachings but is also psychologically harmful.

The Bible declares, *"Cursed is the man who trusts in man and makes flesh his strength."* [51]. With this, God warns of the curse that befalls those who believe in humanity. This warning does not imply general misanthropy but rather a caution against idolatry

368

and excessive reliance on other human beings, which can lead to dire consequences.

The Bible also states, *"Because they have forsaken me and offered sacrifices to other gods and provoked me to anger with all the works of their hands."* [52].

The Psalms say, "But thou, o lord, shalt laugh at them; thou shalt have all the heathen in derision." [53] God's mockery of those who trust in the lifeless works of human hands is not cruel or ruthless but rather an expression of deep irony and disapproval at the foolishness of idolizing lifeless visual representations, as Psalm 115 describes.

Does God Contradict Himself?

The concept that human works can be divinely inspired but can also oppose God's will is a tension that is deeply rooted in biblical teaching. The Bible teaches us that God is perfect, unchanging, and righteous in all His ways, meaning He never contradicts Himself or commands anything that He has explicitly forbidden 112 times and approximately 987 times throughout the Bible. This repeated prohibition underscores God's clear and constant stance against idolatry, reaffirming His call for pure and exclusive worship.

The discrepancy between what is genuinely divine and what humans may interpret as such is at the heart of the contradiction in claiming that God inspires some human works. The eternal God does not contradict Himself, and when human works do not align with His revealed principles, they cannot be considered true divine inspiration.

These quotes remind us of that human ideas and works alone are insufficient to attain the truth of the eternal God. Absolute trust in human creations, be they ideas, objects, or people, distances us from the trustworthy source of salvation and wisdom. Only in God do we find a solid foundation of faith and hope, a comforting reassurance in our journey.

Works of art, when crafted with talent, sensitivity, and reverence for divine creation, can indeed be elevated expressions of the human spirit. However, they should never be mistaken for objects of worship or seen as possessing God's power. True divine inspiration is found in creation itself—in the beauty of the natural world, within us, and in our capacity to love, help, create, and transcend.

A Call to the Theological Community

Throughout history and today, many theologians and ideologues have been blind to idolatry. ***They disregard the 987 biblical verses on idolatry,*** a complex phenomenon rooted in various causes. The urgency of addressing this issue, the influence of cognitive biases, the struggle for power and influence, the need for a holistic perspective, and the importance of humility and openness contribute to this difficulty.

Rigor and commitment. Overcoming this blindness requires a sustained effort from the theological community. It is essential to approach this topic with biblical rigor, intellectual openness, and a genuine commitment to truth. An integrated approach encompasses biblical truth, theological dimensions, and psychological perspectives. We can only avoid erroneous interpretations and promote a healthy relationship with images.

Educating and guiding the believer's faith is the key to preventing ignorance and blindness. The theological community, theologians, and believers have a crucial role. It is necessary to foster dialogue and critical reflection in the interpretation of religious texts, leveraging the richness of the biblical tradition to inspire multiple perspectives and offer guidance in navigating the complex challenges of faith and human experience.

This reflection does not imply a denial of human collaboration or the value of interpersonal relationships. On the contrary, it invites us to recognize the importance of maintaining a healthy balance between trust in ourselves, others, and God. This balance is crucial for fostering harmony in our relationships and faith, remembering that ultimate authority lies with the Eternal God.

Faith and experiences with God are deeply personal, but that does not mean there is no objective truth to discover. Everyone carries their faith according to their experiences, understanding of the scriptures, and relationship with God, shaping their faith. While it may not be incorrect, there is room for growth and improvement.

The Wisdom of This World: Folly in God's Eyes

The Bible clearly demonstrates the limitations of human wisdom compared to divine truth. It says, *"For the wisdom of this world is foolishness in God's sight."* This verse reminds us that human understanding, while valuable, often falls short of God's eternal wisdom and purposes.

The Pharisees of Jesus' time exemplify this struggle. They were religious leaders who became overly focused on ritualistic laws and human interpretations of the Scriptures, often missing the spirit and true intent of God's word. They held tightly to the "wisdom" of their interpretations yet usually misrepresented the heart of God's message. Similarly, even well-intentioned theologians and leaders today can fall into the trap of interpreting Scripture in ways that serve personal or institutional purposes rather than remaining grounded in the essence of God's teachings.

The Bible calls us to seek understanding through human interpretation and to have a heart genuinely open to God's guidance. Proverbs encourage us to *"Trust in the Lord with all your heart and lean not on your own understanding; in all your ways submit to Him, and He will make your paths straight."* This means surrendering to God's wisdom rather than relying solely on human perspectives.

Furthermore, Jesus Himself emphasized the Kingdom of Heaven in His teachings, showing that God's priorities often differ from worldly values. By focusing on God's words and aligning our hearts with His teachings, we become better equipped to discern true wisdom from human error.

In our pursuit of faith, we must remain vigilant about the tendency to misinterpret or distort Scripture. This demands humility, prayer, and a commitment to seeking God's truth. By anchoring ourselves in God's wisdom, and the prophets' testimony, and Jesus's, we can better align our lives with the eternal truths that lead us closer to the Kingdom of Heaven.

It bears repeating that man has ceased to use the most common of senses, that is, common sense. Doubts exist, but no one asks! There are answers, but no one answers them! Now, I ask myself, can some hearts understand?

It is essential to reflect on our heritage as heirs of God and how we are grafted into the olive tree by the grace of Christ, destined to inherit eternal life. However, some need clarification, and accommodating interpretations of these teachings distort biblical teaching and logic.

Some of the grafted believe themselves more important than the original olive tree and alter the Bible to suit their convenience. They forget that Jesus Himself said to the Samaritan woman, and consequently to all, "You worship what you do not know; we worship what we know, for salvation is from the Jews." 54

Just as in Jesus's time, many said nothing for fear of the Sanhedrin, the question arises as to **whether there is a biblical right that regulates these matters on earth** despite its absence in the earthly world. It is possible that before God the Father, there exists a just judgment consistent with His teachings and commandments.

God has given us perpetual commandments that cannot be changed or altered. We cannot claim to speak in His name if we contradict or violate His precepts.

God's educational system is faith and truth. He is our oldest and wisest teacher, teaching us through His prophets and son Jesus. We must be willing to listen and learn from His wisdom.

Now, I invite you to express your ideas and concepts. If you are going to give your concept, it is because you have analyzed the entire Bible.

We should celebrate the day of creation and the day of God the Father in the following way.

_____

_____

_____

_____

_____

_____

_____

I think the writer is wrong because.

_____

_____

_____

_____

_____

I think the writer is right because.

_____

_____

_____

_____

_____

"*So be careful to do just as the Lord your God has commanded you; do not turn aside to the right or to the left.*" (**Deuteronomy 5:*32* **).

POEM TO GOD

My God and Lord, the sky is your altar, the clouds are your chariots, the wind your messenger, and the angels, your guardians.

I am enraptured as I behold your marvelous creation: the sky, the clouds, the sea, the animals, the flowers, and the wind and its whispering. Trees and birds lift their song to the heavens in a beautiful Eden.

How small I am compared to your immense greatness.

Lord of the universe, I am left in awe, my soul filled with strength as I gaze upon such beauty.

The sun, the lamp that lights the day and the earth, is a source of life and energy. Yet, I am even more astonished as I contemplate your magnificent creation. With a breath, you gave me soul, heart, and life, making me your weakness, oh, Eternal God, king of my life.

My God and Lord, I know you are with me when I call. My weary arms do not cease to strive for a better world. You come with me, my Lord; for you, I will fight like a friend who cannot be forgotten.

I know I will gain enemies on this path, but for you, it is worth the fight, and in your name, I shall always triumph.

Bernardo A. Arango.

BIOGRAPHY OF BIBLICAL QUOTES

Page 205 1-Proverbs 22:[7] Page 207 1-Matthew 5:[25] Page 242 1-Proverbs 29:[18]

De Donde Viene Dios Padre 1- John 20:[17] 2- Gen 1:[2] 3- Psalm 24:[1]
4- First John 4:[8] 5- Jer 33:[3] 6- Matt 7:[8]

Page 281 1-Matthew 5:[4]

Page 312 1-Psalm162:[13] 2-Romans 2:[6] . 3-Genesis 1:[27] 3 Jeremiah 17:5-[10]

Page 315 1-Génesis 6:[3]

The Circle of Death 1-Gén 2:[7] 2-Eccle 11:[5] 3-Psalm 139:[13] 4-Psalm 139:[16] 5-
John 6:[33] 6-Gén 1:[27]

The Circle of God, Father and Man
1-2nd Peter 3:[5] 2-Gén 1:[20-21] 3-Col 1:[16-20] 4- Deut 10:[14] 5-Luke 9:[50] 6-Matt 10:[29]

THE OFFENSE TO GOD THE FATHER

1* Gen 1:[29-30] & Gen 9:[2-3]	
1-John 6:[38-39] 2-John 14:[28] 3- Acts 13:[33-35] 4-Matt 3:[17] 5-Isa 42:[1-4]	28-Matt 6:[9-13]
6-Luke 4:[18-19] 7-John 5:[19]	29-John 20:[17] 30-John 14:[9] 31-John 14:[11] 32-Matt 5:[45] 33-1ra John 4:[15]
8- Acts 2:[32] 9- Acts 2:[24] 10- Acts 13:[33] 11- Romans 4:[24-25] 12-Romans 6:[4] 13-Romans 8:[11] 14-Romans 10:[9]	34-Matt 20:[23] 35- Acts 2:[32]

376

15-1 Corint15:[15] 16-Galatians 1:[1]	36- Acts 4:[10]
17-1[ra] Peter 1:[20] [21] 18-Gen 2:[3] 19 -John 10:[30] 20-John 5:[19] 21- Psalm 103:[13-] 22-Isa 53:[1-12] 23-1 John 2:[1] 24-Matt 3[:17] 25-Mark 9:[7] 26-John 6:[38] 27-John 14:[14] .	37-2[da] John 1:[3]
	38 John 14:[28]
	39-Mark 5:[34]
	40-John 20:[17]
	41-Exo 25:[10-20]
	42-Exo Cap 25-31
	43-Matt 5:[17]
	44-1ra John 5:[3]
	45-Matt 5:[16]
	46-John 4:[23-24]
	47- John 17:[5]
	48-Matt 4:[10]
	49-Exo 34:[14]
	50-Exo:20[3-11]
	51-Jer 17:[5]
	52-2-Chro 34:[25]
	53-Psalm 59:[9]
	54-John 4:[22]

«It is a pity and a shame that man grows old and dies without recognizing the greatness of his mental and spiritual capacity. No man should remain blind to such potential but rather explore and fully experience it throughout his life.»

ABOUT THE AUTHOR

Bernardo Arango is a scholar with a rich educational background. He has pursued theological Studies and biblical Hebrew at Loyola University of New Orleans and the Hebrew University of Jerusalem. His academic journey also includes Philosophy, Science, and Religion at the University of Edinburgh, Psychology Studies at Yale University and the University of Palermo, and Positive Psychology at the University of Pennsylvania.

He furthered his knowledge with advanced Neuroscience at Peking University. His professional roles include Family Counselor and Certified Theo therapist. He is a respected lecturer on emotional life, self-improvement, and the Bible.

Focus: Bernardo Arango's work is dedicated to emotional and Inner Healing and Positive Psychology. His lectures on life and personal growth and his role as a Spiritual and Bible Coach have inspired many. His emotional and inner healing workshops have brought hope and transformation to countless lives.

Member of the *"American Academy of Religion"* and the *"Social Psychology Network"* in the USA. Writer of several books, including:

- The Circles of Life
- Workshop on emotional and inner healing.
- Seminar on Total Forgiveness.

He currently lives in Florida, USA, where vocation, he is a theologian, writer, and lecturer on life and bible coaching, giving lectures and workshops on faith, self-improvement, and emotional and inner healing. He discovered in this activity the noblest purpose and mission of his existence, finding his driving force for personal spiritual and experiential growth based on faith. Likewise, you can find healing topics and general interest on his YouTube channel at Bernardo Arango, «A New Knowledge.» To leave your comments and testimonies and learn more about emotional and inner healing, liberation, and other works by the author, visit the sites:

www.tallerdesanacionemocional.com ,
www.socialpsychology.org/member/arango .

Life has no meaning or purpose without emotions. Our successes and problems come from them. Everything has to do with our personal history. We are an impatient, numerous, expansive, and short-sighted species. We poison our emotions and the water we drink, pollute the land that feeds us, and destroy ourselves and what surrounds us.

We must learn to magnify life by creating paths as we walk, leaving a mark worth imitating. This workshop has been an experience, a transformation, and a testimony that it is worth transmitting authentically. This is the contribution I can give to this planet and this life, with the desire to make a better world. Looking back, I can confidently say: "It was worth living! I am ready to go."

"Tikkun Olam." תיקון עולם